Reinventing
the South

Reinventing the South

Versions of a Literary Region

Mark Royden Winchell

University of Missouri Press
Columbia and London

Copyright © 2006 by
The Curators of the University of Missouri
University of Missouri Press, Columbia, Missouri 65201
Printed and bound in the United States of America
All rights reserved
5 4 3 2 1   10 09 08 07 06

Library of Congress Cataloging-in-Publication Data

Winchell, Mark Royden, 1958–
    Reinventing the South : versions of a literary region / Mark Royden Wichell
        p.   cm.
    Summary: "Surveys the revivification and reinvention of southern culture
and literature, and the influence of the Agrarians, Fugitives, New Critics,
and popular writers, including John Gould Fletcher, Robert Penn Warren,
Monroe K. Spears, Walter Sullivan, William Faulkner, Tennessee Williams,
William Humphrey, and Cormac McCarthy"—Provided by publisher.
    Includes index.
    ISBN-13: 978-0-8262-1618-2 (alk. paper)
    ISBN-10: 0-8262-1618-8 (alk. paper)
  1. American literature—Southern States—History and criticism.
2. Southern States—Intellectual life—1865–   3. Southern States— In
literature. 4. Regionalism in literature.   I. Title.
    PS261.W56   2006
    810.9'975—dc22   2005027898

∞™This paper meets the requirements of the
American National Standard for Permanence of Paper
for Printed Library Materials, Z39.48, 1984.

Designer: Stephanie Foley
Typesetter: Crane Composition, Inc.
Printer and binder: Thomson-Shore, Inc.
Typeface: ITC Century Book

61748328

For Walter Sullivan

Contents

Preface

In one sense, what follows is a random selection of essays written over the past twenty years or so. In the midst of this seeming randomness, however, there is an implicit pattern, which says much about the phenomenon we choose to call modern southern literature. By now, the myth of the Southern Renascence has become numbingly familiar. Prior to the War between the States, the South had had a flourishing culture—if not equal in total output to that of New England, then at least competitive and certainly distinctive in character. Then, in the fallow decades after Appomattox, the southern people devoted almost all their energies to keeping body and soul together. Former aristocrats were impoverished by Emancipation and Reconstruction, while poor whites and freed blacks tended to do even worse. The leisure provided for some by a slave economy was gone, and with it the arts had seemed to disappear.

As late as 1920, H. L. Mencken could say of Dixie:

> In that gargantuan paradise of the fourth-rate there is not a single picture gallery worth going into, or a single orchestra capable of playing the nine symphonies of Beethoven, or a single opera house, or a single theater devoted to decent plays. . . . Once you have counted Robert Loveman (an Ohioan by birth) and John McClure (an Oklahoman) you will not find a single southern poet above the rank of a neighborhood rhymester. Once you have counted James Branch Cabell (a lingering survivor of the *ancien regime:* a scarlet dragonfly imbedded in opaque amber) you will not find a single southern prose writer who can actually write. And once you have—but when you come to critics, musical composers, painters, sculptors, architects and the like, you will have to give it up, for there is not even a bad one between the Potomac mud-flats and the Gulf. Nor an historian. Nor a sociologist. Nor a philosopher. Nor a theologian. Nor a scientist. In all these fields the south is an

awe-inspiring blank—a brother to Portugal, Serbia and Esthonia [*sic*].[1]

Although many southern intellectuals would eventually take issue with Mencken, most of them tended to agree with him in the immediate aftermath of World War I.

By 1930, the situation had changed dramatically. For the first time in nearly a century, some of America's most distinguished writers hailed from below the Mason-Dixon line. Even if the Northeast and the heartland each continued to produce more of the nation's major literary figures, those regions did so from positions of cultural strength. If the southern writer was not exactly a contradiction in terms, he (and a growing number of shes) seemed like nothing so much as an idiot savant, a freak of nature from a locale where apparently anything could happen. What was even more scandalous was the fact that a disproportionate number of these gifted southern writers seemed to come from the most socially reactionary elements of the region. Because the phenomenon was too widespread to be a mere hoax played on solemn but gullible Yankee critics, there had to be an explanation for why all these rubes were suddenly so articulate.

One of the most widely held explanations is what Walter Sullivan calls the Götterdämmerung theory of southern literature, first advanced by Allen Tate in his essay "The New Provincialism" (1945). According to Tate: "With the war of 1914–1918, the South reentered the world—but gave a backward glance as it stepped over the border: that backward glance gave us the Southern renascence, a literature conscious of the past in the present."[2] In other words, the insular subculture that had been the traditional South was in the process of being assimilated into the mainstream of American life. It is precisely at this moment of transition when we are able to see a culture most clearly. (Previous generations had either taken it for granted or spent their energies trying to preserve it through rhetoric or strength of arms.) As it was ceasing to be, the Old South became an object most worthy of aesthetic contemplation, and those doing the contemplating were possessed of the proper ironic temperament. It also

---

1. Mencken, *Prejudices*, 2d ser. (New York: Knopf, 1920), 138–39.
2. Tate, *Essays of Four Decades* (Wilmington, DE: Intercollegiate Studies Institute, 1999), 545.

probably helped that the South had lost its own war for independence. If nothing succeeds in life like success, nothing succeeds in literature like failure. The winners may get to write the histories, but the losers, more often than not, have the literature of a given time and place all to themselves.

There were enough gifted writers who exemplified Tate's thesis and enough like-minded critics in positions of cultural power that the South was reinvented as a literary region. It was readily apparent, however, that not all of the talented writers in the southern United States were composing ironic and elegiac tributes to a past way of life. There was, for example, a continuing tradition of southern Gothicism that seemed to exploit the most vulgar and sensational elements of southern life. Because the Gothicists tended to bridge the gap between high and popular literature, they were far better known than the more aristocratic Agrarians. (If Carson McCullers and Truman Capote are the most obvious Gothicists, the most memorable works of Tennessee Williams and a good deal of the writing of William Faulkner also fall into this category.) There were also neoromantics such as Thomas Wolfe and James Agee, who regarded the strictures of the New Criticism as a kind of aesthetic straitjacket. Political liberals such as Erskine Caldwell and Lillian Hellman offered a critique of the traditional South on behalf of the economically disadvantaged and socially marginalized. This was also true of any number of African American writers, who were not part of any "renascence" that the Nashville brethren would have easily recognized. And what is one to make of unabashedly popular writers such as Margaret Mitchell and Hervey Allen? The list could go on, but these few examples are surely adequate to make my point.

By the 1950s, it had become apparent even to neo-Agrarians that the Southern Renascence, as defined by Tate, had pretty much run its course. At the same time, southern writers who fell outside the parameters of the Renascence were making important contributions to American literature. It was only a matter of time before revisionist critics, who were motivated in part by their opposition to the social vision of the Agrarians, began to question whether the Renascence (and perhaps even the South itself) had ever really existed except in the imagination of the Vanderbilt literary mafia. Unfortunately, whatever corrective value might have been served by these revisionists was seriously compromised by their polemical excess.

Clearly, what was needed was a more pluralistic and evenhanded understanding of the variety of literature produced in the modern South. Although not comprehensive enough to be such a study, this book offers preliminary thoughts on a handful of writers both inside and outside the Agrarian canon.

I have chosen to call the first section of this book "The Nashville Renascence" for reasons that should be obvious. While the works of the Fugitives, Agrarians, and New Critics do not constitute the totality of important southern literature written in the twentieth century, they do represent a valuable touchstone against which to measure such literature. No other group tried harder or more effectively to define what it meant to be a southern writer in the modern world. If they were not wholly successful in that effort, their very failure enables us to see the achievement of others in a clearer light.

We begin with what many might consider the most problematic aspect of the renascence—the political views of the Agrarians and their relevance to the world of the twenty-first century. We then look at the enigmatic John Gould Fletcher, who is a case study in southern modernism by virtue of being the only individual to have participated in the imagist, Fugitive, and Agrarian movements. The essay "Renaissance Man" considers some of the roots of the Nashville tradition by examining the influence of William Shakespeare on Robert Penn Warren. The fourth and fifth essays concern Monroe K. Spears and Walter Sullivan—two men who represented the best of the tradition in its long afterglow. We then bring the section to a close by responding to a quarter century of charges leveled against the Fugitives, Agrarians, and New Critics.

By calling Part Two "The Lower South," I mean primarily a geographical location south of Nashville. Nevertheless, the writers considered in this part of the book also aimed at an audience less highbrow than any the Nashvillians would have acknowledged. We begin, appropriately enough, with the position of William Faulkner in the struggle to define modern southern culture. (As the title "The Faulkner Wars" suggests, the legacy of the region's only Nobel laureate is claimed with considerable passion and plausibility by Agrarians and anti-Agrarians alike.) We then join the fray with a reading of the Mississippian's last great novel—*Go Down, Moses*. If the Agrarians thought that Faulkner was well worth claiming, they just as insistently shunned Tennessee Williams, whose myth of the South was radically different from theirs and at least as powerful. In *A Streetcar Named Desire* and *Cat on a Hot Tin Roof*, he gave us original treatments of enduring American archetypes.

While southern literature did not begin with William Faulkner or end with Tennessee Williams, the work of these two men historically spans the period of the renascence. Consequently, the last two figures we consider, William Humphrey and Cormac McCarthy, are post-Renascence (and perhaps even postsouthern) writers. At the beginning of their careers, critics identified both men with the South. Later, they came to seem more western than southern. Perhaps they represent that point in our mythic geography where the South becomes the West.

Most of the following selections have had a previous existence in various forms. "This Land Is Your Land" was originally published in the July 14, 2003, issue of the *American Conservative*. Parts of "Arkansas Traveler" first saw the light of day in the fall 1991 and summer 1998 issues of the *Sewanee Review*. A slightly different version of "Renaissance Man" appeared in Philip C. Kolin's *Shakespeare and Southern Writers: A Study in Influence* (University Press of Mississippi, 1985). "Incarnate Words" includes some material from an essay published in the *Hollins Critic* in February 1990, and part of "'What They Have to Say about Us'" comes from the winter 2002 issue of the *University Bookman*. The original version of "The Faulkner Wars" was published in the spring 2000 issue of the *Sewanee Review*. "Why *Streetcar* Keeps Running" first appeared in Philip C. Kolin's *Confronting* Streetcar (Greenwood, 1992), and "Come Back to the Locker Room Ag'in, Brick Honey!" was originally published in the fall 1995 issue of the *Mississippi Quarterly*. A slightly longer version of "The Achievement of William Humphrey" appeared in 1992 as a monograph in the Boise State University Western Writer's Series. Finally, "Scum of the Earth" was first published in the *Southern Review* in spring 1990. "The Legacy of Monroe K. Spears" and "Family Values in *Go Down, Moses*" appear here for the first time.

I thank Lloyd Davis and the late Ruel Foster of West Virginia University for introducing me to the Vanderbilt literary tradition and to the late Thomas Daniel Young for helping to guide my studies at Vanderbilt. George Core has been a faithful friend and editor for the past quarter century. I am also indebted to Beverly Jarrett and her staff at the University of Missouri Press for believing in my work and helping to bring it before the reading public. As always, my wife, Donna, and my sons, Jonathan and Matthew, have been constant sources of support and encouragement.

Neither this book nor the larger body of work of which it is a part would have been possible without the example of the man to whom it is dedicated. It seems to me that Walter Sullivan has never gotten his due as either a novelist or a critic. But his legacy endures, if only because the written word is the closest that any of us can come to immortality short of the Resurrection itself. As a teacher, I am glad to say, Walter has always been recognized for his extraordinary presence and dedication. Having taught at Vanderbilt for fifty-two years, he was the very embodiment of that school's literary tradition. I once heard a student tell a classmate that "Mr. Sullivan is a good teacher but *kind of set in his ways.*" (Whether intended or not, this was a double compliment.) If, at the end of my career, the same can be said of me, it will be due in no small part to the inspiration of this remarkable man.

Reinventing
the South

Part One

The Nashville Renascence

≋ 1 ≋

This Land Is Your Land

On October 30 and 31, 1980, a group of scholars and other interested persons gathered on the campus of Vanderbilt University to celebrate the fiftieth anniversary of an unusual book. *I'll Take My Stand: The South and the Agrarian Tradition* had been published by Harper and Brothers in November 1930. The driving forces behind this volume were four poets who had been associated with each other at Vanderbilt a decade earlier and had been instrumental in publishing the *Fugitive: A Magazine of Poetry* from 1923 to 1925. Up until 1925, John Crowe Ransom, Allen Tate, Donald Davidson, and Robert Penn Warren had been primarily interested in literature and largely indifferent to economic and social issues.

During the second half of the 1920s, however, they became increasingly conscious of their identity as southerners and their social responsibility as southern intellectuals. Although the reasons for this growing regional consciousness were as diverse as the men themselves, the great external catalyst was undoubtedly the scorn heaped upon the South as a result of the Scopes Monkey Trial in the summer of 1925. Thinking southerners either had to agree with the characterization of traditional southern culture as backward and unenlightened or had to formulate a philosophically cogent defense of that culture. The New South liberals of Chapel Hill, North Carolina, and elsewhere chose apology and assimilation. Ransom, Tate, Davidson, and Warren chose explanation and defense.

In addition to the four major Fugitive poets, eight other like-minded southerners contributed to *I'll Take My Stand*. In opposing modernity, especially industrialization, these twelve appeared defiantly out of step with their age. In the best of times, they would have been accused of reactionary sentimentality. Coming thirteen months into the Great Depression, their book was widely scorned as a formula for social and economic disaster. At a time when many desperate people were willing to entertain radical left-wing solutions to the national crisis, the Agrarian program had few adherents.

In one sense, the debate between the Agrarians and their progressive adversaries (including the administration of Vanderbilt University itself) was a variation on the 150-year-old debate between Alexander Hamilton and Thomas Jefferson. By 1930, the Hamiltonian vision had triumphed everywhere in the United States except for the South and a few isolated pockets of rural culture elsewhere in the country. Advocates of the New South wanted to make that victory total. The Agrarians, however, believed that the Faustian bargain being offered to the South would result in the region giving up too much for too little. (It is doubtful that even they could have imagined the contemporary Sunbelt, with indistinguishable shopping malls stretching from Phoenix to Atlanta and a landscape of highrise hotels with revolving restaurants on top.) Although their warning went largely unheeded at the time, *I'll Take My Stand* remains in print more than seven decades later, even as more topical social manifestos have been largely forgotten.

If Agrarianism had seemed quixotic in 1930, it was virtually incomprehensible to the politics of 1980. The movement was originally understood to be an extreme manifestation of southern conservatism. On the Tuesday after the Vanderbilt symposium, however, the first president elected from the Deep South since James K. Polk was defeated for reelection by the widely acknowledged conservative candidate. One suspects that the Agrarians would have been troubled by both Jimmy Carter and Ronald Reagan. A nuclear engineer and agribusinessman, Carter was clearly a product of the New South. (Eugene McCarthy once called him a "third-generation Snopes.") Reagan, on the other hand, was the favorite of industrialists, who talked the talk of laissez-faire capitalism while walking the walk of corporate welfare. During a discussion session at the 1980 conference, Lyle Lanier (one of three surviving contributors to *I'll Take My Stand*) made several favorable references to the environmental scientist Barry Commoner, presidential candidate of the ultra-left-wing Citizen's Party. One might have wondered whether the extreme conservatism of 1930 had become the cutting edge radicalism of 1980.[1]

In 1930, industrialism and progress were widely considered to be synonymous. Thus, anyone who opposed industrialism was conservative, if not downright reactionary. But as the ravages of pollution and urbanization became apparent, those who preached concern for the natural and human environment increasingly came to be labeled as socialists or worse. Socialism, however, depends on centralized solutions to national problems. Like most traditional southerners, the Agrarians favored local control of local communities. One is tempted to think of Agrarianism as an early example of Left Conservatism (which, according to Norman Mailer, involves thinking "in the style of Marx in order to attain certain values suggested by Edmund Burke"), except that the Agrarians were more radical than Marx and more conservative than Burke. If Marx detested capitalism, he saw it as a necessary and inevitable prelude to socialism.[2] Precisely because they agreed with that analysis, the Agrarians were not content with conserving the existing consensus—they wanted to turn the clock back to a time before huge economic power had been concentrated in the hands of corporate capitalists and government bureaucrats.

By 1933, the Agrarian movement seemed dead in the water. Critics were no longer saying even bad things about *I'll Take My Stand*. They were simply ignoring it. And the primary spokesmen for the group had neither the money nor the contacts necessary to create a political infrastructure. Then, when things seemed hopeless, the Agrarians found a sympathetic ear in the New York editor Seward Collins. From 1933 to 1936, they published more than seventy articles and reviews in his magazine, the *American Review*. A man of intense but transitory enthusiasms, Collins was briefly attracted to Agrarianism as an alternative to the seemingly doomed system of

1. For an edited transcript of the proceedings of this conference, see William C. Havard and Walter Sullivan, eds., *A Band of Prophets: The Vanderbilt Agrarians after Fifty Years* (Baton Rouge: Louisiana State University Press, 1982).

2. Mailer, *The Armies of the Night: History as a Novel, the Novel as History* (New York: New American Library, 1968), 185. For a historical discussion of the southern conservative critique of capitalism, see Eugene D. Genovese, *The Southern Tradition: The Achievement and Limitations of an American Conservatism.*

democratic capitalism. When he switched his allegiance to Italian fascism, however, the Agrarians cut their ties with Collins and began looking for new allies. The result was a liaison with the Kentucky journalist Herbert Agar.

While serving as London correspondent for the *Louisville Courier-Journal* from 1929 to 1933, Agar discovered the British Distributist movement. Although the Agrarians had probably never heard of the Distributists at the time they published *I'll Take My Stand*, the two groups shared several key principles. These included opposition to the dehumanizing effects of industrialism and a fear that greater economic centralization would result in diminished personal liberty. Because the Distributists (G. K. Chesterton, Hillarie Belloc, and others) were overwhelmingly Roman Catholic, they attributed the excesses of capitalism to the spirit of Protestant individualism. In 1936, a coalition of Agrarians, Distributists, and other economic devolutionists published a collection of essays called *Who Owns America? A New Declaration of Independence.*

With twenty-one essays, *Who Owns America?* was a more diverse collection than *I'll Take My Stand.* Because Herbert Agar (who coedited the volume with Allen Tate) was consciously trying to influence the Roosevelt administration, the book is filled with the policy wonkery of a bygone age. Nevertheless, the passion for decentralization that runs through its pages is as timely today as it was in 1936. (The Intercollegiate Studies Institute issued a handsome reprinting of the book in 1999.)[3] This is true in large part because it helps to explain divisions in the conservative movement that are far more apparent in the early twenty-first century than they were when the Agrarians celebrated their semicentennial in 1980.

One of the fundamental differences among conservatives since the breakup of the Reagan coalition has been over the size and power of government. Historically, southerners have distrusted centralized authority in Washington. If that used to be the universally held conservative position, such is no longer the case. Neoconservatives and other establishment figures see themselves as nationalists and internationalists. If southerners are not the only people who argue for decentralization, they are the only ones who fought a war

---

3. Agar and Tate, *Who Owns America? A New Declaration of Independence* (1936; reprint, Wilmington, DE: ISI Books, 1999).

over that principle. It is surely no accident that the battle flag of the Confederacy has become the unofficial banner of devolutionists from the breakaway states of the former Soviet Union to the Quebec separatists in Canada.

As several of the Agrarians and their allies sought to break up concentrations of wealth and property, others focused on the dangers of concentrated government. Two years after the appearance of *Who Owns America?* Donald Davidson published a book of essays called *The Attack on Leviathan: Regionalism and Nationalism in the United States.* In 1989, Russell Kirk recalled happening on this book while browsing through the library at Michigan State College as an "earnest sophomore" more than fifty years earlier. "It was written eloquently," Kirk notes, "and for me it made coherent the misgivings I had felt concerning the political notions popular in the 1930s. The book was so good that I assumed all intelligent Americans, or almost all, were reading it." In fact, *The Attack on Leviathan* was remaindered after selling only a few hundred copies in the decade after publication. It has been reissued at least twice, however, most recently in 1991 by Transaction Publishers, as part of Kirk's Library of Conservative Thought.[4]

One of the essays anticipating *The Attack on Leviathan* had been Davidson's contribution to *Who Owns America?* Its title, "That This Nation May Endure: The Need for Political Regionalism," ironically alludes to Lincoln's obsession with preserving the political integrity of the Union but offers a much different prescription for achieving that end. By this point in his career, Davidson had become convinced that the United States was neither "one nation indivisible" nor an association of sovereign states, but a congeries of regional cultures. National unity could be preserved only if that fact were acknowledged and respected. Although the issue of secession had been settled by the War between the States, regional differences had not been obliterated. The subjugation of the South by the federal army was a military act with political consequences, but it could not impose an alien culture on a conquered territory. To use a distinction popular in our own time, the Unionists were authoritarians interested only in political control. The totalitarian sensibility, however,

---

4. Kirk, "*The Attack on Leviathan* and the South's Conservatism," *Heritage Foundation*, lecture 206 (July 11, 1989): 1.

insists on controlling the hearts and minds of people, as well. In the 1930s, Nazism and communism unmistakably posed that threat by joining the totalitarian sensibility with the brute power of the state. But totalitarianism is perhaps even more insidious when it wears a benign and genial face. The Agrarians believed that industrialism, with its promise of the good life, did wear such a face.

Nearly seven decades after Davidson wrote his defense of regionalism, one is struck by his celebration of cultural diversity. By the last decade of the twentieth century, that concept had become a shibboleth of the cultural Left. In practical terms, "diversity" all too often came to mean a racial and ethnic spoils system enforced by the protocols of political correctness. The idea of a "national" or American culture, which had once been championed by political liberals, now came to be seen as a conservative (or perhaps neoconservative) notion. It is interesting, though probably pointless, to wonder whether Davidson would have altered his vocabulary had he lived to see the cause of multiculturalism extolled by black race hustlers, radical feminists, and militant homosexuals.

We now live in an age when a reconstituted remnant of the Old Right (the so-called paleoconservatives) are questioning the rapacity of multinational corporations, which subordinate every other human value to the profit motive. These same paleoconservatives are also challenging a concept of nationalism that requires uniformity at home and imperialism abroad. In performing their cautionary role, however, they find themselves at odds with what passes for the national conservative consensus. (Norman Podhoretz has written that the paleoconservatives have been on the wrong side of all the important cultural issues because they are too heavily influenced by T. S. Eliot and the Agrarians, "who despised capitalism, industrialism, and bourgeois democracy.")[5] In this battle, the Agrarians can provide much intellectual sustenance.

Though we should certainly go back and rediscover Agrarianism for ourselves, its principles have never totally disappeared from conservative thought. Richard M. Weaver, who is considered one of the founding fathers of modern conservatism, was influenced by John Crowe Ransom and Donald Davidson at Vanderbilt and by Cleanth Brooks and Robert Penn Warren at Louisiana State University.

5. Podhoretz, "Letters from Readers," *Commentary* (June 1996): 16.

(Weaver is sometimes called the Saint Paul of the Agrarian movement—too young to have been one of the original twelve but the most effective evangelist of the cause.) M. E. Bradford studied under Davidson at Vanderbilt and did more than any other scholar of our time to demonstrate the relevance of traditional southern values to contemporary political issues. As we have seen, Russell Kirk, who taught us all that there is such an thing as a conservative mind, was a northern admirer of the Agrarians.

Certainly, one of the challenges currently facing any political philosophy is finding a way to achieve harmony in an increasingly pluralistic society. Properly understood, the qualities of diversity and tolerance are more natural to a conservative than to a schematic leftist mind-set. Among his "six canons of conservative thought," Russell Kirk identifies an "affection for the proliferating variety and mystery of traditional life as distinguished from the narrowing uniformity and equalitarianism and utilitarian aims of most radical systems."[6] Decentralization—political, cultural, and economic—is one way of maintaining and enhancing that proliferating variety. As the copperhead poet Robert Frost reminds us, "Good fences make good neighbors."

6. Kirk, *The Conservative Mind: From Burke to Santayana* (Chicago: Regnery, 1953), 7.

Arkansas Traveler

If one were to write a historical novel about Anglo-American poetry during the first third of the twentieth century, the ideal narrator would be someone who was at the important places and knew the important people, while remaining something of a peripheral figure in his own right. Perhaps what is needed is not so much a Marlow or Nick Carraway as a high-modernist version of Charlie Schuyler, the observer whom Gore Vidal uses as a guide through American political history from the age of Washington to that of U. S. Grant (a "progression" that Henry Adams claims disproved Darwin). During his troubled life and protean literary career, John Gould Fletcher came close to being such a figure. For that reason, literary scholars have always had trouble distinguishing Fletcher the poet and critic from Fletcher the paradigm.

A century after his birth, the University of Arkansas Press posed that dilemma for us once again when it began a decadelong project, which included the publication of Lucas Carpenter's critical study of Fletcher, Ben F. Johnson III's biography of the poet, and a selection of Fletcher's correspondence, along with the reissue of four of his most important books. The impulse to promote Fletcher as Arkansas's most distinguished poet is understandable, especially when one considers that his closest rival is probably Maya Angelou. There are two problems with this effort, however. One is the uneven nature of Fletcher's work. The other is summed up nicely in the first sentence of Johnson's biography: "John Gould Fletcher was a difficult individual to know and regard kindly."[1]

---

1. Ben F. Johnson III, *Fierce Solitude: A Life of John Gould Fletcher* (Fayetteville: University of Arkansas Press, 1994), xiii.

If Fletcher was a man whom not even a biographer could love, he was also eventually estranged from friends and family. Although he idolized his distant and forbidding father, Fletcher detested his mother, and he regarded his sisters as little more than sources of needed cash. He began his romance with his first wife, Daisy, at a time when she was married to another man. After persuading her to divorce her husband, he gradually tired of her and her children and freed himself from them with a financial settlement from his annuity. (Cleanth Brooks once told me that his chief reason for disliking Fletcher was the savage way in which he depicted Daisy in his autobiography.) When his literary benefactress, Amy Lowell, died, Fletcher wrote to another sometime friend John Cournos: "I felt curiously relieved— as if something for which I was partially responsible, and did not care to be responsible for, had vanished at last."[2]

By the mid-1930s, Fletcher had alienated all of his fellow Agrarians except for Donald Davidson, and he was pointedly excluded from the second Agrarian manifesto *Who Owns America?* He embarrassed even Davidson by picking a fight with Lambert Davis, editor of the *Virginia Quarterly Review*, over his rejection of an article by Davidson. Fletcher publicly attacked Davis at a literary conference in Baton Rouge in the spring of 1935. (Ford Madox Ford, who also spoke at the conference, recalled "the figure of Mr. John Gould Fletcher from Little Rock, Arkansas, prowling at the back of the audience asking them why they do not lynch me.") Three years later, after Robert Penn Warren had rejected several of his poetry submissions to the *Southern Review*, Fletcher wrote a letter of protest to the magazine's nominal editor, Charles W. Pipkin. "The 'Southern Review,'" he fumed, ". . . is being run in the interests of a clique—engaged in proving that Donne was a better poet than Shakespeare!— and that T. S. Eliot and his imitators are the only modern poets worth reading!" Eliot was another early friend and patron with whom Fletcher had broken.[3]

Almost everything that has been written about Fletcher has focused on him as either imagist or Fugitive-Agrarian, although he was at the center of neither movement. Even his autobiography, which

2. Ibid., 146.
3. See Mark Royden Winchell, *Cleanth Brooks and the Rise of Modern Criticism* (Charlottesville: University Press of Virginia, 1996), 102.

was published in 1937, stops a full decade and a half before his death. Prior to Johnson's biography, the only published record of Fletcher's final years was the fictionalized one in *Johnswood*, a novel by his second wife, Charlie May Simon. With the exception of winning a totally unexpected Pulitzer Prize for his *Selected Poems* in 1938, those final years were ones of obscurity and despair. If Fletcher did not become a more likable figure before his death, he became a more pitiable one. He saw his literary stock plummet even as he became increasingly unable to produce new work. His last book was a moderately interesting history of Arkansas, and much of his waning literary energy was devoted to collecting Ozark folklore. (Several years after his death, his friend and colleague Vance Randolph told an interviewer that Fletcher "was a goddamn fool, but I thought he was a great man somehow.") The relative tranquility of his second marriage was not sufficient to bring rest to his perturbed spirit. In the summer of 1944, he even contemplated divorce because Charlie May was becoming too much of a "modern woman." Fletcher changed his mind, however, when he was stricken with dysentery later that year. "As the doctor bills mounted up," he wrote to a friend, "I discovered that after all, my love for Charlie May amounted to more than I thought."[4]

The last sentence of Fletcher's autobiography reads: "I have not so far lived my life, that I need ever fear death." A dozen years later he was dead by his own hand. In discussing the incidence of mental illness and suicide among southern writers, Bertram Wyatt-Brown notes the influence of cold and domineering fathers. He also cites the "late nineteenth-century transition from a primitive planter culture to a more modern and secular style."[5] If this sense of historical discontinuity was particularly acute in the South, it was hardly unique to the region. Fletcher's friend Van Wyck Brooks had much the same experience as a New Englander. He too went insane and even tried to commit suicide by eating pieces from the broken crystal of his watch. Brooks solved his dilemma by retreating into an arcadian past in a series of best-selling books on antebellum New

4. Johnson, *Fierce Solitude*, 251.
5. Wyatt-Brown, "Creativity and Suffering in a Southern Writer," in *W. J. Cash and the Minds of the South*, edited by Paul D. Escott (Baton Rouge: Louisiana State University Press, 1992), 57.

England. Fletcher's Agrarianism represented a similar impulse with less profitable results.

Fletcher's autobiography (originally published in 1937 under the maudlin and misleading title *Life Is My Song*) can be read as a kind of Agrarian parable. Born in 1886, the son of a former Confederate officer and successful businessman, Fletcher grew up in Little Rock, Arkansas, where he lived in the historic house of Albert Pike, one of the state's most prominent early citizens and its first poet of note. In 1903, he left Little Rock for Harvard, where (in the familiar rite of passage of sensitive youth everywhere) he lost his religious faith but acquired a priestly dedication to art. He read Nietzsche, the French symbolists, and the decadent poets of the British fin de siècle. A year after his father's death in 1906, Fletcher dropped out of Harvard. By 1908, he was in Europe as one of the twentieth century's first American expatriates.

Between 1909 and 1913, Fletcher took the first tentative steps toward realizing his vocation as a professional writer. This included publishing, at his own expense, five volumes of his verse in a single month in 1913. That spring, Fletcher met Ezra Pound in the Closerie des Lilas cafe on the Left Bank of Paris and began an association that would make him one of the six poets most prominently identified with the imagist movement. Although Pound soon abandoned imagism for the even more revolutionary and exotic vorticism, Fletcher remained with the group for the balance of the decade. It was during this period, when Amy Lowell had transformed the new poetry into what Pound derisively called "Amygism," that Fletcher wrote the verse for which he would be best remembered.

By the early 1920s, Fletcher was far removed from both his American and his southern origins, a thoroughly cosmopolitan poet married to a British wife. In 1922, however, while lecturing on American poetry at Oxford, he met the Rhodes scholar William Yandell Elliot. A Vanderbilt graduate and minor Fugitive, Elliot introduced Fletcher to the work of the Nashville poets. The next year, Fletcher contributed two poems to the *Fugitive*. He met with the group while visiting Nashville in 1927 and, in 1930, became one of the twelve contributors to *I'll Take My Stand*. In 1933, Fletcher returned to the United States. Having divorced his wife and taken up residence in Little Rock, he married Charlie May Simon in 1936. He spent the last years of his life at Johnswood, a home he built on a bluff outside of Little Rock, where he wrote poetry about the South and, in 1947, his history of Arkansas.

It is tempting to interpret Fletcher's life as that of a man who found his true vocation and his true happiness only after he rediscovered his regional roots. Unfortunately, the facts suggest otherwise. Fletcher's best poetry was written during his most deracinated years, and the peace he found back home in Arkansas was marred by periodic bouts of depression that eventually led to his suicide in 1950. Given the professional and personal decline that Fletcher experienced during his final years in Arkansas, it is ironic that promotional flyers from the University of Arkansas Press would later describe him as "the prototype of the Southern modernist" and "perhaps the most representative poet of his generation."

One unfamiliar with Fletcher's life and work should begin with his autobiography. It is a very readable narrative, which captures the character and personality of some of the major imagists and Fugitives. Consider, for example, Fletcher's initial assessment of Pound: "Internationally Bohemian in aspect, he yet laid claims to be a great scholar in early Provencal, Italian, and Latin. Keen follower of the *dernier cri* in art and letters, his own poetry was often deliberately archaic to a degree that repelled me."[6]

It is significant that among the Fugitives, Donald Davidson appealed most to Fletcher. Regarding John Crowe Ransom as something of a cold fish and Allen Tate as prematurely world-weary (he was thirteen years Fletcher's junior), the autobiographer responded to Davidson as a kindred spirit. (Davidson returned the favor by writing what is perhaps the best single essay on Fletcher in a posthumous tribute published in *Poetry* magazine.) Davidson "was more interested in the South on the emotional side than on the intellectual," Fletcher discovered, "and for this reason, my heart warmed to him. He was capable of an unstudied frankness in regard to his ideals and beliefs, on many occasions, where Ransom would have employed all his resources of mental reserve; and for just this reason, Davidson was, like myself, far more discontented and unhappy at bottom than Ransom."[7]

6. Fletcher, *The Autobiography of John Gould Fletcher* (1937; reprint, Fayetteville: University of Arkansas Press, 1988), 63.

7. Ibid., 348–49.

The only major character in the autobiography about whom Fletcher seems to lack insight is himself. In his account of his personal and professional life, there is a pervasive air of defensiveness and self-pity. No doubt his first wife, Daisy Arbuthnot, made him miserable; however, he might have expected as much when he began an affair with a married woman whose husband seemed all too eager to be rid of her. Although there is comparatively little in the book about Fletcher's happy second marriage, we do know that Charlie May Simon was also married when Fletcher met her. Whether his experience with Daisy gave him pause about launching this new relationship, Fletcher does not tell us.

As balanced as he is in his presentation of Ezra Pound and Amy Lowell, Fletcher believes that both stole discoveries that were rightly his (in Pound's case the symbolist poets, in Lowell's polyphonic prose). Whether his own lack of assertiveness may have led to his being too easily wronged is a question that seems never to have occurred to Fletcher. Moreover, he is far too quick to blame his lack of recognition on the crass materialism of the age. Facing essentially the same or worse odds, quite a few of his contemporaries managed to survive and even flourish. (One thinks of T. S. Eliot enduring the drudgery of Lloyd's, a bad marriage, and a mental breakdown without resorting to the Miniver Cheevy dodge.) Fletcher's latter-day Agrarianism might have been for him what medievalism was for Henry Adams—a way of dropping out of a world inhospitable to his grandiose ambitions.

The childhood experience that seems to have had the most influence in shaping Fletcher's social views was his father's unsuccessful race for governor of Arkansas in 1901. As a youth of fifteen, Fletcher saw his father, then seventy, denounced as a tool of the special interests, humiliated on the stump, and finally driven out of public life. (Five years later, he was dead.) The winning candidate—named, of all things, Jeff Davis—proved to be a corrupt public official as well as a demagogic campaigner. At the dawn of the twentieth century, it was clear to Fletcher that the New South did not belong to the old aristocracy from which he sprang any more than the emerging New England belonged to the grandson of John Quincy Adams.

To his credit, very little of Fletcher's bitterness comes through in the history of Arkansas he published three years before his death. Although it offers little to the scholar, general readers can be thankful that this lively book is once again available. (The blurb writer might call it "a panorama of Razorback history from Hernando de Soto to J. William Fulbright.") What is most remarkable is that Fletcher did not use this project simply to write a Bourbon tract. One finds him surprisingly sympathetic to persons not of his social class. For example, when describing the plight of the Cherokee Indians on the Trail of Tears, he notes how one white commentator was amazed that the Indians stole "articles of the utmost uselessness . . . from the yards of private residences." To this, Fletcher replies: "Considering that these Indians once had titles to very much more than 'articles of the utmost uselessness,' guaranteed them by the United States—titles now completely broken—the only wonder is that they did not steal the entire town."[8]

When observing poor whites in the Ozarks, Fletcher notes, with perhaps unintended humor: "They do not, unless they are ambitious or notoriously 'trifling,' change their places of abode with great readiness; and this has led to an undoubted amount of interbreeding. Whether this fact is responsible for the not infrequent cases of idiocy to be found, is a question I must leave to biologists." And later in the same paragraph: "It is to be feared that the automobile, which has helped to put them in closer touch with the towns, has also helped to spread venereal disease."[9]

On a more somber note, Fletcher recounts the story of Rubert Byler, an illiterate Ozarker so isolated from civilization that he was uncertain of his own age. When Rubert succeeded in passing a bad check, the sheriff descended on his remote home to arrest him. After the sheriff had placed the handcuffs on him, Rubert somehow wrested the sheriff's gun away and shot him. For the next two months, Rubert and his wife disappeared into the backwoods, surviving on "wild persimmons and whatever they could raid from infrequent corn patches," until they finally gave themselves up. Pondering their condition, Fletcher muses: "Given another environment, who knows where the mother wit that kept Rubert and his wife alive and away from pursuit for two months might not have led? But Rubert was the prisoner of his environment, as are most of the Ozark people today.

8. Fletcher, *Arkansas*, (1947; reprint, Fayetteville: University of Arkansas Press, 1989), 71.
9. Ibid., 264.

They are held captive by the great stillness of the dense wooded hollows, the thunderstorms and tornadoes, the bad roads, the poor schools, the pitifulness of their own living."[10]

Of course, the claims that Lucas Carpenter and the publicists of the University of Arkansas Press make on behalf of Fletcher's literary stature have little to do with his work as a regional historian or his erratic contributions to the Agrarian movement. It is as a southern modernist that we are asked to judge Fletcher. Certainly, the only poet to have been involved with the imagist, Fugitive, and Agrarian movements is uniquely both southern and modern. But, Carpenter argues, the variety of his poetic influences and associations has probably been more a hindrance than an aid to Fletcher's proper recognition. Rather than seeing him as a kind of literary chameleon who never found his proper identity, we should regard Fletcher as, first and last, a southern poet—one who helped define southern modernism and launch the Southern Renascence a decade before the *Fugitive* appeared on the scene.

There are several problems with Carpenter's thesis. To begin with, his identification of Fletcher as an early southern modernist, who was actually less cosmopolitan than he appeared to be, is based on little more than the importance of memory and an aversion to city life in Fletcher's early quasi-symbolist and protoimagist poetry. Although these themes can be found in most modern southern literature, they are also present in the work of nonsoutherners. Except for a few incidental regional references, Fletcher's early verse could have been written by a New Englander. His technique was far different from that of the local colorists who dominated southern poetry at the time. And, unlike the Fugitives, he never expressed a conscious intention to turn southern verse away from the magnolia-and-moonlight tradition. Until discovering the Fugitives, he did not seem to regard himself as a particularly southern (or even American) poet.

What is more to the point, the most distinctive qualities of Fletcher's poetry, both before and *after* his alliance with the Fugitive-Agrarians, are far different from those we associate with southern modernism. Under the leadership of John Crowe Ransom, the Fugitives attempted to recover the tradition of seventeenth-century

10. Ibid., 277.

metaphysical poetry. (Here they were following Eliot's lead.) Like the imagists, they were reacting against the emotionalism and abstractions of romanticism. Where they broke with the imagists was in their insistence on including intellectual and moral values in poetry. In *The World's Body* (1938), Ransom argues that the imagists' aversion to intellect and morality resulted in a purely "physical poetry," which was far removed from the significant concerns of human life. The poetry Ransom preferred was characterized by irony, wit, paradox, and fully developed metaphor. If one considers the verse actually written by both the Fugitives and the generations of younger poets (not all southern born) who came under Ransom's influence, it is clear that the metaphysical sensibility did represent the main current of southern modernism for the balance of Fletcher's life.

Lucas Carpenter may prefer to see Fletcher's career as a seamless web of southern modernism, but Fletcher himself clearly did not. At least by August 1927, when he published "Two Elements in Poetry" in the *Saturday Review of Literature*, Fletcher was openly repudiating imagism and taking his stand with the Fugitives. Speaking in the first-person plural, he states: "We are anti-romantic, because we do not believe that our deepest feelings are incommunicable, or that beauty is more than truth, or that to be incoherent is to be artistic, or that perfection is attainable by any other path than by the path of a persistent grappling with reality." Later in the same essay, he argues that "the movement which a few poets in America and England have fostered of a return to intellectualism, should . . . be encouraged, for to make poetry more metaphysical in subject-matter as well as more exact in concrete detail, is to make it more the arbiter, not of taste, but of destiny." Unfortunately, this important critical document, which William Pratt regards as the best single comparison of the imagist and Fugitive schools, is not included in Lucas Carpenter's otherwise invaluable edition of Fletcher's *Selected Essays*.[11]

There was little in Fletcher's early career to foreshadow his wholehearted embrace of Fugitive poetics. Although his verse sequence "Ghosts of an Old House" (published in 1916) was inspired by a brief visit to Little Rock, the technique is imagistic (or as close to imagistic as Fletcher would ever get). It is true that his most famous poem

---

11. Fletcher, "Two Elements in Poetry," *Saturday Review of Literature* (August 27, 1927): 65–66.

develops a simile (between trees and jade elephants), but the effect is less paradoxical and ironic than decorative and emotional.

Apparently, Fletcher saw the Fugitive movement as representing a new direction not only for poetry in general but also for his own vocation in particular. One of the ironies of Fletcher's contradictory career is that this did not prove to be the case. As sincere as his intellectual adherence to Fugitive dogma may have been, his poetic sensibility was finally more romantic than modernist. Despite being associated with the two most important schools of modern poetry, Fletcher was at home in neither. More orthodox imagists (Richard Aldington, Hilda Doolittle, and even Pound himself) understood imagism as implying a specific doctrine of the *image*—namely, a hard visual impression rendered in an instantaneous moment. In contrast, Fletcher exploited the musical devices of poetry (assonance, consonance, alliteration, and the like) to paint a suggestive picture. (As he notes in "The Impulse of Poetry," the object of poetic art is to use words to approximate both music and painting.) During his Fugitive-Agrarian years, Fletcher's technique did not become more metaphysical. Rather, as William Pratt notes, it "tended to devolve into diffusion and verbosity."[12]

From his return to Little Rock in the mid-1930s until his suicide in 1950, Fletcher's romantic impulses caused him to identify himself ever more passionately with the Agrarian myth of the South—the society that supposedly existed before his father's humiliation at the hands of Arkansas's Jeff Davis. (It is no accident that he found Donald Davidson to be the Fugitive most like himself.) Consequently, Fletcher's poetry dealing with the South is more aptly characterized as Agrarian than Fugitive. This distinction becomes clear if one compares Fletcher's "Elegy in a Civil War Cemetery" with Tate's "Ode to the Confederate Dead." Both poems are set in a Confederate graveyard in the fall, both describe the weathered tombstones and the autumn leaves ("scattered" in Fletcher's version, "splayed" in Tate's), and both lament the indifference of the modern southerner to the valor of his forebears. Tate, however, transforms these materials into

---

12. Pratt, "John Gould Fletcher: Imagist Poet, Fugitive and Agrarian Critic," in *The Vanderbilt Tradition: Essays in Honor of Thomas Daniel Young*, edited by Mark Royden Winchell (Baton Rouge: Louisiana State University Press, 1991), 66.

a meditation on solipsism as the curse of modern man. His image of the serpent in the mulberry bush is far richer and far more ominous than Fletcher's mocking bird in the magnolia boughs. And there is nothing in Fletcher's poem to compare with Tate's jaguar leaping at his own reflection in the jungle pool. That image, which was meant to represent modern man in general, seems—in retrospect—prophetically relevant to Fletcher, who drowned himself in a cattle pond on his farm.

Except for reissuing *Arkansas*, the Fletcher project has done nothing to reacquaint us with the Agrarian social critic. (In the aftermath of the cold war, it would be interesting to judge the prescience of Fletcher's comments about the United States and Russia in *The Two Frontiers* [1930].) With Carpenter's edition of Fletcher's *Selected Essays*, however, most of the important commentary of the Fugitive literary critic is between hard covers for the first time. As Pratt has pointed out, Fletcher was not a New Critic in the sense of being a close reader of individual texts. Instead, he was a remarkably lucid and perceptive theoretician. In "The Impulse of Poetry," "Herald of Imagism," and several lesser-known pieces, Fletcher clarifies difficult issues without minimizing their complexities. It is as a critic that he has been most slighted.

In his affectionate tribute to the recently deceased Fletcher, Donald Davidson compared his friend to Faulkner's Sartoris family. (Fletcher's father certainly resembled Colonel Sartoris.) Like the doomed aristocrats of Yoknapatawpha, Fletcher "was born into a world that no longer offered a good field for the exercise of . . . gallantry; but he did not, like the Sartorises of William Faulkner's novels, waste his strength in jousting in lists where victory would be a worse calamity than defeat. He gave his strength to the cause of art and to those who were enlisted in that cause."[13]

As true as this may be, one cannot help thinking that there is an even closer resemblance between Fletcher and Quentin Compson. Both left their provincial homes for Harvard. Both were haunted by the myth of a South that was gone, that may never have existed as they imagined it to have been. Both were plagued by insanity, and both took their own lives by drowning. Because Fletcher was a real

---

13. Davidson, *Still Rebels, Still Yankees, and Other Essays*, (1957; reprint, Baton Rouge: Louisiana State University Press, 1972), 40.

person, we will never know as much about him as we do about Quentin Compson or any fictional character. However, we can come a step closer to understanding both his life and his art if we see John Gould Fletcher as a southerner undone by modernity. In this respect, he may well have been the representative southern modernist.

⚛ 3 ⚛

Renaissance Man

The study of literary influence is fraught with pitfalls. One can follow the path of what Gore Vidal calls the "scholar-squirrel" and get caught up in the cataloging of adventitious parallels and pointless verbal echoes, or one can indulge in the sort of cryptic psychocriticism popularized by Harold Bloom. The problem becomes even more acute when dealing with William Shakespeare, because one could argue that within the past four centuries those English-speaking writers who have *not* been influenced by the venerable bard are in the minority. With Robert Penn Warren, however, the study of Shakespeare's influence is not only useful but also virtually indispensable.

When we think of Warren, we are apt to think of the author of *All the King's Men*, of one of the most important American poets of the twentieth century, of the editor, textbook author, and influential literary critic. But Warren also spent the bulk of his adult life as an academic. And from his early days as a Rhodes scholar at Oxford to his last days as a professor at Yale, his primary teaching interest was in the literature of the English Renaissance. In an interview he gave in 1978, Warren maintained that the most satisfying courses he had ever given were seminars in "Elizabethan literature, Renaissance, and Shakespeare." Elsewhere, he has acknowledged Shakespeare as the single greatest influence on his writing.[1]

To appreciate the degree to which Warren was devoted to Shakespeare, one need only consider his reaction when his old mentor,

---

1. Floyd C. Watkins and John T. Hiers, eds., *Robert Penn Warren Talking: Interviews, 1950–1978* (New York: Random House, 1980), 267; and Charles H. Bohner, *Robert Penn Warren* (New York: Twayne, 1964), 160.

John Crowe Ransom, submitted his essay "Shakespeare at Sonnets" to Warren and his coeditor, Cleanth Brooks, at the *Southern Review* on October 18, 1937. Because this was to be the final selection in a volume called *The World's Body*, which Scribner's intended to publish in the spring of 1938, Ransom hoped that his essay could find a place in the winter number of the review. As a frequent contributor to the magazine and a friend of its editors, Ransom probably expected a routine acceptance. Thus, the reaction he got from his former students must have been quite a shock.

Because that reaction has not been preserved, we do not know precisely what Warren and Brooks had to say about Ransom's treatment of Shakespeare. We do know, however, that Ransom was exercised enough about their letter to enclose it with one he sent to Allen Tate on November 4, 1937. Here he observes: "The boys deal pretty pedantically with my poor paper, you will see. . . . I wrote them a pretty warm letter but after thinking over it withheld it and wrote another. I also revised the thing, adding a bit, taking account of points of theirs which seemed to me worth anything, generally improving it; I wanted to do this anyway." Ransom concludes that he "stepped on their toes a little come to think about it. For Red [Warren] is a Shakespearean and would not like my irresponsible knocks for the comfort of the Philistines."[2]

In this particular instance, Shakespeare (particularly as a writer of sonnets) becomes a touchstone for measuring the widening gulf between Ransom's critical sensibility and that of Brooks and Warren. Although it is possible to speak of generational conflicts and to interpret the whole matter in Freudian terms, we are perhaps on safer ground simply to consider the ideas involved. As one of the seminal forces in southern modernism, Ransom represented a radical turning away from the romanticism of nineteenth-century southern letters (the Fugitive fleeing from the high-caste Brahmins of the Old South). Part of that romanticism was a kind of bardolatry. Although he greatly admired Shakespeare as a dramatist, Ransom was more than capable of finding fault with the construction of his sonnets. To those schooled in the old literary pieties, such an observation was virtual sacrilege. It was a measure of Ransom's iconoclasm that he stated his position without fear or favor.

2. Thomas Daniel Young and George Core, eds., *Selected Letters of John Crowe Ransom* (Baton Rouge: Louisiana State University Press, 1985), 233–34.

Ransom found fault with Shakespeare's minor poetry for its tendency to accumulate a series of undeveloped associations rather than pursue the implications of a single metaphor. Ransom is quick to point out, however, that the antimetaphysical tendency of Shakespeare's verse is not a flaw when that verse is confined to the context of drama. Analyzed as a metaphysical poem, for example, Macbeth's "To-morrow, and tomorrow, and to-morrow" speech is an incoherent hodge-podge of mixed and imprecise metaphors. Dramatically, however, it possesses undeniable power. Thus, Ransom concludes that "Shakespeare could put a character into a situation that called for a desperate speech, and give him one. But he could not seat his character at the table to compose a finished poem, and then let him stand up and deliver it."[3]

Brooks and Warren shared Ransom's disdain for fuzzy romanticism and for knee-jerk bard worship. They too argued for the place of intellect in poetry. And they probably agreed with Ben Jonson that Shakespeare should have blotted many more lines than he did. Nevertheless, they were not willing to give logic the sort of primacy that Ransom insisted upon. For them, what was all important was not the poem's paraphrasable prose content but its psychological coherence. Because they saw *all poems* as minidramas, they were more willing than Ransom to accept illogic in poetry *as long as it was contextually appropriate.* Brooks and Warren extended to lyric poetry the sort of indulgence Ransom showed toward Macbeth's speech. Moreover, in their critical writing, they were constantly referring to passages in Shakespeare's plays as *poems.* This was true not only of Brooks's famous essay on *Macbeth* in *The Well-Wrought Urn* but also of the discussion of a crucial speech from act 5, scene 2 of *Antony and Cleopatra* in Brooks and Warren's classic textbook anthology *Understanding Poetry.*

The critics begin by reminding their reader of the circumstances in which the speech is delivered. With Antony recently dead, Cleopatra is now at the mercy of the conquering Octavius. As Octavius's emissary Dolabella seeks to arrange the terms of Cleopatra's surrender, the Egyptian queen remembers the days of her former happiness with Antony. "I dreamed there was an Emperor Antony," she begins, and her entire speech is couched in dream imagery that

3. Ibid., 302.

paints a picture of Antony "in shocking contrast to what any human being might be."

Brooks and Warren continue:

> Cleopatra starts with a comparison so extreme as to break any ordinary logic—Antony's face as the very heavens, with eyes like sun and moon lighting the little earth. But the violation of logic is an index to the force of feeling that now breaks out. We feel a dramatic grounding for the violence and elevation of the utterance—with its sense of dreamlike release and apocalyptic grandeur—which is not like the language of, say, the Book of Revelations, another attempt to utter the unutterable.

In the second section of her speech, Cleopatra appears to be attempting a systematic description of Antony. But, as Brooks and Warren point out, "this systematic description breaks into a series of images which have no consistent relation to the main image with which the passage begins."[4] Far from finding this lack of systematic coherence to be a flaw, the critics see it as yet another index of the dramatic urgency of the situation.

The definition of *poetry* with which Brooks and Warren operate is much broader and more inclusive than any that Ransom would comfortably allow. Ransom believed that feeling, unless it were rigorously shaped by logic, had no proper place in poetry. Brooks and Warren were much more willing to let feeling itself serve as a shaping agent. For this reason, they defended Shakespeare's use of mixed metaphor as both dramatically and *poetically* appropriate to Cleopatra's speech. Indeed, consistent development of imagery and metaphor would seem—in this context—sterile, artificial, and psychologically implausible. Cleopatra's speech is quite properly a poetry of discontinuity. As even Ransom would probably concede, Shakespeare did not seek to write metaphysical verse and fail. Rather, he attempted and achieved totally different, but equally valid, poetic ends.

Warren's views on the nature of poetry are most fully articulated in his essay "Pure and Impure Poetry," first published in 1942. Although

---

4. Brooks and Warren, *Understanding Poetry: An Anthology for College Students*, 3d ed. (New York: Holt, Rinehart, and Winston, 1960), 291.

we cannot be certain why he chose this particular title, we do know that the distinction between dramatic poetry and lyric, or "pure," poetry had been made by Ransom five years earlier in "Shakespeare at Sonnets." In his essay, Warren takes an approach toward poetic theory that is much more eclectic than Ransom's and even cautions against the limitations of critical strategies and labels. "Poetry wants to be pure, but poems do not," he begins. "At least most of them do not want to be too pure. . . . They mar themselves with cacophonies, jagged rhythms, ugly words and ugly thoughts, colloquialisms, clichés, sterile technical terms, headwork and argument, self-contradictions, clevernesses, irony, realism—all things which call us back to the world of prose and imperfection."[5]

Warren illustrates his point by citing an example that only appears to be pure and lyrical—the balcony scene in *Romeo and Juliet*. Here we seem to have the spiritualized essence of true love, unsoiled by the dross of everyday life. But Warren reminds us that "beyond the garden wall strolls Mercutio . . . , who is always aware that nature has other names as well as the names that pure poets and pure lovers put upon her." If the presence of such a bawdy wit as Mercutio's beyond the garden walls were not harmful enough to the "purity" of this scene, we find prosaic elements introduced within the garden itself. When Romeo swears his love by the moon, Juliet replies, "O! swear not by the moon, the inconstant moon, / That monthly changes her circled orb." In effect, she challenges Romeo's "pure poem" by questioning the aptness of his metaphor, thus injecting "the impurity of an intellectual style" into the scene. Warren also notes that, within the house, we have Juliet's nurse, "the voice of expediency, of half-measures, of the view that circumstances alter cases—the voice of prose and imperfection."[6]

Warren concludes that the garden scene would not have been more effective had Mercutio and the nurse been further removed or had Juliet been more sympathetic to her lover's choice of metaphor. "The effect might even be more vulnerable poetically if the impurities were purged away. Mercutio, the lady, and the nurse are critics of the lover, who believe in pure poems, but perhaps they are necessary. Perhaps the lover can be accepted only in their context. . . . The

5. Warren, *New and Selected Essays* (New York: Random House, 1989), 4–5.
6. Ibid., 7.

poetry arises from a recalcitrant and contradictory context; and finally involves that context."[7]

The most extensive critical observations that Warren has written about Shakespeare are—technically speaking—not his at all but those of Slim Sarrett, a character in his second novel, *At Heaven's Gate* (1943). Obviously, we cannot take these observations at face value: Sarrett is a character in a novel, and one who is far from embodying a moral norm. It seems significant, however, that Warren has inserted in almost the exact middle of his novel nearly three pages of fairly sophisticated Shakespearean criticism. At the very least, Sarrett's insights can help us better understand the novel in which they are contained, as well as some of the themes most often used in Warren's other fictional and poetic narratives.

To begin with, Sarrett argues that one ought not to make facile assumptions about Shakespeare's moral and philosophical views based solely on the action of his plays. All intelligent critics are wary about accepting the statements made in a drama as "content-absolutes." Such critics rightly note that "because Lear says so-and-so, I am not to infer that Shakespeare meant so-and-so; we must remember that Lear is a character in a play." Unfortunately, those same critics do frequently assume that character and plot are content-absolutes. They infer "from what happens to Richard III that Shakespeare believed in and depicted a universe operating according to a moral order." But once those same critics look broader and deeper, they see that Shakespeare's supposed moral order is not always consistent: "The [simplistic] moral critic forgets, or blandly neglects, the tissue of negative instances surrounding the central character— good men brought to ruin, etc.—ah, where are the pretty little princes in the Tower? Although Shakespeare may never have painted vice as prosperous . . . , he did something far more reprehensible; he painted virtue brought to misery."[8]

The problem with moral critics is not so much that they misread Shakespeare's plays, Sarrett argues, but that they misdirect the focus of their reading. For Shakespeare, "the tortured residuum of the Christian tradition . . . is simply part of the stuff available—like Plutarch or Holinshed or Marlowe's mighty line or the condition of language."

7. Ibid.
8. Warren, *At Heaven's Gate* (New York: Harcourt, Brace, 1943), 194.

Such elements, in other words, are the materials with which Shakespeare worked, but they are not themselves the end product of that work. What is of supreme importance to Shakespeare's tragedy is the central theme to which all of the constituent elements of the tragedy are subservient: the necessity for self-knowledge. According to Sarrett: "The tragic flaw in the Shakespearean hero is a defect in self-knowledge. . . . Bacon wrote: Knowledge is power. Bacon was thinking of knowledge of the mechanisms of the external world. Shakespeare wrote: Self-knowledge is power. Shakespeare was thinking of the mechanisms of the spirit, to which the mechanisms of the external world, including other persons, are instruments." Although Shakespeare was interested in the success that comes with self-knowledge, "his tragedy is concerned with failure. . . . The successful man . . . offers only the smooth surface, like an egg. In so far as he is truly successful, he has no story. He is pure. But poetry is concerned with failure, distortion, imbalance—with impurity. And poetry itself is impurity."[9]

If we consider the entire context of Warren's novel, we can see that his characters—like Shakespeare's—almost all suffer from deficient self-knowledge. Although such a condition is common to much of humanity and is not a peculiarly Shakespearean concern, Warren's literary preoccupation with the theme of self-knowledge can be traced—at least in part—to his study of Shakespeare. (Sarrett's commentary is derived practically verbatim from the lectures on Shakespeare that Warren's fellow Fugitive poet Walter Clyde Curry delivered at Vanderbilt.)[10] One of the crowning ironies of Warren's novel is the fact that Slim Sarrett can deliver such a perceptive discourse on self-knowledge in Shakespeare yet fail to realize that he, too, is living a lie. Although able to unmask and analyze his friends with an almost voyeuristic detachment, he is himself eventually revealed as a bisexual poseur. He has manufactured a romantic past, in which his father is a riverboat captain and his mother a prostitute rather than the bland middle-class folk they actually are, and has disguised his sexual ambivalence by taking Sue Murdoch as his mistress and devoting himself to boxing.

Although *At Heaven's Gate* is more influenced by Dante than by

---

9. Ibid., 195, 196.
10. L. Hugh Moore Jr., *Robert Penn Warren and History* (The Hague: Mouton, 1970), 38–39.

Shakespeare, we can find a few affinities with the bard's work that go beyond anything suggested in the critical musings of Slim Sarrett.[11] To begin with, the novel's principal female character, Sue Murdoch, plays Cordelia in an amateur production of *King Lear.* Despite being a more-than-competent actress, Sue is incapable of analyzing the character she portrays. Her relationship with her own father, Bogan Murdoch, is a vulgarization of the more purely tragic bond of Lear and Cordelia. Sue banishes herself from her doting father more in petulant rebellion than in moral steadfastness. And Bogan, who lacks any of Lear's virtues, resembles Shakespeare's king only in being a socially prominent man brought to ruin. If we continue to search *At Heaven's Gate* for perverse parodies of Shakespeare, we might find a suggestion of the story of Romeo and Juliet in Sue Murdoch's romance with Jason Sweetwater, the labor leader who challenges Bogan Murdoch's business empire. Finally, in the wisecracking choric figure of Duckfoot Blake—who enjoys privileged status as a sort of court jester in Murdoch's firm—one could even see an updated version of the Shakespearean fool. If the other characters in Warren's novel demonstrate the limits of Baconian knowledge and power, Blake rises above their follies with a hard-boiled cynicism that disdains the "mechanisms of the external world."

True to his critical principles, Warren has written poetry that frequently mars itself with cacophonies, jagged rhythms, colloquialisms, irony, realism, and other things that call us back to the world of prose and imperfection. As Louis D. Rubin Jr. has noted, Warren's imagination eschews the lapidary smoothness for which Ransom and Tate so assiduously strived.[12] This is not because of careless craftsmanship so much as conscious intention. A living and inclusive poetry is, by definition, impure. Accordingly, some of Warren's most representative early verse is characterized by the sort of emotional extravagance and violent imagery that Ransom found so objectionable in Shakespeare.

11. In his introduction to the Modern Library edition of *All the King's Men*, Warren notes that all the major characters in *At Heaven's Gate*, like those in the seventh circle of Dante's Hell, are violators of nature. See Robert H. Chambers, ed., *Twentieth-Century Interpretations of "All the King's Men"* (Englewood Cliffs, NJ: Prentice-Hall, 1977), 95.

12. Rubin, *The Wary Fugitives: Four Poets and the South* (Baton Rouge: Louisiana State University Press, 1978), 357.

Essentially, Ransom possessed a classical temperament. For him, order, regularity, logic, and symmetry were of primary importance. Warren, however, represents a romantic strain of modernism—one that embraces discontinuity, individuality, psychology, and distortion. Although this fact alone is not enough to demonstrate that Shakespeare significantly influenced Warren's poetry, more is involved than the truism that Shakespeare was the literary godfather of romanticism and that every quasi-romantic writer to come along since has somehow worked in his shadow. The distinctively *Shakespearean* imprint on Warren's verse is unmistakable in the years of his apprenticeship.

The poetry Warren wrote during the first twenty years of his career is relatively closed and formal in structure and often suggests Elizabethan models. (After these first two decades, there is an eleven-year gap, from 1943 to 1954, followed by the more open and personal verse of Warren's later years.) In a single volume from that early period, *Eleven Poems on the Same Theme* (1942), the influence of Shakespeare is most noticeable. One of the eleven poems, "Terror," depicts the spiritually catatonic modern man, whose inability to formulate "an adequate definition of terror" causes him to seek ever more lurid dangers and thrills. Such an individual is unable to "heed the criminal king, who paints the air / With discoursed madness and protruding eye." This "criminal king" is Macbeth, and modern man's inability to share his sense of terror reflects the banality of our present age.[13] Like T. S. Eliot and other reactionary modernists, Warren uses analogies from both our historical and our literary past to shed light on the here and now.

Elsewhere in *Eleven Poems* we find "Revelation," a psychologically acute rendering of a boy's traumatic sense of guilt at having spoken harshly to his mother. In the course of that poem, the boy imagines all of nature to be profoundly altered by his deed:

> When Sulla smote and Rome was racked, Augustine
> Recalled how Nature, shuddering, tore her gown,

13. Warren, *Selected Poems, 1923–1975* (New York: Random House, 1976), 284. The allusion to *Macbeth* was pointed out to me by Victor H. Strandberg in personal correspondence dated December 7, 1980. I am indebted to Professor Strandberg for his insights concerning Shakespeare's influence on Warren's poetry.

And kind changed kind, and blunt herbivorous tooth dripped
   blood;
At Duncan's death, at Dunsinane, chimneys blew down.

But since his mother "was kinder than ever Rome / Dearer than Duncan," the cosmic ramifications of this lad's sin are correspondingly more horrible.[14] Because of the obviously ironic tone of this poem, Warren's use of Shakespeare here is essentially mock-heroic.

Finally, we come to "Love's Parable"—a rich, bold metaphysical poem in which quite a few readers have seen traces of Shakespeare's influence. John L. Stewart, for example, begins by noting some parallels between Warren's poetic strategies and those of John Donne but then goes on to say:

> The diction and the other images show that Shakespeare, particularly through his sonnets, was a more important agent in Warren's imagination. The poem could have been written only by one who had steeped himself in Shakespeare's works. The strength of Warren's affinity for that work is suggested by the images of morbid conditions of the flesh. . . . Like Shakespeare, Warren was obsessed with the canker rotting the substance beneath the winsome surface, and henceforth he used some form of that metaphor many times in his works to suggest a secret evil within the most innocent seeming occasion.[15]

In the ten stanzas of this poem, Warren speaks of the failure of a love affair, but instead of giving us the mimetic particulars of the situation, he piles one elaborate simile on top of another. Although some of these similes remind one of Donne, Warren's refusal to follow any of them through in an extended and systematic way is more characteristic of Shakespeare. At various points in the poem, the relationship of the lovers is compared to that of a conquered people and a benevolent despot, two suns, and iron and a magnet, whereas their misfortune calls to mind the fate of "blockhead masons" who tear down ancient monuments to build their hovels, a "wastrel bankrupt," victims of an infectious disease, and a "pest-bit whore."

14. Ibid., 301.
15. Stewart, *The Burden of Time: The Fugitives and Agrarians* (Princeton, NJ: Princeton University Press, 1965), 465–66.

As Stewart has indicated, Warren's fondness for images of rotting flesh is also vintage Shakespeare. Consider, for example, the following lines:

> But we have seen the fungus eyes
> Of misery spore in the night,
> And marked, of friends, the malices
> That stain, like smoke, the day's fond light,
> And marked how ripe injustice flows,
> How ulcerous, how acid, then
> How flesh on the sounder grows
> Till rot engross the estate of men;
>
> And marked within, the inward sore
> Of self that cankers at the bone.[16]

During the eleven-year period in which he published no short poetry, Warren produced two novels, two volumes of short stories, and—in 1953—*Brother to Dragons*, a book-length "tale in verse and voices." Regarded by some critics as his poetic masterpiece, *Brother to Dragons* clearly marks a departure from the Fugitive verse of Warren's early career. Moreover, from both a thematic and a technical standpoint, it reveals aspects of Shakespearean influence found nowhere else in Warren's poetry. The story Warren tells is based loosely on a grotesque incident in the lives of Thomas Jefferson's nephews Lilburn and Isham Lewis. "On the night of December 15, 1811," Warren explains in his foreword, "—the night when the New Madrid earthquake first struck the Mississippi Valley—Lilburn, with the assistance of Isham and in the presence of his Negroes, butchered a slave named George, whose offense had been to break a pitcher prized by [Lilburn's dead mother, Lucy Jefferson Lewis]."[17] Because there is no historical record of Jefferson's reaction to his nephews' brutality, Warren has created an imaginative one in a poetic dialogue, which transpires at "No place" and in "Any time."

In a discussion of the use of history in Warren's fiction, L. Hugh Moore Jr. makes an observation equally germane to *Brother to Dra-*

16. Warren, *Selected Poems, 1923–1975*, 311–12.
17. Warren, *Brother to Dragons: A Tale in Verse and Voices* (New York: Random House, 1953), ix.

gons. "Just as a comparison of Shakespeare's plays with their sources in Holinshed and elsewhere reveals the magnitude of his imagination," Moore points out, "a comparison of Warren's novels with their sources merely makes one realize the greatness of his achievement." Like Shakespeare, Warren is interested less in historical facts than in the timeless truth derived from a study of the past.

To be sure, countless writers other than Warren and Shakespeare have reconstituted historical events for paradigmatic purposes. Moreover, the theme of self-knowledge, which is central to *Brother to Dragons* and which Warren has identified as the key motif in Shakespeare's plays, is a nearly universal concern of the literary artist. Nor can one claim even that the nexus between historical drama and domestic tragedy is unique to Warren and Shakespeare. Rather, what is crucial here is the *form* in which Warren has cast his poetic narrative. Strictly speaking, *Brother to Dragons* is not a drama; however, as a dialogue among sharply defined characters, it possesses dramatic qualities. In addition, that "dialogue" is only in part a conversation; its extended speeches resemble nothing so much as the introspective reflections found in Shakespeare's soliloquies. Finally, the poetry itself is written in blank verse, in which Randall Jarrell has found "conscious echoes of Shakespeare."[18]

When we consider the poetry that Warren wrote during the last three decades of his life, we do not find the accumulation of undeveloped similes and the archaic diction of "Love's Parable" or the blank-verse drama of *Brother to Dragons.*[19] We find instead other influences and the emergence of an increasingly distinctive poetic voice. Still, it is clear that during the long years of his apprenticeship,

18. Moore, *Warren and History,* 44; Jarrell, "On the Underside of the Stone," *New York Times Book Review,* August 23, 1953, 8. The prominence of domestic tragedy in Shakespeare's history plays is discussed at length in John Wilder, *The Lost Garden* (Totowa, NJ: Rowman, 1978).

19. There have been numerous theatrical productions of Warren's verse dialogue, including a 1955 dramatic reading for the BBC (which Warren had no part in), a staging at Harvard, a Broadway production canceled on opening day, reworkings in Seattle and at the American Place Theater in New York, and two productions directed by Adrian Hall in Providence in 1968 and 1973. See Margaret Mills Harper, "Versions of History and *Brother to Dragons,*" in *Brother to Dragons: A Discussion,* edited by James A. Grimshaw Jr. (Baton Rouge: Louisiana State University Press, 1983), 230. Finally, in 1976, Warren's text of *Brother to Dragons: A Play in Two Acts* was published in the *Georgia Review.*

Warren's poetry owed much to the fact that it was indeed written by a "great Shakespearean."

Although Warren's poetry eventually outpaced his fiction, he is still best known to the general public as the author of *All the King's Men* (1946). One of the great novels of American literature, this book tells the story of Jack Burden, a young newspaper reporter who undergoes a profound spiritual transformation while witnessing the rise and fall of a complex, demagogic politician named Willie Stark. In addition to his obvious and much discussed resemblance to Louisiana's legendary Huey P. Long, Stark calls to mind recognizable Elizabethan antecedents. To begin with, *All the King's Men* was not originally a novel at all but a verse play called *Proud Flesh*. In speaking of his initial conception of this work, Warren invokes Shakespeare's *Julius Caesar* by referring to the assassin of his politician as a "self-appointed Brutus." Elsewhere, he notes that "Huey Long and Julius Caesar both got killed in the capitol" and that he himself was teaching Shakespeare in Louisiana at the time of Long's death.[20] There is even a hint of Spenser in the fact that the character in *Proud Flesh* who would later become Willie Stark was named Willie "Talos," after the iron groom in the *Faerie Queen*.

Essentially, however, Willie Stark is a unique creation, not a fictionalized Huey Long or an updated Julius Caesar. Thus, when we belabor an analogy between Stark and any other figure—historical or literary—that analogy breaks down. Rather than being cloned from a single donor, Stark's personality more nearly resembles a mosaic of influences. One can see in him as much of Brutus as of Caesar. Like Brutus, Willie starts out as an idealist who rises to power by displacing a regime that he perceives to be unjust (albeit Stark's triumph is the bloodless one of electoral victory). Also like Brutus, Stark is initially recruited by conspirators who believe that his assistance

20. Watkins and Hiers, *Robert Penn Warren Talking*, 60. Elsewhere, Warren says of Huey Long: "The only time that his presence was ever felt in my classroom was when, in my Shakespeare course, I gave my little annual lecture on the political background of *Julius Caesar*; and then, for the two weeks we spent on the play, backs grew straighter, eyes grew brighter, notes were taken, and the girls stopped knitting in class, or repairing their faces" ("*All the King's Men:* The Matrix of Experience," in *Robert Penn Warren: A Collection of Essays*, edited by John L. Longley Jr. [New York: New York University Press, 1965], 75).

will aid their cause. In addition, we see that increasing political involvement destroys the marriages of both men. Finally, both Stark and Brutus are undone by their attempts to achieve good ends through evil means.

The recognition that Willie Stark's story is rooted at least in part in Warren's knowledge of Elizabethan tragedy helps supply a needed corrective to some superficial misreadings of that story. Because of Stark's similarity to Huey Long, many early reviews of *All the King's Men* were less discussions of the novel than arguments about Long himself. As Robert B. Heilman points out, the authors of such reviews were so obsessed with topicality that they seemed incapable of reading tragedy. "One may doubt whether *Macbeth* would have been improved," Heilman continues, "if it had been conceived as a recipe for the curtailment of royal abuses." Even those persons perceptive enough to realize that Willie Stark is more than a thinly disguised Huey Long sometimes make the mistake of reading *All the King's Men* as a solely political novel. Such a reading, however, raises more questions than it answers. We must wonder, for example, why the domestic conflicts of Jack Burden's life play such a large role in another man's story.[21] If Warren is concerned primarily with Willie Stark, then much of what we learn about Jack is peripheral and irrelevant. For this reason, critics who find *All the King's Men* to be an artistic success tend to regard Burden as more than a mere Ishmael or Nick Carraway but as the novel's central character. For that reason, the most intriguing Shakespearean analogue for us to consider may be not *Julius Caesar* but *Hamlet.*

The Hamlet story would have had obvious appeal for a southern American writer of Warren's generation. As Leslie Fiedler maintains in his essay "Caliban or Hamlet: A Study in Literary Anthropology," the Hamlet image "has most obsessively concerned our writers, all the way from *The Power of Sympathy*, whose appearance coincided with our birth as a nation, to *The Hamlet of A. MacLeish* or even Hyman Plutzik's Horatio poems." Among the pantheon of American Hamlets, Fiedler cites Melville's Pierre Glendinning, Poe's Roderick

21. Heilman, *The Southern Connection* (Baton Rouge: Louisiana State University Press, 1991), 220. Arthur Mizener has noted "interesting similarities between *All the King's Men* and Shakespeare's 'dark' comedies, *Measure for Measure* and *Troilus and Cressida.*" See Richard Gray, ed., *Robert Penn Warren: A Collection of Critical Essays* (Englewood Cliffs, NJ: Prentice-Hall, 1980), 54.

Usher, "the Dimmesdale-Coverdale melancholiacs of Hawthorne," and Bellow's Herzog. For our purposes, however, the most suggestive figure he mentions is Faulkner's Quentin Compson.[22]

Quentin's obsession with the disparity between the myth of the Old South and the reality of the New South (most evident in *Absalom, Absalom!*) and his more general love-hate relationship with his home region is simply a pathological exaggeration of what many young southern intellectuals felt during the cultural upheaval that began in the 1920s. The Agrarian movement, of which Warren was a part, consisted of sons of the Old South who saw their mother region repudiating past loyalties in favor of the whoredoms of industrialism. (All of their polemical efforts were directed toward upholding the honor of the old culture and convincing the motherland of the error of her ways.) Like Quentin Compson, Warren's Jack Burden is a neurotic young man who is caught in the middle of the South's cultural transformation. He comes from the dying aristocracy and is employed by a quintessential embodiment of the rising class—the redneck Willie Stark. (Although Warren never actually worked for Stark's model, Huey Long, the Louisiana "kingfish" was indirectly responsible for supplying the money with which he and Cleanth Brooks started the *Southern Review*.)[23] Still, Jack's most deep-seated conflicts are generated less by the wider society than by the impact of that society on his own family situation.

In discussing *All the King's Men* as a modern tragedy, Heilman notes its "intra-family confrontations and injuries, the repercussions on generation upon generation, as with Hamlet and Orestes."[24] It is within the matrix of family strife that Jack Burden has developed the personality that speaks to us in the novel. Like Hamlet, Jack is a brood-

---

22. Fiedler, *The Collected Essays of Leslie Fiedler* (New York: Stein and Day, 1971), 2:290. Warren himself has noted the appeal of the Hamlet story for another modern southern writer. See "A Note on the Hamlet of Thomas Wolfe," in *Selected Essays*, by Warren (New York: Random House, 1958), 170–83.

23. In his story "Knight's Gambit," Faulkner has Gavin Stevens tell his nephew Chick Mallison that "Huey Long in Louisiana had made himself founder, owner and supporter of . . . one of the best literary magazines anywhere, without ever once looking inside it probably nor even caring what the people who wrote and edited it thought of him" (*Knight's Gambit and Other Stories* [New York: Random House, 1949], 229–30). The most definitive discussion of the original series of the *Southern Review* can be found in Thomas W. Cutrer, *Parnasus on the Mississippi: The "Southern Review" and the Baton Rouge Literary Community, 1935–1942* (Baton Rouge: Louisiana State University Press, 1984).

24. Heilman, *The Southern Connection*, 213.

ing philosophical young man who lacks a clear direction in life. (Both young men have interrupted their university studies.) Jack communicates his view of himself and his world in interior monologues, the novelistic equivalent of the dramatic soliloquy. Among other things, these monologues tell us that at the beginning of the novel Jack is a radical subjectivist, who is blinded to any reality separate from his own perceptions and neuroses.

Although we do not have enough information about Hamlet's childhood to do more than speculate on the influences that shaped his personality, his ambivalent relationship with his parents seems to be of fundamental importance. Based on a much fuller depiction of Jack Burden's youth, we can say that a similar ambivalence lies at the heart of his malaise. As Louis D. Rubin Jr. notes, Jack's decision to work for Willie is "an attempt to deny the sense of futility, of aimlessness, of unreality that he felt . . . as a child."[25] The man whom he first knew as his father deserted the family when Jack was six. Although his mother brings a succession of new husbands into the house over the years, none of these men can replace Ellis Burden, the father whom Jack has lost. Instead, they simply become rivals for his mother's affection. Growing up in this environment, Jack looks upon his mother as a shallow and promiscuous woman who is incapable of true love.

It takes no great psychological insight to predict that Jack's upbringing will cause him serious difficulties in his later dealings with women. Although his youthful romance with Anne Stanton ultimately flounders because of her disgust with his lack of purpose and vocation in life, things begin to fall apart when he refuses to take her sexually. Later, his marriage to Lois fails when he is revulsed by her overt sensuality. To identify the source of Jack's arrested development, one need only consider the fact that the closest approximation of a truly erotic scene in the novel comes in the following passage:

> She . . . took me by the sleeve of the forearm and drew me toward her. I didn't come at first. I just let her pull the arm. She didn't pull hard, but she kept on looking straight at me.
> I let myself go, and keeled over toward her. I lay on my back, with my head on her lap, the way I had known I would do. She let her left hand lie on my chest, the thumb and forefinger holding,

25. Rubin, *Wary Fugitives*, 123.

> and revolving back and forth, a button on my shirt, and her right
> hand on my forehead. . . . She had the trick of making a little is-
> land right in the middle of time. . . .
>   Then she said, "You're tired, Son."[26]

When we analyze Hamlet's situation, we also find an unconventional mother-son relationship. At a conscious level, Hamlet's main
grievance against Claudius is that he has murdered the elder Hamlet
and usurped his throne. As Ernest Jones and others have pointed
out, however, the prince's anger seems to be aroused more sponta-
neously by the marriage of Claudius and Gertrude.[27] In the famous
bedroom scene with his mother and elsewhere in the play, Hamlet
dwells incessantly on the physical reality of Gertrude's copulation
with her new husband. The tone here is less that of an aggrieved son
than of a spurned lover.

Although the schizophrenic nature of Hamlet's courtship of Ophelia
and his ultimate rejection of her love is probably the result of complex motivations, it is clear that his general view of women has been
colored by his ambiguous feelings toward his mother. The misogynistic animus of his "Get thee to a nunnery" speech is certainly not
evoked by anything that Ophelia has done. For Hamlet, she seems to
exist as a mere pawn in the game he is playing with Gertrude. When
he lays his head in Ophelia's lap at the performance of *The Murder of
Gonzago*, it is simply to taunt his mother. Like Jack Burden, Hamlet
has a thing about laps.

In terms of the action of the play, Hamlet's more important parent
is his father; after all, the revenge dilemma that bedevils Hamlet is
caused by his father's death. Also, because he is bereft of his real father, he must create an ideal one out of his memory and his imagination. This ideal father appears to Hamlet, either in fact or in fancy,
and places him under filial obligations. Thus, Hamlet is not searching for a father in the literal manner of a Telemachus, but is striving
instead to establish, or reestablish, a bond with the past by doing his
father's bidding. His misgivings about that task are what create the
central dramatic tension of the play.

Jack Burden's identity as a son is even more complex than Hamlet's because Jack is dealing with three father figures. When the first

---

26. Warren, *All the King's Men* (New York: Harcourt Brace, 1946), 119.
27. Ernest Jones, *Hamlet and Oedipus* (New York: Norton, 1949).

of these fathers (Ellis Burden) deserts his family, Jack is plunged into the aimlessness and ennui of his formative and early adult years. This period in his life ends when Jack goes to work for Willie Stark. In signing on with Willie, who in effect becomes his surrogate father, Jack is rejecting the past—for Willie is a man of the future, a Machiavellian upstart whose political movement is largely an insurgency against the oligarchy of the Old South from which Jack is fleeing.

Jack's admiration for Willie is not unlike Hamlet's envy of the assertive Fortinbras. His work on Willie's behalf ironically leads to Jack's discovery of his true father. Told to dig up some dirt on Judge Irwin, Jack uncovers a scandal in the judge's past and confronts him with the incriminating evidence. Rather than submit to political blackmail, Irwin commits suicide. At this point, Jack's mother reveals that Judge Irwin was her son's real father. Like Hamlet, Jack has lost a father as a result of political intrigue, but, unlike Hamlet, he does not immediately contemplate revenge.

An instructive contrast to Jack is provided by the character of Adam Stanton. Adam serves as a foil to Jack in much the same way as Laertes does to Hamlet. Adam is moved to seek vengeance because Willie Stark has wronged his family, first by discovering scandal in the administration of the late Governor Stanton and second by taking Anne Stanton as his mistress. Similarly, Laertes is moved to avenge his father and sister, both of whom are victims of Hamlet's madness. Forsaking rational deliberation, both Laertes and Adam Stanton instinctively seek violent retribution. When Jack feels tempted to do much the same, he is stopped in his tracks by the realization of his own complicity in all that has occurred.

Jack cannot even bring himself to expose Tiny Duffy's role in the assassination of Willie Stark because he is unnerved by Duffy's assumption that Jack will work for him now that Stark is dead. Rather than failing at revenge, Jack turns his back on its imperatives. This process becomes complete when he is finally reunited with his original father figure, Ellis Burden—now a street-corner evangelist. Unlike Hamlet, Jack has found a father who is neither usurper nor pagan revenge god. Out of the materials of tragedy, Warren has emulated another, more affirmative, type of Shakespearean drama—a comedy of forgiveness.[28]

---

28. For a discussion of this concept, see Robert Hunter, *Shakespeare and the Comedy of Forgiveness* (New York: Columbia University Press, 1965).

Still, the mere existence of thematic resemblances between *Hamlet* and *All the King's Men* does not make a sufficiently striking case for direct influence. Nor does the available external evidence close the deal. To my knowledge, the only Shakespeare play that Warren has ever mentioned in connection with his novel is *Julius Caesar.* Beyond that, we know only that he was reading Elizabethan tragedy at the time he was writing *All the King's Men.* A couple of affinities in imagery and diction, however, raise the prospect that *Hamlet* was one of those tragedies. To begin with, one of the most famous passages in *All the King's Men* is Willie Stark's folksy articulation of the doctrine of original sin. "Man," he says, "is conceived in sin and born in corruption and he passeth from the stink of the didie to the stench of the shroud."[29] Although Willie's use of Elizabethan diction may suggest a biblical influence, it is not difficult to imagine Hamlet's saying something very similar in the graveyard scene.

In reading the interpolated Cass Mastern story, one is also struck by certain Shakespearean parallels. When he contemplates suicide, for example, Cass ponders some of the same issues that plague Hamlet. Because Claudius has killed the elder Hamlet when his soul was least prepared to be dispatched, the prince thinks it only right that Claudius be killed when circumstances would ensure his damnation. Similarly, Cass feels that his own suicide and subsequent damnation would be the only fitting atonements for his betrayal of Duncan Trice. That he does not kill himself Cass attributes to the fact that "the Lord preserved me from self-slaughter."[30] His word choice may even echo Hamlet's first soliloquy. Here, Shakespeare's protagonist laments the fact that the Everlasting has "fixed his canon 'gainst self-slaughter."

Perhaps more important than the evidence of specific passages, however, is the overall quality of Warren's language. As John M. Bradbury points out, "The 'rhetoric' of Warren's novels, particularly that of *All the King's Men*, has been harshly treated by several competent critics." Although *rhetoric* is a much abused term, Bradbury contends that "it is the proper one for Warren if it be understood in its Elizabethan and baroque-metaphysical sense. In literary temperament Warren is much closer to sixteenth- and seventeenth-century

29. Warren, *All the King's Men*, 54.
30. Ibid., 193.

ideals than to modern simplicity cults."[31] Not only his rhetorical predilections but also the very catholicity of his achievement suggest that Warren was indeed a throwback to another age. If the breadth of his intellect and the boldness of his imagination bespeak an Elizabethan sensibility, it is not surprising that his work has been influenced from time to time by that of the greatest Elizabethan. In a specific as well as a generic sense, Robert Penn Warren was truly a Renaissance man.

31. Bradbury, "Robert Penn Warren's Novels: The Symbolic and Textural Patterns," in *Robert Penn Warren*, edited by Longley, 14.

≋ 4 ≋

The Legacy of Monroe K. Spears

I rose at six on the morning of March 20, 1993. For most people
that would be unremarkable, but for a notoriously late riser on
vacation, it was an extraordinary act of will. Spring break was
over, and I had a long and uncertain drive ahead of me between St.
Petersburg Beach, Florida, and Valdosta, Georgia, where I was to
catch an afternoon flight for Charleston, South Carolina. That evening, Monroe K. Spears was to be inducted into the South Carolina
Academy of Authors. It was an occasion I did not want to miss. An
entire generation of southern writers and critics was passing from
the scene. Robert Penn Warren and Walker Percy had fallen victim to
cancer only a few years earlier. Cleanth Brooks, whose biography I
was writing, would be gone in little more than a year. And Andrew
Lytle was past ninety. Monroe Spears was not as well known as any
of these men, but he had done important work as an editor, critic,
and mentor of young writers.

Perhaps Spears had been born too late to be immortalized in histories of southern literature. When he first saw the light of day in
Darlington, South Carolina, on April 28, 1916, the poets who would
later call themselves Fugitives had already begun meeting on Nashville's Twentieth Avenue. *I'll Take My Stand* was published the year
he turned fourteen. By the time he completed his master's degree at
the University of South Carolina in 1937, Cleanth Brooks and Robert
Penn Warren had already founded the *Southern Review* and published their first textbook. Spears finished his Ph.D. at Princeton in
1940, a year after John Crowe Ransom founded the *Kenyon Review*.
When he finished four years of service in the U.S. Army during World
War II and began teaching at Vanderbilt in 1946, the only one of the
original brethren still left in Nashville was Donald Davidson. Al-

though he wrote poetry, Spears was no latter-day Fugitive, and his literary interests seemed firmly rooted in eighteenth-century scholarship.

More than a half century later, Spears's students at Vanderbilt remember him as an imposing presence and a demanding teacher. (By the end of the semester, he expected graduate students to be able "to distinguish the couplets of John Dryden from those of Alexander Pope, without reference to their content.") According to Henry Hart, Spears "liked to pose as a dandy by wearing a camel hair topcoat to class, puffing at a cigarette in a long black holder, and jumping up to gaze out the window as if searching for ideas in the heavens. He dashed around the classroom, leapt toward the blackboard to write down a sudden thought, and stared fixedly at students when they spoke, quizzing them about their remarks with utter seriousness."[1]

One day, Spears's wife, Betty, who was teaching freshman English, began grading a stack of papers on Edward Donaghue's "Head by Scopas" from Brooks and Warren's *Understanding Fiction*. One paper seemed so much better written and more sophisticated than the rest that she suspected plagiarism. When she brought it to Monroe to read, he detected a couple of minor flaws that convinced him the paper was nonprofessional. "But most importantly," Spears recalls, "it was a far better essay than anything the student could have found in print." Betty Spears introduced her husband to this remarkable student, James Dickey, and a lifelong friendship ensued. Like Spears, Dickey was a southerner, a lawyer's son, and a veteran of World War II. Although both young men were interested in poetry, Spears's tastes ran toward the neoclassical poets and, among moderns, W. H. Auden, whereas Dickey preferred romantic and visionary poets such as George Barker, Kenneth Patchen, Dylan Thomas, Hart Crane, and Theodore Roethke. While not trying to alter Dickey's aesthetic preferences, Spears did urge him to make his poetry less obscure. When he once asked Dickey why he did not make his narrative more dramatic, the poet replied: "Because it didn't happen that way." To this, Spears responded: "Well, what difference does that make? It would be so much better if you did it that way."[2]

1. Hart, *James Dickey: The World as a Lie* (New York: Picador, 2000), 146.
2. Spears, *One Writer's Reality* (Columbia: University of Missouri Press, 1996), 69; Dickey, *Self-Interviews*, recorded and edited by Barbara Reiss and James Reiss (Garden City, NY: Doubleday, 1970), 33.

Spears made such a lasting impression on his student that, on April 24, 1981, Dickey wrote the following tribute, "To Posterity":

> Dear Sir—if so I may address all the millions who compose you now and the billions who will compose you—I should like, as one assured of your continuous and deepening attention, to place, for my works in poetry, in the novel, in literary criticism, in advertising, in film-making, in speech writing, in political controversy, in interviews, in private conversations and dreams and reveries, to the entire credit of Monroe K. Spears: to his early influence when he was my first real teacher—and incomparably the best—and to his continuing presence in everything my mind conceives. In the parlance of the football field, it was Monroe Spears who threw the key block for me: who opened up the whole field upon which all kinds of running were possible. I would wish for every writer to have such an angelic blocker ahead of him, but there is only one Monroe.[3]

Immediately following Spears's induction into the South Carolina Academy, Dickey came up to his old teacher and said, "It's not over yet, Monroe." In a little more than five years both men were dead.

After six years at Vanderbilt, Spears assumed the editorship of the *Sewanee Review* in 1952. Located at the University of the South in Sewanee, Tennessee, that magazine had been founded sixty years earlier by William Peterfield Trent. (Its first issue had contained a review of the recently published *Tess of the D'Urbervilles.*) Despite its longevity, this magazine had rarely risen above somnolent respectability during its first half century of existence. All of that changed, however, in the mid-1940s. When Louisiana State University suspended publication of the *Southern Review* in 1942 because of alleged wartime austerity, the two major literary quarterlies in the United States were the *Partisan Review* in New York City and the *Kenyon Review* in Gambier, Ohio. Sensing the need for a first-rate southern magazine to take the place of the defunct Baton Rouge quarterly, University of the South vice chancellor Alexander Guerry decided to remake his school's magazine into a major force in the Republic of Letters.

3. Hart, *James Dickey*, 130.

Although he was unable to snare Cleanth Brooks, who had already cast his sights on a professorship at Yale, Guerry did secure the services of Allen Tate. (Andrew Lytle was already on the faculty at Sewanee and was serving as managing editor of the review.) When Tate assumed the editorship of the *Sewanee Review* in 1944, he redesigned the format of the magazine, began paying contributors, introduced prize competitions, and quadrupled the circulation of the review. The magazine began publishing fiction for the first time in the 1940s and greatly increased the space devoted to poetry. Also, some of the most distinguished critics in the United States and England began appearing in its pages. The *Southern, Kenyon,* and *Sewanee* reviews exemplified a kind of publication that had scarcely been seen in America before. From the 1920s on, "little magazines" had appeared and disappeared as modernism began to assert itself as the dominant literary mode of the new century. But, as Spears pointed out in a talk he gave at the end of his tenure at Sewanee, a little magazine is not the same as a critical quarterly. According to Spears, little magazines such as *Broom, Blast, Transition,* and the *Little Review* "were founded to publish experimental poetry and fiction, and most of them paid little attention to criticism. They were intense and impudent, carefree about deadlines and business arrangements, living very much for the moment."[4] The literary review, in contrast, is a grown-up enterprise that is meant to be around for the long haul.

"The literary quarterly or critical review," Spears notes, "is a noncommercial magazine, uncompromisingly highbrow in character, which publishes criticism of literature and to some extent the other arts in the form of essays, book reviews, and chronicles, together with fiction and poetry selected according to the kind of high standards defined and employed in the criticism." Such a definition places the literary review somewhere between the little magazine and the scholarly journal. The literary review is descended from such European prototypes as the *Edinburgh Quarterly* and the *Nouvelle Revue Française.* The early decades of the twentieth century provided such transitional models as T. S. Eliot's *Criterion* (1922–1939), "which gave most of its space to discussion of fundamental

4. Spears, *American Ambitions: Selected Essays on Literary and Cultural Themes* (Baltimore: Johns Hopkins University Press, 1987), 111.

issues in literary and cultural criticism, and the *Dial*, which in its second incarnation (1920–29) was strongly aesthetic in emphasis."[5] The *Criterion* was published in London and the *Dial* in New York. By the mid-1940s, however, critical fashion was being set not in London and New York but in a rural village in north-central Ohio and a small town in the Tennessee mountains.

Despite his invaluable contributions to the *Sewanee Review*, Tate was gone by 1946 (dogged by charges of sexual harassment). Although Alexander Guerry once again tried to lure Cleanth Brooks to Sewanee, Brooks was already on his way to Yale. John Palmer, however, was a veteran of World War II looking for a job. Because Palmer had served with distinction as managing editor of the *Southern Review*, Brooks recommended him for the job at Sewanee. For six years, Palmer followed the editorial example set by Tate. However, he remained an officer in the naval reserve and was called back to active duty during the Korean War. After his efforts to edit the *Sewanee Review* from his station in London proved unworkable, Palmer turned over the reins of the magazine to Monroe Spears.

As the fifties wore on, the *Kenyon Review* began to run out of steam. (Many observers believe that it was never the same after managing editor Philip Blair Rice was killed in a car wreck in 1956.)[6] Thus, by the middle of the 1950s, the American critical quarterly that best exemplified what the *Southern Review* had been in the thirties and the *Kenyon Review* had been in the forties was the *Sewanee Review* under Monroe K. Spears. As might be expected, Spears proved to be hospitable to both southern writers and the New Criticism. He published the work of such established southern luminaries as Allen Tate, Robert Penn Warren, John Crowe Ransom, Cleanth Brooks, and Flannery O'Connor, along with such relative newcomers as Walker Percy, Madison Jones, George Garrett, Louis Rubin, and his

5. Ibid., 110, 111.

6. In the 1950s, two independent quarterlies in the Northeast were pursuing very different agendas. Since the late thirties, the *Partisan Review* had published socially engaged cultural criticism by anti-Stalinist intellectuals, many of whom were Trotskyites or former Trotskyites. In 1948, the *Hudson Review* was founded as a more or less conscious alternative to the *Partisan Review*. Its ideological stance was not just apolitical but antipolitical. If the *Partisan Review* seemed dominated by Jewish critics who were primarily interested in a literature of ideas, contributors to the *Hudson Review* were equally distinguished WASPs, committed to high modernism in literature and the other arts.

own young protégé, James Dickey. (Dickey's criticism appeared so frequently in the *Sewanee* that many readers mistakenly thought him the magazine's poetry editor.) Once, after Cleanth Brooks published an essay on Faulkner in the review, Spears indicated in a contributor's note that Brooks was writing a book on Faulkner. Although Brooks had no such intention, he thought it such a good suggestion that he produced *William Faulkner: The Yoknapatawpha Country.* Spears also published a special issue in 1959 to commemorate Allen Tate's sixtieth birthday.

At the same time that the *Sewanee Review* was perpetuating the Southern Renascence, it featured such nonsouthern writers as T. S. Eliot, Francis Fergusson, Lionel Trilling, Philip Wheelwright, R. P. Blackmur, Malcolm Cowley, Robert Lowell, Jacques Maritian, Arthur Mizener, Howard Nemerov, Sir Herbert Reed, Mark Van Doren, and Eliseo Vivas. Moreover, in his inaugural editorial, Spears made it clear that his magazine would not simply be a house organ for the New Criticism:

> Criticism is essentially an effort to make sense of literature and relate it to the rest of human experience; it always operates upon religious, philosophical, political assumptions, however unconscious the critic may be of them. The hypothesis that criticism can be purely literary was a valuable corrective, and necessary to the great achievements of the past thirty years. But the hypothesis has only an operational validity; it is time to recognize that impurity is one of the justifications of criticism. The point has been made, the lesson learned, and we have plenty of critics able to do good formal analysis. We need now, in addition, a consciously impure criticism which will seek coherent answers to questions of theory and will interpret literature in relation to the rest of man's concerns.[7]

The burden of editing a quarterly magazine (with inadequate clerical support), teaching part-time, and trying to do some writing of his own took such a toll on Spears that he stepped down from the helm of the *Sewanee Review* in 1961. (Andrew Lytle, who had just finished a thirteen-year stint as a professor of creative writing at the University of Florida, edited the magazine for the next twelve years.)

7. Spears, editorial, *Sewanee Review* 60 (Fall 1952): 748.

Although his only book at that time was an edition of the writings of Matthew Prior (which he coedited with H. B. Wright), Spears's interests had shifted from eighteenth-century literature to modern poetry. Consequently, in 1963, he published *The Poetry of W. H. Auden: The Disenchanted Island*, a work that Allen Tate called "the best book by anybody on a living poet." Although the statement appeared in a back-cover blurb, it was made by a man who once said that he would have no trouble telling Jesus Christ if he had written a bad poem.

In many respects, Spears's book on Auden is the sort that one might expect from a traditional literary scholar rather than a New Critic. Anyone looking for a close and extended reading of any single poem is likely to go away disappointed. (Anthony Hecht's *The Hidden Law: The Poetry of W. H. Auden* [1993] is far more useful in this regard.) Spears is more concerned with stepping back from the individual trees in order to see the shape of the forest. We find a bold example of this impulse late in the book, when Spears describes Auden in relation to three key predecessors:

> The work of both [Auden and Dryden] exhibits a superb virtuosity in all the techniques of poetry. Auden, like Dryden, writes much for music, collaborates frequently, and spends a good deal of time in translating and adapting; he is a major critic as well as a poet. If one superimposes on the figure of Dryden that of Lord Byron, to contribute audacity, rebelliousness, comic vigor and cosmopolitan sophistication; and then adds the spectre of Coleridge to bring in magic and the supernatural, an affinity with Germany and a concern for abstruse questions of aesthetics and theology, the composite image is close to Auden. Though this quadruple portrait is more than fairly absurd, it does at least suggest Auden's continuity with the tradition, his deep sense of his relation to the whole of English literature.[8]

Because so much has been said against Auden's later, religious, poetry, Spears spends much of his book providing a revisionary interpretation (and defense) of that poetry. The case that has frequently been made against Auden is that he produced some important poems in the thirties but essentially sold out in his later career. Not

8. Spears, *The Poetry of W. H. Auden: The Disenchanted Island* (New York: Oxford University Press, 1963), 338.

only did he stop writing socially conscious left-wing poems in favor of more orthodox Christian verse, he also revised some of his better-known earlier poems in ways that seemed to blunt their original ideological force. In his *Collected Poetry* (1945), for example, he reprints his classic poem of the Spanish civil war, "September 1, 1939," but deletes the stanza that ends with that poem's most famous line, "We must love one another or die." Whereas the earlier Auden scholar Joseph Warren Beach had concluded that the stanza was deleted because its statement was "not made in specifically and unmistakably religious terms," Spears argues that the poet simply found it to be "too explicit and facile."[9]

Although Spears's book is in no sense a biography, it is arranged chronologically in four sections, beginning with Auden's birth in 1907 and taking us up to 1962. Each section begins with a chronology of important events and publications in a particular period of Auden's life and ends with a substantial section of endnotes. To the charge that Auden's return to the Anglicanism of his youth represents an opportunistic defection to the Right, Spears argues that Auden's politics have remained liberal and that the depth and sincerity of his religious conviction are beyond question. Some critics, however, see his later poetry as essentially frivolous because, unlike Gerard Manley Hopkins and T. S. Eliot, he does not make personal issues of guilt and salvation essential themes in his poetry. Spears suspects that the problem may simply be that, in his later verse, Auden regards poetry as a public and social art rather than the language of some existential vision—either religious or secular.

In an essay published in 1982, Spears went so far as to suggest that Dante's *Divine Comedy* might actually be a useful paradigm for conceptualizing Auden's career. Thus, his early angrier poems (those written up through 1939) correspond to *The Inferno*. With "New Year Letter," which is dated January 1, 1940, Auden moves into a phase that corresponds to *The Purgatorio*. Here, Dante is explicitly chosen as Auden's "judge-confessor in the imaginary tribunal all writers face." Throughout this poem, and much of the other verse of this middle period, Auden presents the drama of salvation in psychological terms. Hell becomes a possibility only if we deny the law of consciousness and the reality of suffering. Spears argues that a third

9. Ibid., 155.

period in Auden's canon begins in 1947, when "there is an apprehension of the Sacred and the celebration of Joy, communal as well as individual, that suggests a parallel to the *Paradiso*." Unlike Dante, however, Auden gives us a very human and terrestrial view of paradise. Without explicitly rejecting the Christian notion of an afterlife, the closest that he can get to heaven in his poetry is a vision of human community. Perhaps for that reason, Spears is forced to revise his paradigm and conclude that Auden's "spiritual journey corresponds only to the central one of Dante's three."[10]

In a memorial service for Auden celebrated a month after his death, Spears argued that the two Christian themes most prominent in his poetry were the experience of Pentecost and the redemption of time in the cycle of the church year. In a sense, community is the common denominator of both. In *A Certain World* (1970), Auden remarks:

> It is extraordinary that sects of religious enthusiasts, from the Montanists down to the Catholic Apostolics, should have imagined that to make verbal noises which nobody else could understand was evidence of Divine Inspiration, a repetition of the miracle of Pentecost. What happened at Pentecost was exactly the opposite, the miracle of instantaneous translation—everybody could understand what everybody else was saying.[11]

A realization of the peculiarly Christian concept of time is perhaps best rendered in Auden's Christmas oratorio *For the Time Being* (1944). Here the poet juxtaposes the uniqueness of the Incarnation with the annual celebration of the nativity and the daily attempt of Christians to experience incarnation in their daily lives.

In 1964, Spears left Sewanee to become Moody Professor of English at Rice University. That same year, Prentice-Hall brought out his edited collection of essays on Auden. Then, in 1965, he published a study of Hart Crane in a series of monographs on American writers sponsored by the University of Minnesota Press. One could hardly imagine two poets of the same generation (Crane was born eight years earlier than Auden) more different in their approach to their art. Auden was a social and public poet, known for wit, irony, and in-

10. Spears, *Countries of the Mind: Literary Explorations* (Columbia: University of Missouri Press, 1992), 86, 90, 100.

11. Auden, *A Certain World* (New York: Random House, 1970), 170.

tellect. Many of his themes were taken from domestic life, and even his religious imagery was closer to earth than to heaven. Crane, on the other hand, was a mad visionary—always trying to find mythic significance in the most ordinary and sordid aspects of everyday life. At the same time, his was not a totally undisciplined talent. Craftsmen as exacting as Allen Tate and Yvor Winters applauded his lyric gift, while regretting his philosophical indebtedness to the airy mysticism of Emerson and Whitman.

In his forty-one-page monograph on Crane, Spears does more close textual analysis of individual poems than he had done in the 330 pages of his book on Auden. In his very choice of poems to discuss (particularly, "Chaplinesque," "Black Tambourine," "Praise for an Urn," "The Wine Menagerie," and "Possessions"), he identifies those works that seem to him "central to Crane's achievement." Of his two long poems (both of which are examined in detail), Spears finds "Voyages" (1926) to be superior to *The Bridge* (1930). In trying to make the latter poem into an epic of the United States, Crane wrote brilliant individual passages about urban life while falling victim to structural and philosophical incoherence. Although he possessed an abundance of both craft and vision, Crane finally lacked the intellect that might have made him a great poet. In a telling comparison, Spears states: "Yeats's system enabled him to 'hold reality and justice in a single thought'; Crane's allowed him too often to transcend, or to ignore, both."[12]

When Monroe Spears's *Dionysus and the City: Modernism in Twentieth-Century Poetry* appeared in 1970, it soon became indispensable reading for an entire generation of graduate students. This is not to suggest that the book was without interest to seasoned professionals, only that it possessed a singular appeal for readers who needed a framework for understanding what might otherwise seem to be discrete and even inexplicable literary phenomena. Graduate students facing a comprehensive examination on the entire canon of English literature clearly constituted such a group of readers. (Edmund Wilson's *Axel's Castle* [1931] had served a similar function for a much larger audience of general readers four decades earlier.)

One of the problems, of course, was the built-in obsolescence of

12. Spears, *Hart Crane* (Minneapolis: University of Minnesota Press, 1965), 46.

the term *modernism* itself. The concept had existed in the English tradition at least since Swift's "Battle of the Books." What made the modernism of the early twentieth century different was that, in addition to mere novelty, it introduced the notion of apocalypse. Not only was the contemporary epoch different from anything that went before, but it was also the end of the road. As Virginia Woolf put it, "On or about December, 1910, human nature changed."[13] If the Renaissance saw civilization emerge from the Dark Ages, we now seemed to be heading into another dark age—one characterized by despair, not faith.

Spears begins *Dionysus and the City* by identifying four types of discontinuity that plagued artists and intellectuals in the decades surrounding World War I. Metaphysical discontinuity, as he describes it, is the belief that those gaps that separate the natural, the human, and the supernatural are finally unbridgeable. This frame of mind is a valuable guard against both naturalism and Gnosticism; however, carried to an extreme, it can lead to a profound sense of alienation. The angst of metaphysical discontinuity pervades Eliot's *The Waste Land* and countless other works of the modernist era. It is a rejection of the facile humanism that sometimes afflicts both the classic and the romantic minds. Those of a theological bent might well equate it with a belief in original sin. Secular philosophers would be more inclined to call it man's existential condition.

The concept of aesthetic discontinuity suggests a further cleavage—one dividing art from life. Although this notion did not originate in the twentieth century and is not shared by all modern artists, it has achieved greater currency as the artist has become progressively alienated from the community in which he lives. No longer a spokesman for that community, he is now an isolated egoist expressing a private vision. One of the consequences is a rejection of art as mimesis and an increase in nonrepresentational artworks, "the creation of a heterocosm, a world parallel to but distinct from the 'real' one."[14]

The primary technique used to assert a division between art and life in modern literature is rhetorical discontinuity. If there is no

13. Spears, *Dionysus and the City* (New York: Oxford University Press, 1970), 29.
14. Ibid., 25.

longer an agreed-upon truth, then the conventional language ordinarily used to convey such a truth becomes obsolete, whereas elliptical, imagistic, and fractured language can at least express the cognitive dissonance of modern life. Although it can be argued that the use of fragmented language to depict fragmented reality is itself a kind of mimesis, the result is representation based on discontinuity, not on conventional notions of harmony, beauty, and wholeness. Even if one shores the fragments against his ruin (as Eliot's speaker does in *The Waste Land*), they are still visible reminders—almost sacraments—of that ruin.

Finally, temporal discontinuity denies the existence of a bond uniting the living, the dead, and the yet unborn. It can be seen as a liberation from the dead hand of the past and a source of optimism about the future. (We get a sense of this in Emerson's talk about a party of hope and in the nineteenth-century view of the American as a new Adam in a new Eden.) However, as Spears notes, "most serious writers and artists of the present century have exhibited the other reaction, . . . regarding the break with the past as disinheritance or Fall. This historical catastrophism has been a central theme of modern art and the concomitant view of the present as a waste land, now that civilization is destroyed and human nature changed, becomes, with its wrenching sense of loss, the dominant myth."[15]

Spears argues that the ancient Greek gods Apollo and Dionysus (symbolizing the clash between reason, order, and decorum, on the one hand, and madness, energy, and excess, on the other) represent a polarity sufficiently inclusive to describe any time or place. In literary history, however, it seems that one or the other deity tends to dominate particular eras. In the English tradition, for example, the Dionysian Renaissance is followed by the Apollonian eighteenth century, which itself gives way to an even more Dionysian romanticism. According to this scheme of things, modernism is a Dionysian reaction to the Apollonian Victorian era, which succeeded the romantic revolution.

Although Spears is not altogether comfortable with what he calls "such large and mechanical generalizations," his paradigm makes at least as much sense as Eliot's notion of the dissociation of sensibility (even as it was elaborated at book length by Cleanth Brooks in

15. Ibid., 33.

Modern Poetry and the Tradition [1939]). In fact, Spears's understanding of the relation of modernism to the rest of English literary history is an implicit rebuke of Eliot's antiromanticism. Not only did the dawn of modernism mean the return of Dionysus, but certain cultural developments in the late nineteenth and early twentieth centuries helped to bring him back with a vengeance as well.

By the time that modernism became a self-conscious force in twentieth-century literature, Nietzsche, Freud, Frazer, and Marx (one is tempted to add Darwin to the list) had collectively created a radically new image of humanity: "Man is not a rational animal able to understand and control his world and himself, but a mysterious being of unknown heights and depths, subject to forces within and without that he comprehends only in part. Naturally, then, the imagination of the pioneering modern artist tends to be apocalyptic, seeing both the end of a cultural era and the end of all things."[16]

Underlying the rejection of Apollonian norms in modern art is a wholesale repudiation of liberal humanism. I suspect that this process may actually have been more incremental than one would infer from Spears's account. If the philosophy of progress was official dogma during the Victorian era, then the most prophetic writers of that period had the sense that they lived in a time of transition between unrealistic optimism and an ominous future (as Matthew Arnold put it in "Stanzas from the Grande Chartreuse": "Wandering between two worlds, one dead, / The other powerless to be born"). By the early twentieth century, that future was unmistakably here, and the reaction against everything officially Victorian was intense.

In addition to profound developments in the realm of philosophy, simple economic and technological factors effected changes in the arts. One of the most obvious hallmarks of modernism was a widening gap between art produced for the masses and the kind intended for a sophisticated few. Spears argues that the perfection of photography eliminated the market for representational painting, whereas the invention of the phonograph greatly reduced the audience for live musicians. By the same token, film (and later radio and television) provided a means of telling stories that was more immediately apprehensible than print. As a result of these transformations, "serious" painting, music, and literature all became more experimental

16. Ibid., 42.

and less mimetic in form. In poetry, for example, free verse finally became dominant in the modernist era.

The controlling trope for Spears's book comes from Walter Pater's observation that Greek tragedy began when Dionysus entered "the city." The image of the city is here used to represent an Apollonian ideal of civic order, which is disrupted by the deity of riot and excess. "In a different sense," Spears explains, "modernism may be said to have begun when Dionysus entered the city, meaning by it this time the literal and physical city which dominates the modern environment and is both cause and symptom of our characteristic maladies. The city is the literal environment and scene, and hence a part of the subject, of most modern literature; it is the background which produces the typical modern man and the stage upon which he acts."[17] Even when the modern Dionysus operates in creative tension with an Apollonian ideal, he does so more to maintain the memory or hope of that ideal than to express confidence that it will prevail. Philosophically, this is the respect in which the most vital modernist writers most differ from the official spokesmen for Victorian optimism.

Rather than disrupting a preexisting order (as he does in Greek tragedy), the modern Dionysus is the prophetic spirit who observes and renders the disorder that has already overtaken the modern city. Although one can cite classic city poems from earlier periods (Blake's "London," Wordsworth's Westminster Bridge sonnet, and James Thomson's "City of Dreadful Night" are among those mentioned by Spears), it was not until the twentieth century that the urban landscape came to dominate poetry. Poets as diverse as William Carlos Williams, E. E. Cummings, Wallace Stevens, Hart Crane, W. H. Auden, and Robert Lowell (along with a host of lesser lights) are all preeminently poets of the city. The master of the genre, however, is T. S. Eliot.

In such early poems as "Rhapsody on a Windy Night," "Portrait of a Lady," and "The Love Song of J. Alfred Prufrock," Eliot gave us haunting images—at once realistic and impressionistic—of the modern city. Although Eliot's own experiences were surely crucial here, Spears is right in pointing out that "it was Baudelaire who first showed him that the experiences of an adolescent in the industrial city could be the material of poetry, and that the sordid aspects of

17. Ibid., 70–71.

the modern metropolis might be fused with the phantasmagoric."[18] To be sure, Eliot's masterpiece—and the central poem of the modernist era—is called *The Waste Land*, not *The City*. Nevertheless, that masterpiece is filled with—mostly harrowing—images of urban life, which show the continuing influence of Baudelaire and, less directly, of Dante. (By the same token, Spears notes, the most important novel of the twentieth century—James Joyce's *Ulysses*—is a study of city life.) Even as we move into the post–World War II era, the famous dialogue in "Little Gidding" between the air raid warden and the composite ghost of his long-dead master takes place on a war-torn urban landscape that seems to be a modern equivalent of the Inferno.

In Spears's judgment, the formative years for literary modernism were 1909–1914. Ezra Pound, who is generally acknowledged to have been the seminal figure in the new movement, had arrived in London the previous year. The extreme aestheticism that had emerged in the 1890s as a brief but intense reaction against high Victorianism had collapsed with the early death of several of its major figures and the trial of its most notorious exponent, Oscar Wilde. The last Victorian poets of any note—Algernon Swinburne and George Meredith—both died in 1909, A. E. Housman had fallen into a prolonged silence after the publication of *The Shropshire Lad* in 1896, and the school of "physical force" (as represented by Rudyard Kipling, Alfred Noyes, and Henry Newbolt) was ascendant. In contrast, however, painting and music were both in the midst of revolutionary change. Cubism came in 1907 and the collage in 1912. At the same time, Igor Stravinsky, Arnold Schoenberg, and others seemed intent on reinventing sound. The real experiments in literature were in the impressionistic novel, as seen in the late work of Henry James, the early novels of Joseph Conrad, and the continuing influence of Ford Madox Ford.

While Spears is careful not to exaggerate the enduring impact of the imagist movement, he does quote the following observation by T. E. Hulme: "This new verse resembles sculpture more than music; it appeals to the eye rather than the ear. It has to mould images, a kind of spiritual clay, into definite shapes. . . . It builds up a plastic image which it hands over to the reader, whereas the old art endeavoured to influence him physically by the hypnotic effect of rhythm."[19] Most of the poets Spears discusses in connection with the

18. Ibid., 76–77.
19. Ibid., 116–17.

beginnings of modernism (Pound, Wallace Stevens, D. H. Lawrence, and Cummings) seem to fit this description. The two who most emphatically do not are Eliot, who was more influenced by music, and W. B. Yeats, whose sensibility was shaped by his experience in the Abbey Theatre. Of course, the fact that Eliot and Yeats are generally regarded as the two most important English poets of the twentieth century may actually make Spears's case about the transitory influence of imagism.

In his fifth chapter, Spears jumps across the ocean from London to Nashville to discuss the three major Fugitive poets—Ransom, Tate, and Warren. In doing so, he seems to be following the example of Cleanth Brooks, who had included a similar chapter in *Modern Poetry and the Tradition*. Although cynics might accuse both Brooks and Spears of undue tribal loyalty, their emphasis can be defended on its merits. For one thing, the poets who would later call themselves Fugitives began meeting and writing about the time that the imagist movement was breaking up. Many reputable critics consider the imagists and Fugitives to have been the two most influential *groups* of poets in the twentieth century. And finally, between them these two groups brilliantly represent the Dionysian and Apollonian impulses in poetry. (As I have suggested elsewhere in this volume, that contrast is evident in the odyssey of John Gould Fletcher, who was involved with both movements.) Certainly, the pervasiveness of modernism is demonstrated by the fact that poets in provincial Nashville were reacting to some of the same pressures and influences felt by artists in more cosmopolitan settings.

One of John Crowe Ransom's primary concerns as both poet and critic was with the condition that Eliot called a dissociation of sensibility. For Ransom, however, this phenomenon was not an occurrence in English literary history but an endemic human affliction that has gotten only worse with the triumph of science in the modern era. Ransom believed that science encouraged abstract utilitarian thinking, which was fine as far as it went. Unfortunately, this mind-set represents only the mechanistic side of what it means to be human. Much of the enjoyment of life comes from those things we do that are not required to put bread on the table and (as Ransom reminds us in his essay "Forms and Citizens") may actually delay our eating it. If our customs, games, and mores define who we are as human beings (not just as efficient economic animals), our literature and religion do so to an even more profound degree.

Of all the original Fugitives, Tate had the earliest and most substantial awareness of the modernist revolution going on outside Nashville. Though lamenting the historical and metaphysical discontinuity that produced this revolution, he regarded the techniques of modernist poetry as the inevitable literary response. As much as one might prefer to live in a different era, when more classical literature was possible, the modern writer had no choice but to accept the hand that was dealt him. Rather than adopting Eliot's notion that symbolism somehow represented a recovery of what the metaphysical poets had been doing in the seventeenth century, Tate argues that poetry inevitably exists in a tension between the metaphysical and symbolist impulses. In his book *On the Limits of Poetry* (1948), he argues:

> The metaphysical poet as a rationalist begins at or near the extensive or denoting end of the line; the romantic or Symbolist poet at the other, intensive end; and each by a straining feat of the imagination tries to push his meanings as far as he can towards the opposite end, so as to occupy the entire scale. . . . It would be a hard task to choose between the two strategies, the Symbolist and the metaphysical; both at their best are great, and both are incomplete.[20]

In a kind of logical progression, Warren—who was the youngest of the major Fugitives—was also the most contemporary. If he was not as close as Tate to the heart of early modernism, he was the only one of the group to go beyond modernism and fully participate in the even newer direction that American poetry began to take after the mid-1950s. Spears argues that the reason Warren was able to make this transition (after a near decade of poetic silence from the midforties to the midfifties) was that his conception of poetry was never limited by the constrictions of high modernism to begin with. In such essays as "Pure and Impure Poetry" and "A Poem of Pure Imagination" (1946), we see that he regards irony not as a mere technical device for distancing the poet from his subject matter but as an index to the moral complexity of actual life. The fact that Warren was also a popular novelist made it that much easier for him to write narrative verse, something the high modernists generally avoided doing.

20. Tate, *On the Limits of Poetry: Selected Essays, 1928–1948* (New York: Swallow, 1948), 86.

In a concluding paragraph, Spears succinctly justifies the space he has devoted to Ransom, Tate, and Warren in a study of poetic modernism:

> Each of the three incorporates in himself, as well as perceives in the outside world, the forces of disorder that we have symbolized as Dionysian. Each has a distinctive version of the tension between this and the opposing Apollonian principle: Tate, the most radical in language and structure, is most conservative in prosody and genre; Warren, striving in his later verse for increased intimacy, directness, spontaneity, loosens his rhythms and flattens his language, while retaining regular forms and employing a special private but systematic group of symbols, sometimes surrealistic. Ransom, simplest on the surface, but fundamentally dualistic, produces cosmic and moving ironies through masterful control of language and tone in a deliberately minor art.[21]

In his final two major chapters, Spears takes us beyond modernism to consider the literary situation at the time he was writing, which is to say the mid- to late 1960s. Because both modernism and the New Criticism were not considered passé until the midfifties, Spears had only a decade's worth of evidence from which to educe what would come next. In a chapter called "The Newer Criticism," he stresses the continuing importance of the conflict between Apollo and Dionysus by asserting that Frank Kermode and Northrop Frye "are the two most considerable critics to emerge since World War II."[22] When one considers that the major New Critics and New York intellectuals had all "emerged" prior to the war and that the French theorists who would dominate literary criticism during the final third of the twentieth century were not yet widely known, Spears may well be right in assigning preeminence to Kermode and Frye. If nothing else, their work tells us a good deal about the modernism that was.

Kermode's hugely influential book *Romantic Image* (1957) was published at a time when American (and to a lesser extent British) poetry was becoming more defiantly romantic in reaction to the doctrine

---

21. Spears, *Dionysus and the City*, 196.
22. Ibid., 199.

of impersonality advanced by T. S. Eliot. Kermode's novel, though entirely plausible, thesis was that Eliot's criticism—along with the symbolist poetry it extolled—was at least implicitly romantic because of its preference for the imagistic over the rational powers of the mind. In other words, Eliot denounced romanticism while exhibiting some its defining tendencies.

In thus attempting to discredit Eliot as a critic, Kermode hoped to rehabilitate Milton and other poets whom Eliot had accused of a dissociation of sensibility. In fact, Kermode believes that the whole notion of the dissociated sensibility was simply a back-projection of symbolist doctrine into literary history. (C. K. Stead argues that Kermode had it backward—that the doctrine of the image was, in fact, a reaction to the experience of psychological dissociation.)[23] In affirming the rational over the occult or imagistic powers of the imagination, Kermode clearly represents the forces of Apollo. He nevertheless possesses sufficient critical intelligence to write with perception and sensitivity about the American symbolist Wallace Stevens.

If Kermode was an accomplished practical critic and literary historian, Northrop Frye was a revolutionary theoretician who seemed bent on doing nothing less than remake literary criticism from the ground up. One might even argue that Frye was finally interested not in literature at all but in a generic structure of myth that was breathtakingly all-inclusive. The very audacity of his theories, codified in *Anatomy of Criticism* (which, like Kermode's *Romantic Image*, was published in 1957), accounts for the cult following that Frye enjoyed. If the New Critics were close readers who focused on the text, Frye was the classic distant reader who could see the pattern of which the text was a part. One was never entirely sure, however, if that pattern corresponded to a verifiable reality.[24] Consequently,

---

23. Ibid., 201.

24. W. K. Wimsatt puts the matter well: "The Ur-Myth, the Quest Myth, with all its complications, its cycles, acts, scenes, characters, and special symbols, is not a historical fact. And that is not only in the obvious sense that the stories are not true, but in another sense, which I think we tend to forget and which mythopoeic writing does much to obscure: that such a coherent, cyclic, and encyclopedic system, such a monomyth, cannot be shown ever to have evolved actually, either from or with ritual, anywhere in the world, or ever anywhere to have been entertained in whole or even in any considerable part. We are talking about the myth of myth" ("Northrop Frye: Criticism as Myth," in *Northrop Frye in Modern Criticism: Selected Papers from the English Institute*, edited by Murray Kreiger [New York: Columbia University Press, 1966], 97).

Frye managed to elevate the critic to equality with the creative writer while allowing him to abjure any responsibility for aesthetic evaluation.

Spears sums up the impact of Kermode and Frye by arguing that, at their worst, they "represent a pulling apart of qualities that the best New Critics maintained in balance or tension. Kermode, especially in his earlier work, maintained what seems to me an excessively rationalist position, denying any essential difference between poetry and prose; Frye, on the other hand, is a complete irrationalist, whose only articles of faith are the occult 'tradition' and the Imagination." What these men offer are radically different correctives to the excesses of the New Criticism. Kermode has helped to restore Milton and the romantics to their rightful place in the literary canon, while emphasizing the importance of historical considerations in literary study. Frye, on the other hand, has reminded us of the origins of literature in myth. In doing so, he has added context and significance to what might otherwise be a sophisticated game of acrostics. While stopping short of saying that Kermode and Frye represent older criticism repackaged, Spears does concede that "there is no Newer Criticism."[25]

Although he does not use the term *postmodern* in referring to the verse that has been written in the aftermath of modernism, Spears is almost as uncomfortable with such adjectives as *neomodern, open, naked,* or *confessional.* The problem may simply be that, by the mid-sixties, it was not yet clear which of the manifold reactions against modernism would prevail. Whatever the newer verse might ultimately prove to be, it was most emphatically a rebuke to the notion that poetry must be intellectually difficult, impersonal, ironic, and paradoxical. If the poetry of high modernism was written for the eyes of a coterie rather than the ears of the masses, the Beat poets read their work in coffeehouses—often to musical accompaniment. If anything, poetry may have been late in involving the audience in the total aesthetic experience. As Spears notes, the playwrights Samuel Beckett and Eugene Ionesco had already gone a long way toward breaking down the barriers between audience and performance in the theater of the absurd.

I suspect that one of Spears's problems in discussing the poetry written in the immediate aftermath of modernism was its resistance

25. Spears, *Dionysus and the City,* 227, 228.

to the model of literary history adumbrated earlier in the book. If modernism represented the triumph of Dionysus, the reaction to it should have been Apollonian. To be sure, some contemporary poets seemed to fit that description. One thinks of the later Auden, of individual American poets such as Richard Wilbur and Howard Nemerov, and of a host of British poets of the 1950s—for example, Philip Larkin, Thom Gunn, John Wain, and Donald Davie—reacting against the Dionysian excess of Dylan Thomas. (Although few would have anticipated it at the time, the American neoformalists, who began making their mark in the 1980s, would constitute a similar Apollonian response to the anarchy of free verse.) The main current of contemporary verse, however, seemed to be even less Apollonian than modernism itself—as if the earlier "revolution" had not gone nearly far enough. If Eliot served as a kind of negative model for many of these newer poets, he was replaced as a culture hero and father figure by William Carlos Williams and (at a further remove historically) by Walt Whitman.

If the Beats commanded the most attention in the midfifties (Allen Ginsberg's *Howl* was published in 1956), a far more profound indication of change in the poetic landscape could be found in the new styles adopted by two more established poets—Robert Penn Warren and Robert Lowell. As Spears had already noted in an earlier chapter, the more open and personal style of Warren's later poetry began with *Promises* (1957). In *Life Studies* (1959), Lowell abandoned the elliptical and ironic style of his earlier verse (acquired at least in part from Allen Tate) for a poetry of direct statement, which often resembled prose broken into lines. When he was not mining his own experience (including recurring bouts with mental illness), he deliberately distanced himself from that experience by writing imitations of poems from other languages. In doing so, Lowell may have been reflecting the influence of Pound, whom the newer poets (particularly Charles Olson and the Black Mountain school) were willing to accept as mediated through Williams rather than Eliot.

After a brief discussion of Theodore Roethke and John Berryman (two older poets who seem to have anticipated certain aspects of the newer verse), Spears turns his attention to a pair of representative contemporary poets—England's Ted Hughes and his own former student James Dickey. In addition to the obvious personal connection, Dickey also illustrates the tension between Dionysus and Apollo at the heart of Spears's argument. "The basic perception that lies behind" Dickey's poetry is "often Dionysian, more than human," Spears contends. "Though his central concern is with vision, not form, he is aware that the problem of form is inescapable. . . . Dickey began as an extremely difficult and often obscure poet; his striving toward greater openness and accessibility may be regarded as an Apollonian quality."[26]

In the short final chapter that he calls "In Place of a Conclusion," Spears returns to the question of modernism's vexed relationship with romanticism. The problem is compounded by the fact that so many critics who tackle the problem do so with a hidden agenda. (The attempt to prove that Eliot was really no classicist but a self-loathing romantic has become something of a cottage industry.) Perhaps the best that one can do is to admit that not only does modernism come after romanticism historically but it also could not have existed without the precedent of the earlier revolution. Beyond that, we should perhaps limit ourselves to identifying particular affinities between key modernist poets and certain romantic predecessors. (Three years after Spears's book, Harold Bloom would add a further measure of Freudian complexity to this exercise with his study *The Anxiety of Influence*.)

About the only thing that Spears can say with certainty about the newer poetry is that it achieved a kind of critical mass in the mid-fifties and that it seemed primarily to be a reaction against the rhetorical discontinuity of modernism. Its basic impulse was "toward statement, toward poetry conceived of as not something uttered by a *persona* or a fragment of a drama but as direct confession or revelation or prophecy by the poet undisguised. . . . The poem is no longer timeless artifact, but [is] designed to draw the reader into time, immerse him in immediate experience."[27] Perhaps for that reason, Spears is drawn to the label that Robert Langbaum used to describe the dramatic monologue—poetry of experience.

If we accept Spears's dates, modernism began no earlier than 1909 and lasted no later than 1957. Thus, in 1970, it was still the most important literary movement in recent memory. As we reach the midpoint of the first decade of the twenty-first century, however, we

26. Ibid., 258.
27. Ibid., 265.

realize that modernism has now been gone for as long as it was here. The reason it is so hard to make sense of what has come in its aftermath is that an apocalypse (even one that did not come) is a tough act to follow. The new poetry seems less an advance over modernism than a series of attempts to find a more usable past. If Whitman and Williams represented one such past for the poets of 1957, Longfellow and Frost would constitute an equally valid tradition for a later generation of neoformalists. By rejecting what seemed to be the bankrupt legacies of romantic and Victorian excess, the pioneers of modernism may simply have made it possible for aspects of those movements to be resurrected at a later date. That would be only fitting, given the fact that the original resurrected god was Dionysus himself.

Spears's next major project after *Dionysus and the City* was to be a study of modern poetry in terms of space and time. Unfortunately, that project never got beyond an introductory lecture delivered at Texas Christian University in April 1971, which was published as a monograph by that university's press the following November. Because this lecture is both suggestive and incomplete, one can only regret that the promised book was never forthcoming. Spears's basic argument is that twentieth-century verse can be divided into poetry of space and poetry of time. Of course, by its very nature, literature is a temporal art. Whereas spatial arts such as painting and sculpture are meant to be perceived in a single instant, it takes time to sing songs, tell stories, and act out plays. Nevertheless, experiments in language (rhetorical discontinuity and the like) can so disrupt the reader's sense of the orderly progression of time that one can get the sense of perceiving discrete fragments of language. Poets such as William Carlos Williams and E. E. Cummings further this illusion through their arrangement of words on the page. Such poems are meant to be seen as well as heard and depend for their very existence on modern typography.

Spears begins his discussion by reaching back into ancient Greek metaphysics to identify Zeno with the philosophy of space and Heraclitus with that of time. Those two dimensions remained relatively fixed until the early twentieth century, when theoretical physicists such as Max Planck, Werner Heisenberg, and Albert Einstein demonstrated their essential relativity. The artists who sought to "spatialize" music and literature were responding to much the same zeitgeist, if not to the discoveries in physics themselves. (The philosopher Henri Bergson was probably a more direct influence.) Along with these experiments in form, one also saw space and time becoming more explicit themes in verse. Beginning with the imagists (whose poems seemed like nothing so much as verbal equivalents of still-life painting) and ending with Robert Lowell (who was generally regarded as America's foremost living poet in 1971), Spears throws out a multitude of ideas that seem to demand greater elaboration. For example, all that he says of "The Dance" by Williams is that it is a poem about a painting, whose "effect is achieved largely through rhythm."[28] In fact, this poem is a complex demonstration of the relativity of space and time. It is based on Brueghel's painting *The Kermess*, which is itself an attempt to capture the kinetic energy of temporal activity in a spatial artifact. It is a crowded and busy canvas with the action "bleeding" beyond the frame. In addition to rhythm, Williams uses repetition (for example, the first and last lines of the poem are identical), enjambment, and several other rhetorical devices to achieve the effect of time imitating space imitating time.

If Spears was not to give us another self-contained book such as *Dionysus and the City*, he continued publishing essays and reviews in magazines aimed at the intelligent general reader. A collection of twenty of these pieces appeared under the title *American Ambitions* in 1987. It is more than a little ironic that this was the same year that Russell Jacoby published *The Last Intellectuals*, a kind of requiem for the plainspoken man of letters, who wrote in lively and lucid prose for an audience of nonspecialists. Such public intellectuals flourished in the early decades of the twentieth century, when the United States could boast a strong literary culture independent of the academy. By the 1930s and '40s, however, many of the independent magazines and publishing houses that had supported this earlier generation of critics no longer existed. Consequently, the intellectuals born around 1920 (Alfred Kazin, Mary McCarthy, Irving Howe, and others) were forced to moonlight in the university. The literary quarterlies allowed them to continue writing in a public idiom rather than becoming academic drones. Having been born in 1916, Monroe

---

28. Spears, *Space against Time in Modern American Poetry* (Fort Worth: Texas Christian University Press, 1972), 14.

Spears belonged to this generation. Although he was a conventionally trained academic, he managed to write like the freelance critics whose proudest boast was their lack of an advanced degree.

In *American Ambitions*, Spears wrote perceptively and engagingly on a wide range of topics, including contemporary poetry (Robert Lowell, Daniel Hoffman, James Dickey, and Robert Penn Warren), the state of criticism (Allen Tate, R. P. Blackmur, Cleanth Brooks, Warren again, Rene Wellek, Randall Jarrell, Helen Vendler, and Ursula Le Guin), southern fiction (George Garrett, Madison Jones, Walker Percy, and John Kennedy Toole), and the various nooks and crannies of our general culture (visual art, the Jewish intellectuals of New York, and black English). Reaching back into our history, Spears opens his book with essays on two very different figures who helped shape the American character—Cotton Mather and William James.

Though detesting Mather, Spears gives the Puritan devil his due and, in the process, tells us some unsettling things about ourselves. The piece on James is a more wholehearted appreciation of an American culture hero. Throughout much of his discussion, Spears points to fascinating affinities between James and that ultimate British culture hero, Samuel Johnson. His conclusion—which is surely a minor heresy for a literary academic schooled in eighteenth-century studies—is that "James is more profound than Johnson, more fully aware of the mystery of fact and the unfathomableness of ontology, the otherness of people and things."[29]

Although no single section of Spears's book is devoted to Vanderbilt writers, six and a half of the twenty essays concern the Fugitive-Agrarians and their literary progeny. The oldest of these is an extended review of Allen Tate's *The Limits of Poetry*, published in the *Sewanee Review* in 1949. Coming early in his career, when he was still immersed in eighteenth-century scholarship, Spears already displays the critical intelligence that would distinguish all his subsequent writing. As one might expect, he praises Tate for identifying positivism as the central philosophical malaise of our time. This is a theme running through Tate's poetry and criticism (and, one might add, his single novel, *The Fathers*). He yearned for the cultural unity that can be provided only by a traditional society. While extolling the virtues of the traditional South, he realized as early as his participa-

29. Spears, *American Ambitions*, 22.

tion in *I'll Take My Stand* that the one essential thing that society lacked was a religion appropriate to an agrarian economy. Instead, the region was saddled with what Tate called a "non-agrarian and trading religion that had been invented in the sixteenth century by a young finance-capitalist economy."[30] To try to assert the values of tradition without affirming their roots in religion (as the neohumanists attempted to do) was a futile exercise. Unfortunately, as Spears points out, this was the position in which Tate found himself. He would later resolve this dilemma by joining the Roman Catholic Church. Until he was able to make that commitment, however, he was a brilliant physician unable to cure himself.

Spears is far less restrained in his appreciation of Cleanth Brooks. At the time that he originally published "Cleanth Brooks and the Responsibilities of Criticism," the subject of his essay was seventy years old and recently retired from Yale. Although he would have another eighteen years of active lecturing and publishing ahead of him, Brooks's reputation was already well established. (In contrast, Tate was only fifty at the time that Spears first wrote about him and seemed still to be a writer in midpassage.) The title of Spears's essay is an apparent allusion to F. O. Matthiessen's "The Responsibilities of Criticism," which was originally delivered as a lecture at one of John Crowe Ransom's summer schools of criticism. Matthiessen, who was a fully engaged cultural critic, was trying to stress the obligations of the critic to the larger society of which he is a part. This is, of course, one area in which New Critics such as Brooks were often seen as deficient. Spears challenges this canard by showing Brooks's writing to be deeply historical and fully contextual. (In making this point, his two major texts are *William Faulkner: The Yoknapatawpha Country* [1963] and *A Shaping Joy* [1971].) Moreover, even in his role as close reader, Brooks performs a valuable *social* function by alerting us to the power of language to benefit or corrupt our culture.

Among his own contemporaries, the one American writer whom Spears seemed to hold in the highest regard was Robert Penn Warren. Perhaps because of the sheer breadth of his achievement, Warren is the only writer to merit two essays in *American Ambitions*. In the first of these, Spears considers the poetry Warren had published

30. Tate, *On the Limits of Poetry*, 316.

since *Dionysus and the City* appeared. This includes three separate volumes of new verse since 1967, followed by *Selected Poems, 1923–1975*. This last book begins with ten previously unpublished poems and then moves backward in reverse chronological order. Fewer than half of Warren's *Selected Poems* from 1944 have been preserved. In fact, 268 of the volume's 325 pages contain work from 1954 or later. It is more than a bit ironic that Warren, who was the youngest and most precocious of the Fugitives, should have begun writing his best verse at age forty-nine. Following Warren's own lead, Spears devotes the bulk of his discussion to the ten most recent poems—all written in 1975 and grouped under the title "Can I See Arcturus from Where I Stand?" This astronomical query is the final line of the final poem in the sequence, a truly visionary meditation called "Old Nigger on One-Mule Cart Encountered Late at Night When Driving Home from Party in the Back Country."

Most seventy-year-old poets with a fifty-two-year career behind them might be content to rest on their laurels. Instead, Warren won a Pulitzer Prize with his next volume of verse, *Now and Then: Poems, 1976-1977*. (He had previously won a Pulitzer in fiction for *All the King's Men* and one in poetry for *Promises*.) Although Spears mentions this book only in passing, he discusses Warren's next three volumes of verse—*Being Here* (1980), *Rumor Verified* (1981), and *Chief Joseph of the Nez Perce* (1983)—and four critical studies of the poet's work. In a play on words, Spears calls Warren a "Hardy American"—arguing that his verse resembles Thomas Hardy's in "its religious attitude of yearning unbelief coupled with grim irony and . . . metrical virtuosity based on stretching traditional forms."[31] The one other respect in which Warren might remind one of his British counterpart is his longevity and his persistence in writing poetry well into old age. Although Warren died two years after the publication of *American Ambitions*, he lived long enough to become America's first official poet laureate and continued writing and publishing almost to the end.

Because of Warren's distinction as a poet and his popularity as a novelist, less attention has been devoted to his achievement as a literary critic. Thus, one of Spears's most useful contributions is his discussion of Warren's criticism. If Cleanth Brooks is the paradigmatic (though not stereotypical) New Critic, his old friend and col-

31. Spears, *American Ambitions*, 97.

laborator does not fit the mold. Like Brooks, he realized that students at Louisiana State University (and elsewhere) needed to know how to read literature as literature before they could presume to talk about it in other terms. Nevertheless, Warren did not do the sort of close reading one finds in Brooks's *The Well-Wrought Urn*. Nor did he engage in polemical warfare with the old guard and avant-garde enemies of the New Criticism. Instead, he preferred to write theoretical essays such as "Pure and Impure Poetry" and long philosophical meditations on works as diverse as Conrad's *Nostromo* and Coleridge's *Rime of the Ancient Mariner.*

Although Warren wrote criticism intermittently throughout his career, there was a final burst of activity from 1970 to 1975. During this time, he published editions of the poetry of Melville and Whittier, along with substantial critical introductions to these poets, a long essay on Hawthorne, and a short book on Dreiser. At the same time, he collaborated with Cleanth Brooks and R. W. B. Lewis on a monumental two-volume anthology of American literature. (The commentary in this textbook constitutes one of the best critical histories of American literature ever published.) Warren finished this half decade of activity by giving the annual Jefferson lecture, which he expanded into a monograph called *Democracy and Poetry.* In all of these studies of American writers, Warren is a model of the fully engaged cultural critic. Although Brooks was also capable of playing that role, he was always leery of making literature into a substitute for religion, in the manner of Matthew Arnold. Perhaps because he subscribed to no orthodox creed, Warren did mix aesthetic and religious impulses in ways that took his criticism far beyond the bounds of explication. For that reason, Warren's criticism often sheds light on both its ostensible subject and his own creative work.

Although Spears devotes a modest amount of space to reviewing books by two other Vanderbilt writers (Randall Jarrell's *Letters* [1985] and Madison Jones's *A Cry of Absence* [1971]), he is far more detailed and expansive in his commentary on James Dickey's *The Zodiac* (1976). Spears begins by placing his former student in the broader context of twentieth-century southern literature. Although Dickey came to Vanderbilt far too late to have been directly influenced by the Fugitive and Agrarian movements, both traditions left an indirect mark upon his sensibility. Largely because of the Fugitives, writing has always been taken seriously at Vanderbilt. If the austere formalism of Ransom and Tate was of little interest to Dickey, he could feel a kindred spirit in the later Warren, who published a positive review of *The Zodiac* in the *New York Times Book Review*. (Though having very little in common with Dickey, Tate thought him the best southern poet since the Fugitives were in their prime.) Dickey also shared the Agrarians' reverence for nature and has paid homage to *I'll Take My Stand* in his own book *Self-Interviews* (1970).[32]

The heart of Spears's essay is an analysis of *The Zodiac*, an imitation of a poem by the major Dutch literary figure Hendrik Marsman. Although the original poem is not well known in the United States, a fairly conventional translation by A. J. Barnouw appeared in the *Sewanee Review* in 1947, when Dickey was a student at Vanderbilt. By loosening the language, Dickey makes his version of the poem longer and more distinctively his own. Like Dickey, the speaker is a drunken poet who seeks the meaning of earthly life in the mystery of the stars. (Not long before writing the poem, Dickey completed a correspondence course in celestial navigation.) According to Spears: "Dickey's essential affirmation is the same one made by his predecessors in the visionary line from Blake to Hart Crane and the Dylan Thomas of *Altarwise by Owllight:* the analogy, or identity, of the poetic imagination and the divine power that created the stars. . . . The subject of *The Zodiac*, then, is not astrology but the nature of reality and its relation to the poet's creative imagination, treated not in post-Kantian philosophical terms but dramatically and mythologically."[33]

This essay on Dickey seems to have grown over the years. Originally, Spears was commissioned to review *The Zodiac* for the *New York Review of Books*. When that review was not published, the material on Dickey as a southern writer was added to a lecture given at the University of South Carolina on the occasion of the poet's sixtieth birthday. At such a function, it must have seemed appropriate to say something nice about Dickey's most recent work. Unfortunately, a discussion of the domestic muse that informs Dickey's *Puella* (1982) is jarringly out of place in an essay subtitled "Southern Visionary as Celestial Navigator." Spears's comments about the impulse behind *Puella* and what it might mean for the direction of Dickey's

32. Dickey, *Self-Interviews*, 33.
33. Spears, *American Ambitions*, 81.

career are plausible enough. The suggestion that Hopkins was an influence on the language of the poem also seems astute. What is lacking is the aesthetic evaluation one finds in Spears's evenhanded discussion of *The Zodiac*. In many quarters, *Puella* was greeted not as a triumph of originality but as a parody of Dickey's worst excesses.[34] It would take a critic as brilliant as Monroe Spears to prove that assessment wrong. But on this particular evening, Spears had come to praise Dickey, not to judge him.

After a collection as rich and various as *American Ambitions*, one might have expected a decade to pass before Spears was capable of producing another book of comparable size. Nevertheless, a mere five years later, he published *Countries of the Mind*, a gathering of thirty essays on topics as diverse as Montaigne, Tocqueville, Stephen Hawking, Delmore Schwartz, and Mary Lee Settle. Although several of the pieces in this new volume predate *American Ambitions*, the majority originally appeared in 1987 or later. A few of the selections were first delivered as lectures. Most of those that began their life in print were initially published in literary quarterlies (the *Hudson*, *Gettysburg*, and *Sewanee* reviews), fortnightly magazines (the *New Republic* and the *New York Review of Books*), and the Sunday book page of a major metropolitan newspaper (the *Washington Post* "Book World"). Only two pieces originated in academic journals *(Contemporary Literature* and the *Journal of Southern History)*. Spears was thus writing (or speaking) to an audience of intelligent general readers, who would typically absorb his discourse in a single sitting. The intensity of effect might not rival what Poe considered essential for a legitimate poem, but such exercises require clarity, concision, and intellectual panache.

The value of the first section of *Countries of the Mind* lies chiefly in demonstrating the range of Spears's interests. The focus moves from sixteenth-century England (*The Lisle Letters* and George Garrett's Elizabethan trilogy) to sixteenth-century France and eighteenth-century America (Montaigne and Tocqueville, especially their relevance to twentieth-century America) and ends with an essay on science for

---

34. For a particularly scathing assessment of *Puella*, see Dana Gioia, *Can Poetry Matter? Essays on Poetry and American Culture* (St. Paul, MN: Graywolf, 1992), 190–93.

the layman ("Cosmology and the Common Reader"). The real heart of the book, however, lies in the second section ("Poets and Critics"). Constituting well over half the text, this unit concentrates on literary figures who made their mark after the decline of early modernism. The one apparent exception is a lecture on Eliot delivered at Miami University in 1988, the year of the poet's centennial. But the purpose of this speech is not so much to place Eliot historically as to rehabilitate him as an influence on contemporary poetry.

Although Spears does not frame the argument in this way, it would seem that the reaction against Eliot comes from both the poetic Left and the poetic Right. On the one hand, we find the "naked" and "confessional" poets, who regard Eliot as too restrained and indirect in his approach to verse. (In this category, Spears lumps such diverse figures as Ginsberg, Olson, Creeley, Duncan, Ashbery, Merrill, Oppen, and Zukofsky—all of whom are "open, crackpot, occult but secular, prosaic, grandiose.") On the other end of the spectrum are those poets and critics who equate form entirely with meter and reject all free verse out of hand. (From Spears's subsequent essay "The Poetics of the New Formalism," one would get the mistaken impression that this was a widely held belief among poets who write in meter rather than the extreme position of a few disciples of Yvor Winters.) "My preference," Spears notes, "is for poets like Warren, Wilbur, Nemerov, Hecht, Hoffman, Meredith, Dickey, who do not imitate Eliot but are not obsessed by reacting against him; who take poetry with the same seriousness that Eliot did."[35]

Although the concluding section of Spears's book is called "Southern Fictions," it begins with a review of Cleanth Brooks's *The Language of the American South* (1985). One of the purposes of Brooks's study is to celebrate the distinctiveness of the southern idiom. As he had done in his first book (published fifty years earlier and subsequently used by the dialect coach for the film version of *Gone with the Wind*), Brooks shows that the speech of the American South derives from similar provincial dialects in England. At least until very recently, the language spoken in certain parts of the South was closer to Elizabethan English than to the American idiom spoken in the North. This was particularly true of blacks and poor whites, who were uncorrupted by the spelling pronunciations of the New England

35. Spears, *Countries of the Mind*, 79.

schoolmarm. Brooks concludes that much of the charm and vigor of southern literature derives from this rich oral tradition. Writing originally in the *New York Review of Books*, Spears is totally convinced by Brooks's arguments and even defends him against tendentious charges of racism.

Spears's one selection on Warren in *Countries of the Mind* adds little to what had been said in *Dionysus and the City* and *American Ambitions*. Because most of the discussion is focused on Warren's *New and Selected Essays* (1989), Spears does little more than reiterate what he had previously said about Warren as critic—in some cases recycling entire paragraphs word for word. What saves the essay from total redundancy is a prefatory reminiscence of Spears's own acquaintance with Warren over the years. His depiction of Warren as a generous and gracious man, whose considerable talent was matched by genuine humility, has been too often confirmed to be in doubt. What is less easy to know is how much the critic's regard for the man might have influenced his judgment of the work. William Pratt, who greatly admires Spears, has argued that he sometimes heaped unearned praise on writers whom he liked personally.[36] One would think that Warren's achievement was finally too substantial to be damaged by judicious notice of his lapses.

Spears's fond recollection of Allen Tate, elsewhere in the volume, is far less problematic. To begin with, the tough-minded evaluation of Tate as critic that had appeared in the *Sewanee Review* in 1949 leaves little doubt that Spears was capable of seeing his friend's shortcomings as well as his virtues. Perhaps more important, this reminiscence appears in an explicitly biographical context—a joint review of Ann Waldron's book about Tate's former wife, Caroline Gordon, and an edition of the correspondence between Tate and Andrew Lytle.

Spears is particularly impressed by Waldron's refusal to make the philandering Tate into a cardboard villain and the long-suffering Gordon into an equally two-dimensional martyr. Whatever else may be said about Tate, his dedication to art was such that he would go to great lengths to help fellow writers. If Gordon's work was hampered by her domestic responsibilities as Tate's wife, it was also assisted

36. Pratt, "A Critic Who Counts," *South Carolina Review* 27 (Fall 1994–Spring 1995): 362–66.

by his counsel and encouragement. In this regard, Gordon was far from alone, as one can see from a passage about Peter Taylor that Spears cites from Waldron's book:

> Tate encouraged Taylor to send his stories off to magazines and persuaded him to enroll at Vanderbilt that fall. "When I went to Vanderbilt, it happened that I was assigned to Donald Davidson for registration," said Taylor. "I told him I wanted to study under John Crowe Ransom and he said, 'Come on, I'll take you over and introduce you.' We went over to where Mr. Ransom was registering students and Davidson said, 'John, here's a boy Allen has sent us.' That was the way things used to be done."[37]

On Sunday afternoon, September 19, 1993, Monroe Spears chaired a panel on James Dickey's poetry as part of a three-day celebration of Dickey's seventieth birthday in Columbia, South Carolina. After Spears made some opening remarks and sat down, he slipped out of his chair and lay sprawled on the floor, the victim of a massive heart attack. While waiting for an ambulance to arrive, Don Saunders, a cardiologist and director of the University of South Carolina School of Medicine, kept Spears alive with CPR. As he was being rushed to the Baptist Medical Center, emergency personnel tried unsuccessfully to restore a normal heart rhythm. It took an hour and a half after his arrival at the hospital for doctors to stabilize his heart. In the immediate aftermath of this incident, Dickey roamed among the crowd, "groaning to friends: 'I've killed my teacher; I've killed my teacher.'"[38]

In fact, Spears lived another four years and eight months, finally dying of congestive heart failure on May 23, 1998. (He actually survived Dickey by nearly a year and a half.) Two years before his passing, Spears published a final collection of essays. At 124 pages and containing only nine selections, *One Writer's Reality* seems modest in comparison to *American Ambitions* and *Countries of the Mind.* One assumes that Spears was eager to see it in print while he was still alive. During those final years, he lived a restricted existence, rarely leaving the house. But the one thing he continued to do was

---

37. Waldron, *Close Connections: Caroline Gordon and the Southern Renaissance* (New York: Putnam, 1987), 138–39.
38. Hart, *James Dickey*, 724.

write. In an era when literary study seemed to be dominated by theoreticians and ideologues, Monroe K. Spears was a living reminder of an earlier time when critics regarded literature as something more than nonreferential word games or political propaganda. As a young man, he made certain that the *Sewanee Review* would be a forum for public intellectuals and spent the rest of his life fulfilling that role himself. The fact that he was able to do so well into the 1990s suggests that there is still a market and an audience for fully engaged, gracefully written cultural criticism. It would be wrong to eulogize Spears as the last of a vanishing breed. How could public culture be dead when he did so much to keep it alive?

5

Incarnate Words

In his controversial memoir, *Making It*, Norman Podhoretz characterizes the several generations of writers associated with *Partisan Review* as "The Family." It should be clear by now that modern southern literature is also a multigenerational family, with its share of filial loyalties and sibling rivalries. The Vanderbilt branch of that family came into being with the birth of John Crowe Ransom in 1888 and Donald Davidson in 1893. The major figures of the second generation (Allen Tate, Andrew Lytle, Cleanth Brooks, and Robert Penn Warren) first saw the light of day between 1899 and 1906. Walter Sullivan, who was born in Nashville on January 4, 1924, belongs to the third generation of the Vanderbilt clan. Although his education was interrupted by service in the U.S. Marines during World War II, Sullivan completed his bachelor's degree at Vanderbilt in 1947 and his master's in fine arts at the State University of Iowa in 1949. For the next fifty-two years, he taught in the English Department at Vanderbilt, eclipsing by eight years Donald Davidson's record for institutional longevity.

During that time, Sullivan established himself as one of the most astute literary critics in the South. Like the Fugitives before him, his approach to criticism has always been informed by his own experience as a creative writer wrestling with the disciplines of craft. (Although it has been called everything from aesthetic formalism to the New Criticism, that approach was perhaps best described by the title of the composition textbook Sullivan couthored with George Core— *Writing from the Inside*.) At the same time, his fiction is haunted by many of the same issues that dominate his criticism. With the appearance of his long-awaited third novel, *A Time to Dance*, in 1995 and the subsequent reissue of his first two novels, *Sojourn of a*

Stranger and *The Long, Long Love,* by the Louisiana State University Press, it is high time to assess Walter Sullivan's place in contemporary southern fiction.[1]

Sullivan's first novel, *Sojourn of a Stranger,* appeared in 1957, the same year that President Eisenhower dispatched federal troops to desegregate Central High School in Little Rock, Arkansas. Not only was this the first federal invasion of the South since Reconstruction, but the drama was also played out on the new medium of television. Although Sullivan could hardly have anticipated these events when he was writing his novel, they could not help affecting the audience that would receive it. Race was fast becoming America's number-one social problem, and the South was the place where all the action was taking place. The tragic mulatto, who had been a staple of southern fiction at least since the time of George Washington Cable, was the theme of two of the year's most popular movies, *Band of Angels* and *Raintree County* (based on novels by Robert Penn Warren and Ross Lockridge Jr.). The fact that *Sojourn of a Stranger* also dealt with miscegenation should have been enough to ensure that it would be noticed. Surprisingly, however, most of the early reviewers were less concerned with the statement the novel made about contemporary issues than with its success in re-creating the middle Tennessee of a century earlier. (Judged solely in those terms, *Sojourn* is a superbly well-realized piece of fiction.) That is probably just as well, because Sullivan's social and moral vision was not well suited to an age of liberal millenarianism.

Because the novel's protagonist, Allen Hendrick, is the son of a southern aristocrat and a New Orleans octoroon, readers might expect another Faulknerian tale of sexual betrayal and family doom. The aristocrat, however, is no massa-in-the-woodpile but a progressive humanitarian, and the octoroon is neither a slave girl nor a kept woman but his lawfully wedded wife. Everything that Major Marcus Hendrick does is motivated by an admirable sense of social justice. He drops out of a promising law practice when the senior partner wins the acquittal of a man who murdered one of his slaves, he forsakes

---

1. Sullivan, *A Time to Dance* (Baton Rouge: Louisiana State University Press, 1995); *Sojourn of a Stranger* (1957; reprint, Baton Rouge: Louisiana State University Press, 2003); *The Long, Long Love* (1959; reprint, Baton Rouge: Louisiana State University Press, 1999).

real estate speculation when asked to defraud a widow, and he marries his wife when the Kentucky planter whose mistress she has been abandons her. He frees his slaves only to discover that they are even more helpless and shiftless than when they were in bondage. And he dies of apoplexy when he reads that South Carolina has seceded from the Union.

The enlightened modern reader is apt to sympathize with Marcus Hendrick and regret that there were not more like him in the Old South. Yet his goodwill creates problems for others. Speaking of Marcus's marriage, Andrew Lytle notes: "His act is an irresponsible act for two reasons: he ignores the inequalities of the social order without being able to find any concrete means to better the situation. And so he isolates himself and his wife from the society which surrounds him. At least in New Orleans the condition of the kept octoroon gave her a place and a society of a kind, but in violating the mores he not only cut her off from this but himself as well, establishing them both in a social vacuum."[2] The situation seems to be resolved when Marcus's wife insists that the family return to his home turf of Gallatin, Tennessee, believing correctly that her son's grandfather will be so taken with the boy that all will be forgiven. Young Allen does inherit his grandfather's estate and wins the friendship and esteem of virtually everyone in the community. The only thing he lacks is the hand of the woman he loves. The taboo against miscegenation, especially when it is the man who carries the tainted blood, is just too strong for the girl's father to grant his consent.

When Allen's beloved, Katherine Rutledge, is denied permission to marry him, his love for her is gradually transformed into hatred for her father and brother Percy (a sort of headstrong Confederate Hotspur). This hatred sustains Allen through the hardships of the War between the States, until he actually feels deprived by the deaths of old Rutledge and young Percy. Allen returns home after the war to find that his mansion has been burned by a perfidious free black, who had always scorned the way Marcus's benevolence exposed his own inadequacies. Too late, Allen sees his self-destructive animosities more crudely mirrored in the behavior of the black. Katherine is so guilt stricken by the grief that her romance had brought to her father and brother that she refuses to marry Allen, even when she is fi-

2. Lytle, "The Displaced Family," *Sewanee Review* 66 (Winter 1958): 128.

nally free to do so. The only consolation with which he is left is increased self-knowledge.

Sojourn of a Stranger may have suffered from an irrational critical prejudice against historical fiction. At the same time, the tact and restraint with which Sullivan treats the sex and violence inherent in his story may have kept the book from becoming a best-seller. Andrew Lytle believes that, if anything, Sullivan was guilty of too much decorum. Although the romance between Katherine and Allen is the central issue of the plot, it seems to be more postulated than dramatized. The social inhibition that binds the class to which the lovers belong becomes not so much a restraint on passion as a substitute for it. (The feeling between Allen's parents appears more genuine.) One also suspects that the war moves too quickly and with too little consequence in the novel, although drawing it out at much greater length might have upset the equilibrium of the plot.

But these technical quibbles are matters about which reasonable and sensitive readers can disagree. The real test of a historical fiction is whether the author has found a usable past. Ideally, this should involve more than, say, depicting the Salem witch trials as a way of denouncing McCarthyism—as Arthur Miller did in *The Crucible*. Nothing would have been more facile than to write a simplistic attack on southern racism in the guise of a Civil War novel for a sophisticated audience at the dawn of the civil rights era. In praising *The Victim* by Saul Bellow, Leslie Fiedler states: "Our Jewishness or gentileness, Bellow leaves us feeling, is *given;* our humanity is what we must achieve."[3] Substitute the words *Negro* and *white* for *Jew* and *gentile*, and you have a fair description of the moral vision of Sullivan's novel. That vision is more authentic, more fully *earned*, because the novel is unblinking in its depiction of the folly and evil of racial prejudice. As a result, the unwary reader, who thinks he is reading a conventional protest novel, is caught with his complacency showing.

If Allen is shocked by recognizing a kindred spirit in the free black Ben Hill, then what of the enlightened modern reader who has shared Allen's ambitions, loves, and hatreds? The novel finally forces us to pronounce judgment on Allen, but we cannot do so without also

---

3. Fiedler, *The Collected Essays of Leslie Fiedler* (New York: Stein and Day, 1971), 1:235.

pronouncing judgment on ourselves. There is much to admire in Allen and much to detest in his enemies. In an ideal society, neither he nor his mother would suffer discrimination because of their alien blood. Blacks and whites *should* be free to intermarry as their love dictates, and bigoted fathers and brothers should *not* be able to prevent the happiness of others. But it is not the role of the novelist to bring about that ideal society. (As Auden wrote in his elegy to Yeats, "Poetry makes nothing happen.") It would have been easy—and profitable—enough for Sullivan simply to have criticized the inequities of the antebellum South (or for that matter the South of the 1950s), but his primary concern is with the individual—who is always a stranger and a sojourner in this fallen world. Given the realities of the society in which they lived, both Allen Hendrick and his father should have shown greater sensitivity for the values of others and less obsession with abstract justice. Because that simple message is so difficult to accept in an age that has elevated justice above every other social and personal good, *Sojourn of a Stranger* is a more courageous book than any dozen protest novels.

If *Sojourn of a Stranger* achieves its seriousness by refusing to pander to the righteous indignation of its readers, Walter Sullivan's second novel, *The Long, Long Love*, does something even more remarkable: it exposes the limitations of a sacred southern virtue—reverence for the past. It is almost as if Sullivan's first two novels deliberately take the materials of stock antisouthern animus (a racial morality play in one instance and an antinostalgia satire in the other), only to find unexpected complexity in what a lesser writer would reduce to cliché. It is a delicate undertaking to be sure, because the narrative can never stray far from self-parody.

The Long, Long Love is set in present-day (that is, late 1950s) Nashville. The protagonist, Horatio Adams, is a wealthy middle-aged member of the southern aristocracy. After his wife's suicide (prompted in part by cancer and in part by having to live with Horatio), he is plunged into a period of depression and heavy drinking. When he meets and marries a beautiful young woman named Emily, Horatio begins putting his life back together. Unfortunately, his attachment to the past is so overwhelming that he nearly falls apart again when vandals desecrate the grave of his Confederate grandfather on Halloween. In the meantime, Emily and Horatio's son, Tavean, fall in love and run off together.

When Horatio tries to move his grandfather's body to a more secure family plot, he discovers that nobody is buried in the old man's
grave at the Confederate cemetery thirty miles south of Nashville.
Just before the desertion of his wife and son, Horatio dispatches his
daughter's fiancé—a young history professor at Vanderbilt—to find
where the old general is really buried. In quick succession, Horatio
learns that his fleeing son has been killed in a car wreck and that his
grandfather had not fallen on the field of battle but had been appre-
hended in bed with another man's wife. After a humiliating encounter
with a con lady in Florida (who gets him drunk and then rolls him), a
chastened Horatio returns to Nashville and is reunited with Emily,
whose pity he readily accepts as a kind of love.

In this novel Sullivan experiments with different points of view, allowing Horatio, his daughter Anne, and her fiancé, Philip, to tell the
story. Although each voice is convincing on its own terms, the shifting perspectives deprive the book of the overarching critical intelligence necessary to make sense of Horatio Adams's life. In Horatio,
Sullivan has given us a man whose piety for the southern past is
everything that an Agrarian could want. Yet this piety goes a long
way toward making life miserable for both Horatio and those closest
to him. (Faulkner had rendered a more extreme version of this same
phenomenon in the character of Gail Hightower in *Light in August*.)
If, as Jaroslav Pelikan claims, tradition is the living faith of the dead
and traditionalism the dead faith of the living, Horatio is clearly the
victim of a moribund traditionalism.[4] Because he is so firm in his
own sense of tradition, Sullivan avoids turning this cautionary tale
into an anti-Agrarian satire or polemic. By the same token, the younger
people in Horatio's family are not sufficiently shallow or self-
absorbed to make us regard the old guy as the lesser of two evils. We
are finally asked to follow Emily's lead and give him *our* pity as well.

There is much to admire in *The Long, Long Love*. (The title, by the
way, comes from the old Scottish ballad "The Daemon Lover.") The
three narrators are believable and compelling, the action is well
paced, and the thematic conflict between Old South and New is clearly
delineated. If the novel seems to have too happy an ending, it is at
best an ambiguous happiness (who really wants to settle for pity as a
kind of love?) and one that has been purchased with much suffering.

---

4. Pelikan, *The Vindication of Tradition* (New Haven, CT: Yale University
Press, 1984), 65.

Some readers may be put off by Horatio's rhetoric (so florid as to be embarrassing in places), but it is entirely appropriate to his character. Perhaps heeding Lytle's criticism of his first novel, Sullivan has also made Horatio a fully erotic being. As a result, he comes off as a combination schoolboy romantic and dirty old man. Consider, for example, the following description of his second wedding night:

> In a moment or five or ten, we would go to our bedroom. She would remove the negligee under which she wore nothing and I would see—as in my fevered imagination, my distraught mind's eye, I could almost see now—those last inches of flesh which I had never seen, the secret planes and articulations of pale stomach and pale hips and the secret hair, darker than the hair of her head, which the beauticians attended. This, in my fancy, could I almost see.
>
> This and the moment that would follow it, I delayed against.
>
> Because when the desire is very strong, when you are caught up in the simple, aching want, you are like Joshua and the sun stands still, which is to you, in your hiatus of deception, the same thing. There was only Emily and the world did not exist; and not existing, the world did not spin or orbit and there was therefore no night or day, no winter coming.[5]

What finally makes *The Long, Long Love* less satisfactory than *Sojourn of a Stranger* is that the shifting perspectives tell us both too little and too much. Although Tavean and Emily are not inherently implausible characters, we do not know as much as we need to about their motivations. Consequently, in their case character seems molded by plot rather than plot being driven by character. On the other hand, we probably see more than we need to of the inner workings of Horatio's mind. It is doubtful that Gatsby would have been as sympathetic a character had Fitzgerald let him tell any of his own story. The shifting omniscience of his first novel had allowed Sullivan to give us a glimpse into any mind he chose without forcing him to linger there longer than was necessary. Of course, first-person narration creates greater empathy by giving us an identifiable speaking voice. If that was the correct technical choice for *The Long, Long Love*, I would have preferred a single narrator, who was involved

5. Sullivan, *The Long, Long Love*, 68.

enough with Horatio to know his story yet detached enough to put it in perspective. Horatio's daughter's fiancé, Philip Holcomb, might have been such a narrator.

As a southern history professor, Philip is sensitive to the burden of the past in the present. As Horatio's prospective son-in-law, he is around during much of the story and has every reason for wanting to know about things that he has not directly witnessed. (Remember the narrative sleight of hand that Fitzgerald employs to fill Nick in on Gatsby and Daisy's past.) What is equally important, he is sufficiently distanced from the principal characters to analyze and judge all of them. Holcomb does speak in his own voice when he tells us of his quest for Horatio's grandfather's grave site. What is going on in the present is also a mystery, but one that requires the sensibility of a philosopher rather than the instincts of a bloodhound. Like Warren's Jack Burden, Philip Holcomb is a historian who might have been equal to that task.

In his essay "Southern Writers in Spiritual Exile," Sullivan states: "The only way to recreate a South that is hospitable to the production of great literature is to recapture the sacred. I think, paradoxically perhaps, that the best way to do this is to seek the transcendent outside the ambience of southern imagery because the images of the South, familiar and beloved as they are, tempt us to believe that we have not lost our piety."[6] This is a startling admission coming from a writer so steeped in the southern tradition; however, Sullivan was convinced that too much contemporary southern fiction had maintained the regional atmospherics we associate with the great writers of the Renascence, while losing a sense of moral vision and religious commitment. By sounding this theme insistently in his criticism (since at least 1970), Sullivan has also suggested the standard by which his own fiction should be judged. If we look at eight stories he published between 1971 and 2003, we find a writer who is less a neo-Agrarian than a Catholic modernist.

The vision to which I am referring has nothing to do with the theological revisionism also known as modernism. I am thinking instead of those writers who have posited an orthodox Catholic response to

6. Sullivan, *In Praise of Blood Sports and Other Essays* (Baton Rouge: Louisiana State University Press, 1990), 47.

the metaphysical discontinuity depicted by *literary* modernism. In the twentieth century, such writers included François Mauriac, Evelyn Waugh, Muriel Spark, Flannery O'Connor, J. F. Powers, and Graham Greene. Collectively, they articulated what can be regarded as an "antihumanist sensibility." In their fiction, Martin Green points out, "human achievements and modes of being are consistently and triumphantly shown to be inadequate, egotistic, evil, just in being themselves, in being human. Under stress all natural goodness breaks down; only grace-assisted goodness is valid, and grace-assisted badness is perhaps even better."[7] In one sense, then, the fiction of Catholic modernism is almost indistinguishable from secular naturalistic fiction. (Sullivan himself admits to feeling more affinity with a spiritually serious nonbeliever such as Cormac McCarthy than with the facile but shallow Bobbie Ann Mason.) What is needed beyond a sense of natural depravity, however, is a fictively adequate means of depicting redemptive, *superhuman* grace. For more than thirty years, this is a task that Walter Sullivan has set for himself.

Of the eight stories we are examining, five feature a center of consciousness who is forced by the sudden death of a friend, enemy, or family member to reevaluate some of the basic assumptions of his or her own life. Although Sullivan himself does not use the term, these stories exhibit a kind of Christian existentialism. It is possible, even common, for people to live a mundane and unexamined existence for most of their lives. Only in extreme situations are we forced to acknowledge the absurdity of most of what we do and to wonder whether there is a larger meaning that shapes our destiny. Atheistic existentialists are able to live in the face of ultimate meaninglessness—in Albert Camus's phrase, to "imagine Sisyphus happy."[8] Those who find their happiness in Christ do so only after passing through a "dark night of the soul." In Sullivan's fictional universe, grace is not only costly—it is often fatal as well.

Matthew Hood, the central character of Sullivan's "The Penalty of Love" (*Sewanee Review*, Winter 1971), is prepared to face death with a kind of stoic resignation. He has imagined his end coming in the late afternoon with his wife, Patricia, there to send him off after the

7. Green, *Yeats's Blessing on Von Hugel* (London: Longmans, 1967), 74.
8. Camus, *The Myth of Sisyphus and Other Essays*, translated by Justin O'Brien (New York: Knopf, 1961), 123.

priest has given him extreme unction. But his resignation is transformed into foreboding when his wife unexpectedly precedes him in death. As Mr. Hood looks back over his life, we discover that he has frequently made faulty plans and ill-timed choices. He had enlisted in the navy on his seventeenth birthday, November 1, 1918, but had not had time to be shipped overseas before the war was over. Feeling cheated of a great adventure, he insisted on remaining in the service, even though it would delay his marriage. Although he had not asked her to do so, his future wife had waited for him, even after he signed on for a second hitch. For years he had failed to appreciate her patience, as he traveled the world and saw the inside of many different bedrooms. On one occasion, he had mounted a plump woman who was eating an archetypal apple. *"I ain't eat anything all day,"* she said. *"But you come on. A young boy like you ain't going to notice."*[9]

Although he has been an adequate provider, Mr. Hood had stubbornly stayed on the farm too long when there was money to be made working in defense plants during World War II. As soon as she was old enough, his daughter (and only child) moved into a boarding-house, worked as a waitress in a saloon, and married a soldier from St. Louis. When Mr. Hood finally moved to town to reunite the family, it was "too late for the defense-plant money, too soon to get a good price on the farm." Now, in his old age, he is left to meet death alone. Except that he is not alone. The image of his wife keeps appearing to him and then vanishing when he tries to touch her. Only now that it is too late does he realize how much she had loved him and how much he must have loved her. All his priest is able to tell him is that "it's the penalty of love, Matthew. Pay it gladly."[10]

As he leaves the priest's office, presumably to head home, the vision of his wife is so far gone that Mr. Hood cannot even call it up in his imagination. He seems to have reached the nadir of despair:

> He yearned for one small hope, one lovely thing to see, the sound of a voice, someone who knew his name and would call it. But there was nothing to see. Strangely the world was as empty as the sky: the universe had achieved a strange silence. "I'll have to try," Mr. Hood thought. He held to the column he had

9. Sullivan, "The Penalty of Love," *Sewanee Review* 89 (Winter 1971): 57.
10. Ibid., 68.

been leaning against. He boosted himself up with the very last energy that he had, and, turning his back to the heat of the sun, he peered through the doorway into the darkness of the hall. And he saw her there, in her flowered dress, waiting for him.[11]

This final vision comes to Mr. Hood only when he is passive and vulnerable, having given up the effort to achieve enlightenment through his own power. Given the fact that his dead wife is beckoning to him, rather than eluding him, and that his final energy is waning, we might assume that Mr. Hood is on the verge of death. What he sees is no beatific vision (unless his wife is a kind of Beatrice) but only darkness. It is, however, the darkness of a church into which he is summoned.

Uncertainties concerning death also figure prominently in "Sunset and Evening Star" (*Sewanee Review*, Summer 1994). Billy Fisher resides in a nursing home where his friend Leo Stark suffers a heart attack. According to the nurse who administered CPR, the old man had actually been dead for a brief time: "'Like Lazarus,' the nurse said. 'Over and back. He's returned from the nether world.'" This spectacle, combined with a book he has read about near-death experiences, fuels Billy's insatiable curiosity about what is on the other side. He has gotten the book from his spiritual counselor, a female Episcopal priest with the epicene name of Morgan Hall.

As a former activist in the Episcopal Church who became a Roman Catholic when the Episcopalians began ordaining women, Sullivan takes several satirical swipes at the reverend Ms. Not only is Morgan more interested in dispensing bogus comfort than in preaching the Gospel or promulgating the historic dogmas of the church, but she is also a constant source of earthly temptation for poor Billy. "He tried to divert himself by letting his gaze fall, but below her clerical collar, the shape of her breasts showed beneath her shirt and the effect of them was not diminished by the gold cross that lay between them."[12]

Like so many liberal clergy, Morgan does not really believe in sin or judgment. One suspects that she would also have difficulty believing in heaven if she were not certain that everyone was going there. When Billy asks her if "even Hitler didn't go to hell," she replies, "Oh

11. Ibid., 68–69.
12. Sullivan, "Sunset and Evening Star," *Sewanee Review* 102 (Summer 1994): 363.

Billy, hell is just a figure of speech. You need to think positively."[13] Unfortunately, Billy's sense of cosmic justice will not allow him to believe in an afterlife where everyone gets a free pass. Although this may mean that he is more of a traditionalist than his priest, his faith is shallow and superficial for very different reasons. Billy's obsession with the book *We Have Seen the Other Side* reveals him to be a doubting Thomas, who needs empirical proof of the salvation in which he claims to believe. Rather than giving him that proof, the book prompts him to pester Leo about what he has seen on "the other side." The fact that Leo has seen nothing simply fills Billy with apprehension.

The story concludes with Leo's second heart attack. Not only is this one fatal, but he never regains consciousness to be interrogated about what he has seen this time. Consequently, at the end of the story, Billy has nothing to fall back on. The "faith" that Morgan Hall preaches is little more than pabulum for the elderly. Unlike Matthew Hood, Billy has no loved one to lead him through the darkness and no real *evidence* of what lies beyond the grave. Nevertheless, the story does not end on a definitive note of despair. After leaving the dying Leo, Billy reflects on his own lack of faith. "Above the hospital and the busy street, a plane passed, its running lights barely puncturing the vast darkness. Light and dark, Billy thought. Day and night. Years passing. For him they were almost past. . . . He took a deep breath and considered what was to come. He would have to be patient. Before he could know what he wanted to know, he would have to wait through whatever periods were left to him of light and darkness."[14]

The protagonist of Sullivan's "Mortmain" (*Sewanee Review*, Fall 1998) is a woman in late middle age whose consciousness (like Mr. Hood's and Billy Fisher's) is rendered from a third-person-limited perspective. At the outset, the reader is encouraged to feel a sympathetic identification with Lucy, an unattractive woman who has discovered marital happiness with William, an equally unattractive man. They met at a Catholic singles dance and were apparently drawn to each other by their mutual awkwardness. The only thing to mar the happiness of their thirty-year marriage is William's devotion to his

13. Ibid., 368.
14. Ibid., 375.

worthless brother, Marvin. The story opens when Marvin dies during a fire at the nursing home where he lives. (Although only sixty-four and looking fifty, Marvin is brain damaged from a beating he suffered at the hands of a gambler to whom he owed a large sum of money.) Lucy disingenuously prays that Marvin might be relieved of his suffering and is comforted when the nursing home fire seems to answer that prayer.

It is not long, however, before we realize that it is Lucy who wishes to be relieved of Marvin and the demands his presence places on her marriage to William. Marvin keeps popping up at the most inopportune moments, and after he becomes a near vegetable, his care costs William three thousand dollars a month. With him out of the way, Lucy and William can achieve the modest but hard-earned reward of growing old together. What reader could be so hard-hearted as to begrudge this aging couple such a modicum of happiness? Even if William has gone overboard in assisting Marvin, we are led to believe that he too heaves a sigh of relief at his brother's demise. But these assumptions are based almost entirely on the fact that we are seeing things through Lucy's eyes.

Even as we sympathize with Lucy, she inadvertently drops hints of her true nature. Though she is feeling guilty that her prayers might have caused the fire in the nursing home, the very thought that Marvin might be saved produces a flash of anger. Then, when she learns that he was not burned but succumbed to smoke inhalation, she thinks: "Gone with no more than a cough or two. She had been surprised at her own bitterness." She is even annoyed to realize that, after his riotous life, Marvin will be buried in the church. Although she had no objection to the priest's anointing Marvin, she felt that he had gone too far when he "put on his stole and asked Marvin if he were sorry for his sins and taken Marvin's gurgling hee, hee, hee as a proper answer. He had managed to give Marvin communion, though the first couple of times he tried, the host came drooling down Marvin's chin."[15] It is as if the prodigal brother-in-law is getting the royal treatment without having to do penance or even show verifiable contrition. Still, if Marvin is to be buried a Catholic, Lucy is resolved that it be done right. When she discovers that he does not have a rosary, she rushes out of the funeral home and purchases one at a nearby

15. Sullivan, "Mortmain," *Sewanee Review* 106 (Fall 1998): 560.

Catholic bookstore. But, by the time she returns, someone has already slipped a more expensive rosary into Marvin's hands. Thinking this to be one final extravagance of William's, she cannot help being momentarily annoyed. As it turns out, however, it is not William but Marvin's long-lost wife, Lorene, who has shown up and done the honors.

As she observes her husband's awkward behavior with Lorene during the visitation at the funeral home, Lucy remembers the time many years earlier when Marvin and Lorene had lived with her and William. Suddenly, the way that William and Lorene had embraced when she and Marvin made their final exit makes sense to Lucy. Her ugly-duckling husband had once had a dalliance with his brother's beautiful wife. Although it was apparently a one-night affair that began more in compassion than in desire, the news shatters Lucy's view of the world. With her marriage apparently come to an end, she storms out of the funeral home, still holding the sack with the rosary she had purchased for Marvin. "Cursing Marvin in her mind and wishing with all her heart for his damnation, she lowered the [car] window and threw the sack with all the strength she could gather. For a moment it sailed white in the sun. Then the rosary fell out of the sack, caught in the light breeze, climbed briefly before it twisted and dipped and fell fluttering to the pavement."[16]

In every outward respect, Lucy's behavior is morally and theologically correct. She has been a faithful and dutiful wife, and even the severest provocation has never prompted her to take overt action against the hated Marvin. But the miracle of fiction gives us access into her mind and soul. Even though she does not narrate the story in her own voice, the effect is similar to a dramatic monologue by Browning. Lucy condemns herself without realizing it. Although Sullivan does not excuse the adultery of William and Lorene or the more extended misbehavior of Marvin, he obviously realizes that spiritual pride and a lack of charity are far worse transgressions than any sin of the flesh. By the end of the story, we see Lucy as an unreconstructed Pharisee. Living in the same world with William, Lorene, and (especially) Marvin has tested her character and faith. Like an institution bound by the ancient principle of mortmain, she cannot trade or sell what she has acquired—in this case people and the obligations they impose. Like the elder brother in the "Parable of the

16. Ibid., 570.

Prodigal Son," she finally turns out to be too righteous for her own good.

"Love's Mysteries" (*Sewanee Review*, Fall 2001) also focuses on a woman whose life is turned around by the death of a relative and its impact on those who are left behind. Dolores is on a mission to learn what she can about the final years of her estranged brother, Henry. (As one might expect, this quest tells her much about Henry but even more about herself.) All that she or the other members of her large family know is that Henry's life was irrevocably altered when his fiancée, Joanne, broke their engagement years earlier. Henry had returned to his native Nashville and become a successful lawyer. Because he and the rest of his family never again visited each other, news of his fatal illness was concealed until after his death. It is left to Dolores to search out the old family home, which Henry had owned but not occupied for the balance of his life. There she discovers a woman named Jewel, who had rented the house for a call-girl service she ran. Because Jewel had also been Henry's mistress, she is able to fill Dolores in on the sort of man her brother had become.

If the whore with the heart of gold is a stock figure in American literature, the understanding madam is nearly as familiar. Apparently, Joanne had left Henry because of her cultural differences with his family (she is Baptist, and they are Catholic). Because the conflict pulls Henry away from the family even as he loses Joanne, Jewel fills a sizable void in his life. Henry dies outside the church, while living in sin with a woman of ill repute. But that is all part of the prehistory of the story. Sullivan's concern is with the meaning of Henry's fate for Dolores. At first, she is infuriated with him for having given up everything that had been dear to him for the sake of a woman he loses anyway:

> Oh what a fool Henry had been, Dolores thought as she walked back to her hotel. Oh what an idiot. He had been too old to make such a romantic gesture, to give up everything in this world and the next for the sake of a woman. That was a game for young men, for Tristan, for Romeo; and Henry hadn't even had his night of love as they had. For him there had been no consummation, no fulfillment. Mother of God, Dolores thought, how could Henry have abandoned all that had been most dear to him, the religion in which he had been raised, the people whom he loved and who

deeply loved him, out of anger and disappointment? Her heart ached to think of how terribly Henry had been hurt; how utterly profound had been his sorrow. Whether anyone noticed her tears as she crossed the hotel lobby was of no concern to her. At this moment no stranger could think as ill of her as she thought of herself. She was still angry with Henry, but mostly she was ridden with guilt.[17]

That night, Dolores dreams of an event that had happened twenty-five years earlier. During an outing at her parents' summer home, her eighteen-month-old son, Gabriel, had chased a ball into the lake and drowned before Henry could rescue him. Dolores makes intercessory prayers to Gabriel for her brother's soul, even as she realizes that the surviving members of the family must make atonement for their indifference to Henry.

> They wouldn't have to pretend that he hadn't been a fool. They wouldn't have ever to approve of what he had done. But they would have to cherish his memory, and the responsibility for praying for his soul would continue for as long as any of them lived. His death and the circumstances of it had brought him closer to them than if he had lived and died as the rest of his family were trying to do—as unremarkable Christians.[18]

What we may have here is a case of grace-assisted badness serving as a vehicle of salvation.

The principal characters of "Bare Ruined Choirs" (*Sewanee Review*, Fall 2003) are not only Catholics but also members of the clergy. Father Joe Agnelli is a conservative young curate whose supervising pastor seems intent on realizing all of the more radical changes of Vatican II in his own lifetime. Father Tommy Mallard celebrates the most modern and vernacular liturgies available, preaches a theology that dances around the borders of heresy without ever quite crossing the line, and supports people and causes far removed from the institutional church. When he was assigned to St. Bridget's Parish, Father Mallard replaced a more conventional priest who had been forced to retire because of advancing age. Because Father Agnelli has served

17. Sullivan, "Love's Mysteries," *Sewanee Review* 109 (Fall 2001): 508.
18. Ibid., 510.

under both men, he is keenly aware of the changes Father Mallard has wrought—with many of the old parishioners leaving, only to be replaced by a more innovative brand of Catholic. The crowning blow is Father Mallard's plan to replace the existing church building, with its traditional architecture and design, with a more modern and secular edifice.

When Father Mallard suffers a fatal illness, it is too late to undo much of the damage he has already done, but Father Agnelli hopes at least to halt any further modernization. Knowing Sullivan's own traditionalist sympathies, one would assume that Father Agnelli would be the hero of the story with Father Mallard the brunt of its satire. To an extent, this is the case, but Sullivan is finally on to something more sophisticated than ecclesiastical politics, as intriguing as that theme can sometimes be. Agnelli's plans for St. Bridget's are inseparable from his ambitions to become pastor of the parish, and his critique of Father Mallard is inevitably tinged with feelings of resentment and superiority. As much as Sullivan might sympathize with Agnelli's views, he presents the young priest as a flawed human being. Perhaps sensing Agnelli's immaturity and mixed motives, the bishop assigns a more experienced and moderate pastor to replace the dying Father Mallard. Although Agnelli obediently accepts the decision, his vocational pride is clearly wounded.

"Bare Ruined Choirs" ends with a twist that accentuates and resolves the ironies of the preceding action. As Father Agnelli sits among the literal ruins of the partially demolished church, trying to feel contrition for his animosity toward the late Father Mallard, a short, muscular man in an expensive jacket enters the church and expresses surprise to learn of Mallard's death. Because the old priest had once helped him out of a difficult situation by giving him a large sum of money, the man hands Agnelli a wad of bills and instructs him to say some masses for Father Mallard. Given Mallard's theological liberalism, this is probably the last thing he would have wanted done in his memory. To make matters more absurd, it will be Agnelli's responsibility to celebrate the masses for his old nemesis. Although the benefactor is never explicitly identified, he seems obviously associated with the Mob. "You know, Father, in some businesses it doesn't hurt to be Italian," he says. To this Agnelli replies, "Maybe the business I'm in is one of them. Maybe the next pope will be from Italy."[19]

19. Sullivan, "Bare Ruined Choirs," *Sewanee Review* 111 (Fall 2003): 510.

It is not unusual for a modern writer to depict the world in ironic terms. When that writer is also a man of faith, he is saying—in effect—that God has a sense of humor. We are left to speculate about the impact of this final bizarre experience on Father Agnelli. If the bishop has chastened his ambition, this subsequent turn of events has undercut the spiritual certainty with which Agnelli has always judged people and situations. One doubts that either he or Sullivan has become a born-again enthusiast for Vatican II. However, the ability to see beyond one's most cherished assumptions is both a theological and an artistic virtue. As a polemicist, Walter Sullivan would be an articulate ally of Father Agnelli's conservative churchmanship. As an artist, he is able to probe the deeper mysteries of which churchmanship is an outward and visible sign. As a consequence, this story becomes an enactment of its own truth.

Like the preceding five stories, the other three we will examine are narrated from a third-person-limited point of view. (Sullivan seems to have abandoned his experiment in first-person narration after *The Long, Long Love.*) In each case, however, the protagonist is a young woman, and in none of these stories does the plot turn on the issue of death. Sullivan's "Elizabeth" (*Sewanee Review*, Summer 1979) is set in an urban environment that is not recognizably southern. The title character is a young waitress married to an abusive and psychopathic husband. Herman "Lucky" Baker had been a celebrated halfback in high school, but "at under 140 pounds he was too small to play college football." (Sullivan clues us into this quite subtly when he says of Lucky, "He broke for a touchdown, scampering through a hole that future college players made for him.")[20] Like the protagonist of Irwin Shaw's "The Eighty-Yard Run," everything after football is downhill for Lucky. He is too volatile ever to hold a job for very long, goes around with a grudge against the world, and beats his long-suffering wife. After a particularly savage pummeling causes her to lose the child she is carrying, Elizabeth moves out. The story ends when she is summoned to the police morgue to identify Lucky, who has been killed in a barroom brawl.

The sadly misnamed Lucky and the handful of minor characters are all convincingly drawn; however, the crowning achievement of this story is Sullivan's depiction of Elizabeth. He takes us into the

20. Sullivan, "Elizabeth," *Sewanee Review* 87 (Summer 1979): 349.

mind of this troubled woman whose simple faith is shaken by the nightmare of her marriage. Significantly, the institutional church is of little help to her during her time of trial. One day after she has lost her child and left her husband, she enters a church to pray. She no longer has her rosary, which was stolen with her purse, and she does not even bother to light a candle to the Virgin. Sitting in a pew in the back of the church, she feels abandoned by God and man.

Like Blanche Dubois, Elizabeth depends on the kindness of strangers. When she is hospitalized after losing her baby, a young doctor shows her sympathy and gives her five dollars to get home. And Bernie Greenspan, the owner of the bar where she works, is invariably pleasant. But the most loving character of all is Bernie's wife, Leah. She accompanies Elizabeth to the morgue, comforts her, and gives her a large bosom to cry on. While Elizabeth is in the morgue, images of her own life flash through her mind, until she is transported back to a day in her childhood when she and her family put flowers on the graves in the cemetery and prayed for the dead. "She was too weak to do anything but rest in Leah Greenspan's arms and cry and feel her thoughts drift—back to the cemetery, the autumn sky, the praying voices of the women. And she remembered how on that other day she had turned and seen, almost close enough for her to touch, a statue of the Mother of God rising above her."[21] The grace Elizabeth has not found in the church building is ministered to her here by a Jewish mother very unlike the iconographic images of the Blessed Virgin. However, Sullivan leaves no doubt that it is grace that Elizabeth has experienced. She is able to forgive Lucky and reach far enough into her past to recover a faith that is almost literally childlike.

With "Only the Dance" (*Sewanee Review*, Spring 1999), Sullivan makes an uncharacteristic foray into the realm of magical realism. Considerably younger than Elizabeth, Cecilia is the dreamy last-born child of an apparently wealthy family. With her father dead and her older siblings all gone from the nest, Cecilia lives uneasily with her mother, who cannot understand why this able-bodied daughter prefers reading *Don Quixote* to cleaning the pool or wiping bird droppings off the statue of St. Francis of Assisi. After promising to attend to both tasks, Cecilia absconds in the family car to the cemetery where

21. Ibid., 373.

her father is buried. Rather than mourning her father's demise, she sits among the graves imagining a musical comedy in which nuns with mops sing and dance their way through the tombstones. Suddenly, a handsome young man, who knows her every thought, appears and teaches her a dance. The memory of this strange youth sustains Cecilia during the time that her mother grounds her for her irresponsible behavior. After her punishment is completed, she returns to the cemetery and again sees the mysterious boy with whom she resumes the dance. After a final conversation, he refuses her touch and disappears among the tombstones. Upon returning home and attempting (or pretending) to clean the pool, Cecilia loses her balance and falls in the water fully clothed. As the story ends, she continuously swims to the bottom of the pool and rises to the top, spewing water like a dolphin.

Given the moral seriousness of so much of Sullivan's earlier fiction, one hardly knows what to make of such a light, seemingly frivolous, story. One gathers that the young boy Cecilia meets in the graveyard is an angel, although their encounter is much less melodramatic than the typical television episode of *Touched by an Angel*. If she learns anything from him, it is that we are all part of a greater cosmic harmony represented by the image of the dance. Yeats makes a similar point in "Among School Children," when he asks, "How can we know the dancer from the dance?" Sullivan, however, takes his title from T. S. Eliot's explicitly Christian poem "Burnt Norton": "Except for the point, the still point, / There can be no dance, and there is only the dance."[22]

We are apparently meant to conclude that Cecilia's encounter with the angel has led her to the sort of mystical insight described in Eliot's poem. If the immediate practical consequence is to cause her to swim like a dolphin rather than save the world, acquiring a sense of the world's wholeness is no small matter. In terms of personality and temperament, Cecilia is the same flighty bookworm who was reading *Don Quixote* at the beginning of the story. But like Jay Gatsby, she has finally found something "commensurate with her capacity for wonder." Cervantes was a satirical realist because he did not believe that windmills were giants. Sullivan is a literal supernaturalist because he believes that angels can dance.

22. Eliot, *Four Quartets* (New York: Harcourt, Brace, and World), 15–16.

In "Losses" (2001), Sullivan once again enters the mind of a teen-age girl but this time in the world of quotidian reality. Not only is the characterization convincing, but the rendering of young Addie's consciousness achieves a level of irony that is absolutely crucial to the story's meaning. Much is implicit even in the first sentence: "It was true that except for a little heaviness around her mother's waist and hips, she and her mother were the same size, but her mother was forty, the very worst possible age if you didn't count people who were older than that, and there was no way that she was going to wear her mother's dress to the funeral."[23] As readers, we are so immersed in Addie's adolescent vanity and rebellion that we do not immediately look at the situation objectively. As much as she might dislike wearing her mother's dress, the only garments she has in her own closet are a miniskirt, jeans, shorts, and a school uniform, and she is already ten minutes late in leaving for her grandmother's funeral. When she responds to the situation by saying, "Screw that," her mother slaps her hard on the face. This action adds credibility to Addie's ruminations about how neither her mother nor any other adult (especially her late grandmother) has ever understood her. To make matters worse, her father abandoned the family when Addie was so young that she has no clear recollection of him. Thus, she has no other parent to play off against her mother.

This is an ideal story for teaching the importance of point of view. If you take the same situation and render it from the mother's perspective, you would have a story about a single parent trying to instill a sense of traditional values in an impudent and self-absorbed daughter. The measure of the mother's failure is the fact that the daughter does not even show a minimal love and respect for her grandmother on the day of the old lady's funeral. In an effort to skip out on the solemnities as quickly as possible, Addie even allows herself to be picked up by a young man who works for the funeral home. They end up at a bar where Addie proves to be an inexperienced drinker and easy prey for her newfound friend, Frank. Taking advantage of her inebriation, Frank rapes Addie, as she wishes that her mother were there and even shouts out her grandmother's name, which like hers is Adelaide.

23. Sullivan, "Losses," in *The Cry of an Occasion: Fiction from the Fellowship of Southern Writers*, edited by Richard Bausch (Baton Rouge: Louisiana State University Press, 2001), 173.

One could easily read "Losses" as a moralistic tale about what happens to a girl who strays from her proper upbringing. But it is perhaps more appropriately read as a character study of an adolescent who is more traditional than she realizes. Had she been as rebellious as thinks she is at the beginning of the story, Addie would have handled her beer better at the bar and enjoyed her tryst with the young predator from the funeral home. (One might almost see this boy as a demonic counterpart to the angel Cecilia encounters in "Only the Dance," were it not for his total lack of supernatural powers.) Instead, Addie is humbled and violated.

If any good has come from this experience it is a greater degree of self-knowledge and a new appreciation of home. After returning to a locked church, Addie heads to her mother's house at the end of the story. (One suspects that, like Robert Frost's hired man, she has discovered that home is both "the place where, when you have to go there, they have to take you in" and "something you somehow haven't to deserve.") The "losses" referred to in the story's title may actually be paradoxical gains. Rather than insisting upon that point, however, Sullivan simply allows his readers to speculate as to whether Addie has experienced a fortunate fall.

It was not until thirty-six years after the publication of *The Long, Long Love* that Walter Sullivan's third novel appeared in 1995. In that time, the market for literary fiction had shrunk to the point where *A Time to Dance* bore the imprint of the Louisiana State University Press rather than that of a commercial New York publisher. The book was not as widely reviewed as its two predecessors and did not sell as well as Sullivan's next book—a collection of excerpts from the diaries of Confederate women. If such neglect was predictable, it was also unfortunate. *A Time to Dance* is not only Walter Sullivan's best novel but also one of the comic masterpieces of contemporary southern fiction.

The principal characters in this novel are Max and Bunnie Howard, a bohemian couple in their ninth decade. In the year leading up to their sixtieth wedding anniversary, we see Max and Bunnie coping with the burdens of aging as they reflect on the triumphs, disappointments, and manifold indiscretions of their earlier life. After Bunnie suffers a stroke, husband and wife are forced to move from their country home into Nashville, where Bunnie's great-nephew Julien can attempt to look after them. The saga of Max and Bunnie's misadventures alternates with an account of Julien's passion for Shannon, a nurse who cares for Bunnie during a brief hospitalization. Although Shannon is recovering from a youth of drug abuse and Julien is on the rebound from an affair with a mistress in Paris, the young people seem positively tame in comparison to the two old reprobates who dominate the novel. Whether we are to admire Julien and Shannon in their restraint or envy the riotous abandon of Max and Bunnie is an open question.

One of the joys of this novel is its black comedy at the expense of Max and Bunnie. That Sullivan can accomplish this without seeming tasteless or cruel is owing to his obvious affection for these characters. As much as we may disapprove of the way that Max and Bunnie have lived, there is a kind of heroism in the way they rage against the dying of the light. There is also the implicit realization that aging is a universal experience for those who do not die young. So when we laugh at Max and Bunnie, we are also laughing at what we ourselves may become. A dozen pages into the novel, we see Max facing a new day:

> He had decided a while back that the best thing to do in the morning was to get up. If he tried to wait until he was sure where he was, his mind would start flopping around as it did when he awakened in the middle of the night, going from one subject to another, jumbling the past and the present, until there was nothing but a confusion of images in his brain. On good days, once he got himself upright and was sitting on the side of the bed, he would begin to recognize the furniture or the color of the walls or the height of the ceilings. Finding his way to the bathroom helped, and by the time he got to the kitchen he would be sure enough of where he was to turn his attention to what he had done yesterday and what he would likely do today.[24]

Bunnie's memory problems tend to be more intellectual in nature. For example, she keeps getting novels mixed up in her head. "She knew very well that *War and Peace* was about Napoleon's invasion of Russia, but she was certain too that there was a white whale involved somehow.... And there was Becky Sharp, a little schemer

24. Sullivan, *A Time to Dance*, 12–13.

who, Bunnie was sure, had lived in England, but in Bunnie's recollection, she was turning up in rural France." When Bunnie herself decides, late in life, to become a novelist, she cannot seem to get beyond the promising first sentence: "Stately, plump Buck Mulligan came from the stairhead, bearing a bowl of lather on which a mirror and a razor lay crossed."[25]

The combination of Bunnie's physical ailments and Max's general befuddlement makes for macabre slapstick throughout the novel. The story opens with Max discovering Bunnie lying naked and unconscious on the floor of her bedroom in a most indecorous pose. He covers her with a comforter, puts a pillow under her head, and goes to sleep on her bed. When their housekeeper discovers the couple the next morning, Bunnie is sent to the hospital and Max suffers a well-deserved scolding. After Bunnie is discharged from the hospital, she is afflicted with nightmares and insists that Max share her single bed. Unfortunately, the bed is too small to accommodate the two of them, and Bunnie ends up getting pushed onto the floor. When he is unable to lift her, the chastened Max summons the local emergency service to put his wife back in bed. When this happens twice in one night, the harried paramedic tells Max: "We want to be helpful, but this is beginning to look funny on our log. I mean, we can't keep coming back to the same place without transporting the patient."[26]

It is one thing to live hard and die young, but even in their dotage Max and Bunnie continue to swill booze as if it were the very elixir of life. The first time that Julien drives him to the liquor store in Nashville, Max insists on stopping at the convenience store next door for ice and plastic glasses. Max discovers that "the large bottles were too much for him to maneuver with one hand: sometimes he missed the glass entirely. Always liquor splashed—on Max's trousers, on the upholstery, into the ice that melted on the floorboard. Alcoholic vapors would fill the automobile, the odor so strong that Julien's nose tingled."[27]

Max and Bunnie's confusion of past and present makes it that much easier for Sullivan to take us back decades earlier in their life

25. Ibid., 40, 159.
26. Ibid., 67.
27. Ibid., 35.

together. When they were younger, the two were frequently unfaithful to each other. Also, Max's unfulfilled dreams of literary fame cause the couple to forswear having children. This leads to Bunnie's having two abortions, which causes her subsequent infertility. In his midfifties, Max suddenly decides that he needs male progeny and propositions Bunnie's niece Susan (who is also Julien's mother). This crude miscalculation produces a near fatal crisis in Max and Bunnie's marriage. Bunnie flies off to Rome with the intention of leaving Max permanently. When he follows her there and vows to reform, the couple return to Nashville and celebrate a second wedding—this time in the church.

Midway through the novel, we get a flashback to the party immediately after this second wedding. It seems that Max and Bunnie's bohemian friends, who are all well into middle age, are trying one last time to recover their youth. As the evening degenerates into a Dionysian orgy, one of Bunnie's frequent paramours, the novelist John Ross, makes his move on the newly remarried Mrs. Howard. (John assumes that Max is probably cuckolding him at that very moment.) As it turns out, Max is sitting at a decent remove from Edith Ross—discussing theology. She is convinced that Max is a heretic because he reads too much Teilhard de Chardin. Heretic or not, Max has remained true to his renewed vows. When Bunnie says, "We're married for sure now, Maxie," her husband replies: "Yes. . . . We're on our honeymoon."[28]

It is not until we are nearly three-quarters of the way through the novel that we learn what prompted Max to pursue Bunnie to Rome. In his loneliness, he had become nostalgic for a wise and compassionate madam he had known during his days as a newspaperman back in the thirties. Remembering only that she went by the name of Miss Baby, Max phones every escort service in town to find someone by that name. When a woman finally comes to his hotel room, it is not his old companion but a young girl dressed as a nymphet. His protests that it has all been a mistake are taken to be additional evidence of his kinkiness. What follows is a hilarious scene in which Max ineptly fights off the young courtesan, who is trying to undress him. If nothing else, the humiliation shocks him back to a sense of moral balance.

28. Ibid., 101.

> When he was young, living in Mississippi, day had seemed to follow day in a regular order. He had known what was expected of him, known what he could and could not do, known what was right and wrong, good and bad, decent and unthinkable. Everywhere he had turned, there had been someone to advise him, to encourage or to reprimand him: his mother and father, the sisters at his school, the priests at the confessional. Max wasn't foolish enough to believe that he could ever reprise the moral certainty of that time. His life and the world he lived in now were different. But he longed to do something to make his life more orderly.[29]

Again, grace-assisted badness turns a life (and a plot) around.

The one time after their second wedding when Bunnie seems close to slipping up comes when she appears on a literary panel with John Ross in New Orleans. Had things gone according to expectation, he would have come by her room after the session for an all too familiar coupling. As fate (or grace?) would have it, John becomes so enamored with a younger woman on the panel that he stands Bunnie up, pleading loyalty to Max and respect for the couple's newfound fidelity. Bunnie gets drunk that night, oversleeps, and misses her plane. While nursing a terrible hangover, she stops at a church and witnesses parishioners entering the confessional. "She had never understood all this. What she wanted was forgiveness from Max, not absolution from some voice behind a screen. She wanted to go home and put her arms around him. She wanted to do something that would convince him that she loved him."[30]

The presence of Max and Bunnie is so overpowering that it seems something of a letdown when the narrative focus shifts to Julien and Shannon. But it is an essential letdown. The shift is from a kind of absurdist farce to something that more nearly resembles a screwball comedy from the thirties or forties played out against a contemporary backdrop. Had Sullivan wished to write the novel solely about Julien and Shannon, there is enough of potential interest in their past and present lives to make an engaging story. But to emphasize these possibilities any more than he does would have detracted too much from the main action of the novel he has actually written. The fact

29. Ibid., 145.
30. Ibid., 171.

that such an appealing young couple care so deeply for Max and Bunnie speaks volumes about the essential likability of the older pair.

But Julien and Shannon are finally more foils than character witnesses. If we think of young people as wild and hedonistic and senior citizens as mellow and subdued, Sullivan has turned the tables on us. Julien may speak like an impassioned romantic, and Shannon may sound at times like Gracie Allen, but their ultimate objective is to settle down in bourgeois marital bliss. It is altogether fitting that the two story lines come together when the same party is used to celebrate Julien and Shannon's wedding and Max and Bunnie's sixtieth anniversary.

This final party also serves as a contrast to two earlier ones in the novel. Immediately after Bunnie's stroke, Max recalls a gathering in the midforties when he and John Ross's wife, Edith, slipped off for a sexual tryst in the studio of the painter hosting the party. When it turned out that Max was without a condom, all he got for his efforts was a slap in the face. Then, a decade later, there was the riotous debauch after Max and Bunnie renewed their wedding vows. Now, in the midnineties, with their few surviving contemporaries well into their eighties, Max and Bunnie live almost entirely in the past. At one point, Max thinks he sees his mother (who is a young girl again) standing across the crowded party room. Before he can reach her, however, he must stop at the restroom, where he dies on the commode. After the funeral, Bunnie says: "I know that to everybody else he was just an old man lying in a casket, but I could see him when he was young, too. I could see him through all the years we were together."[31]

In a back-cover blurb, Elizabeth Spencer refers to this novel as "our mortal comedy." Both the mortality and the comedy are so evident that inattentive readers might overlook the sense of the sacred that lies at the heart of the novel. The religious themes in Sullivan's short fiction are more transparent, if only because the story must come to closure more quickly. The broader canvas of a novel allows such themes to be developed less obviously. Much of the texture of *A Time to Dance* is owing to Sullivan's acquaintance with the Fugitives and Agrarians. (The characters of Max and Bunnie were

31. Ibid., 192.

obviously inspired by Brainard and Frances Cheney, who were life-long friends of the Nashville writers.) The gift for narrative that was evident in Sullivan's *Allen Tate: A Recollection* (1987) is here put to excellent fictional use in depicting a social milieu that is now largely past. It is Walter Sullivan's conviction that the writer need not be God, but only believe in Him, to make that past come alive again.

6

"What They Have to Say about Us"

In the winter of 2003, alumni all over the nation opened the latest issue of *Vanderbilt Magazine* to Paul Kingsbury's long article on the legacy of the Fugitives and Agrarians.[1] The topic itself was not unusual. True, Vanderbilt had ignored and even opposed its most visionary offspring when they were doing their most distinguished work. But ever since English Department chairman Randall Stewart had invited them back for a reunion in 1956, the university had basked in their reflected glory. And for nearly a half century, it seemed as if the lovefest would go on forever. Beginning with its ambivalent title, "Pride *and* Prejudice," Kingsbury's article proved that that was no longer true. Though paying a kind of grudging tribute to their achievement, Kingsbury depicted the Fugitives and Agrarians as reactionary and racist troglodytes who are now widely ignored even by teachers of southern literature. This characterization was supported by interviews with Michael Kreyling and Kate Daniels, both current professors at Vanderbilt, and John Lowe of Louisiana State University. In fact, the only two scholars to say anything good about the brethren were Walter Sullivan and Paul Conkin, both of whom were retired from Vanderbilt.

The only thing remarkable about Kingsbury's essay was the fact that it appeared in an official publication of Vanderbilt University. None of what he said was particularly new. In their own time, the authors of *I'll Take My Stand* had been dismissed as reactionary dreamers, and political liberals had always suspected a measure of racism in their attachment to the Old South. Given the climate of po-

1. Kingsbury, "Pride *and* Prejudice," *Vanderbilt Magazine* 84 (Winter 2003): 30–39.

litical correctness that had swept the nation's campuses since the
1960s, it should have come as no surprise that the Fugitive-Agrarians
are not in official favor. It had just taken Vanderbilt a bit longer to
come around to the conventional wisdom. Or so the argument went.
The only problem is that the picture Kingsbury paints is far from
complete.

If John Crowe Ransom, Allen Tate, and Donald Davidson are not
safely enshrined on Mount Olympus (next to Robert Penn Warren,
who is seen as the one member of the brotherhood to transcend his
past), very few writers remain at the top forever. (Even Shakespeare
was on the ropes for much of the eighteenth century.) If revisionists
such as Kreyling, Daniels, and Lowe think that the Fugitives and
(particularly) the Agrarians are passé, one wonders why they must
spend so much time and effort saying so. What other fringe group of
the thirties continues to invite such denunciation? How much ink
has been spilled in recent years discussing, say, the poetry of the
Abraham Lincoln Brigade or the critical views of the John Reed Club?

Whatever their shortcomings, *I'll Take My Stand* (1930) and *Who
Owns America?* (1936) have stubbornly refused to stay out of print.
Substantial biographies of Cleanth Brooks, Robert Penn Warren,
Donald Davidson, and Allen Tate were published by major university
presses between 1996 and 2000. The doctoral dissertations devoted
to the Agrarians and their works number in the hundreds. If nothing
else, the continuing (sometimes virulent) opposition their ideas in-
spire is a left-handed tribute to their continuing relevance. This is a
situation that would hardly have been expected as recently as the
1950s. After a period of frenzied activity and controversy in the thirties, many of the Agrarians abandoned the cause for other interests—principally, literary criticism. Despite the continuing interest
the movement elicited among the creative writers and graduate students influenced by Ransom, Tate, Brooks, and Warren, Agrarianism
was slowly assuming the status of a historical curiosity. Then, in
1962, Harper and Row issued a paperback reprint of *I'll Take My
Stand* with an introduction by the southern literary scholar Louis D.
Rubin Jr. The controversy was reignited and continues to rage over
four decades later.

The copyright to *I'll Take My Stand* had been renewed in 1958 by
Donald Davidson, the one charter Agrarian to remain politically
active. At that time, scholarly interest in the Nashville writers had

focused almost exclusively on their work as Fugitive poets. In his introduction to the 1962 reissue of the Agrarian manifesto, Rubin seemed to endorse this emphasis on literary over political considerations. Rubin argued that the book and the vision of the South it articulated were not really political at all, but rather an extended metaphor for the values of religious humanism. Reacting angrily to this notion in a letter to Allen Tate, dated August 12, 1962, Donald Davidson wrote: "I still don't like the notion . . . that all of our agonizing, brooding, studying, discussing, philosophizing, writing about what we have seen, known, experienced, fought-through, lived through, was but a 'metaphor.'"[2]

If it was Davidson's intention to revive debate about the social and political vision of Agrarianism, he got his wish. The first two books on the Agrarians to appear after the republication of *I'll Take My Stand* were sharply critical of the movement. John L. Stewart's *The Burden of Time: The Fugitives and Agrarians* (1965) echoed many of the criticisms leveled against the Agrarians by New South liberals of an earlier generation. The only difference was that Stewart had seen the future and found it far closer to utopia than the spiritual wasteland the Agrarians had predicted. In *Tillers of a Myth* (1966), Alexander Karanikas was considerably more detailed and acerbic in expressing his disdain for the Agrarians. A native of rural New Hampshire, Karanikas had studied at Harvard under the distinguished literary critic and Stalinist naif F. O. Matthiessen. In addition to regarding the Agrarian myth as impractical, he saw it as part of a vast right-wing conspiracy, which extended geographically to Europe and historically back to the nineteenth century. Sounding a note that would become increasingly shrill in later anti-Agrarian polemics, Karanikas saw the aesthetic formalism of the New Critics as an insidious extension of the cultural politics of the Agrarians. Having failed to take over the country, Grant Webster observes, they decided instead to take over the academy.[3]

Stewart and Karanikas were immediately rebutted (if not entirely refuted) by such scholars as Marion Montgomery, M. E. Bradford, Edward S. Shapiro, and Louis Rubin. If anything, the scholarship on

2. This letter is housed in the Fugitive Collection of the Jean and Alexander Heard Library at Vanderbilt University.

3. Webster, *The Republic of Letters: A History of Postwar American Literary Opinion* (Baltimore: Johns Hopkins University Press, 1979), 75.

the Agrarians in the 1970s tended to be overwhelmingly positive. In 1971, Thomas Daniel Young and M. Thomas Inge published a biographical and critical study of their former professor Donald Davidson in Twayne's United States Authors Series. Three years later, Young and John Tyree Fain edited the correspondence of Davidson and Tate. Then, in 1976, Young published his definitive biography of John Crowe Ransom—*Gentleman in a Dustcoat*. In 1977, Louis Rubin brought out yet another paperback reprint of *I'll Take My Stand* with a new introduction partly revising some of the comments he had made a quarter century earlier. The following year, Rubin published his magisterial study *The Wary Fugitives: Four Poets and the South*. The praises of various Agrarians were sung in other important books of the decade, including Radcliffe Squires's *Allen Tate: A Literary Biography* (1971) and *Allen Tate and His Work: Critical Evaluations* (1972), Lewis P. Simpson's *The Dispossessed Garden: Pastoral and History in Southern Literature* (1975), and Walter Sullivan's *Requiem for the Renascence: The State of Fiction in the Modern South* (1976).

While all of this was going on, Cleanth Brooks and Robert Penn Warren were still writing and lecturing, and a new edition of *The Fathers* by Allen Tate appeared in 1977. Then, in August 1979, Clyde N. Wilson organized a conference of fifteen scholars to discuss the future of the South. (Their papers were published two years later under the title *Why the South Will Survive*.) This occasion was followed by a year of celebrations commemorating the semicentennial of *I'll Take My Stand* in 1980. An unwary observer might have prematurely concluded that the Agrarians were finally regarded as prophets who had been vindicated by history. In fact, this was but the lull before the storm. Over the next two and a half decades, a younger generation of literary historians would wage an intellectual jihad against the Nashville Twelve. Their views speak volumes about the culture war itself.

Michael O'Brien, who is a native of Britain, earned a master's degree in history at Vanderbilt and a doctorate at the University of Cambridge. As an intellectual historian, O'Brien has expressed understandable skepticism concerning the Agrarians' description of southern culture. Allen Tate, for example, accounts for the Southern Renascence by saying: "With the war of 1914–1918, the South reentered the world—but gave a backward glance as it stepped over the border: that backward glance gave us the Southern renascence, a literature conscious of the past in the present." From O'Brien's perspective, there are several problems with this account. "It is doubtful," he argues, "that the South's presence in the modern world was drastically altered by the First World War, that the region was any more in and of that world in 1920 than it had been in 1910. Indeed, it is arguable that the Southern economy in 1850, before the decline of cotton, was more a part of a modernizing world than it was to become in 1920."[4] O'Brien goes on to point out that nostalgia, a sense of the past in the present, had been a staple in southern literature at least since the publication of John Pendleton Kennedy's *Swallow Barn* in 1835. If a "Southern Renascence" began in the 1920s, the reasons seemed to lie outside Tate's eccentric interpretation of social and economic history.

As valid as O'Brien's observations may be, they miss the point. The historical situation as it might be perceived by a social scientist is not the same as it is dreamed by a poet. One can only imagine what a literalist such as O'Brien would make of T. S. Eliot's claim to be a classicist, a royalist, and an Anglo-Catholic. Though Eliot might have been attracted to aspects of ancient culture, his writing style was not that of a classicist or a neoclassicist but that of a revolutionary modernist. In an age of constitutional monarchy, royalism could be no more than a sentimental attachment to a political order that had disappeared before Eliot was even born. And Anglo-Catholicism, for all the passionate intensity of its adherents, has always been more of an aesthetic construct than an identifiable sect. Nevertheless, these sociological delusions produced perhaps the most powerful and influential body of poetry to be written in English in the twentieth century.

When Tate and his fellow Fugitive-Agrarians looked at "the South," they saw it from a particular angle of vision. If their perspective was tinged with nostalgia, it was not the nostalgia of John Pendleton Kennedy or Joel Chandler Harris. Theirs was a different response because of the discontinuities of literary modernism. When the Fugi-

4. Tate, *Essays of Four Decades* (1968; reprint, Wilmington, DE: Intercollegiate Studies Institute, 1999), 545; O'Brien, *Rethinking the South: Essays in Intellectual History* (Baltimore: Johns Hopkins University Press, 1988), 162.

tives began writing poetry, they took pains to dissociate themselves from the local-color tradition exemplified by the Poetry
Society of South Carolina. (The assault was led by Donald Davidson, who would later become the most confirmed regionalist of the
entire Agrarian brotherhood.) They desperately wanted to be recognized as modern poets, without any demeaning sectional qualifi-
cation. To the extent that they were aware of H. L. Mencken's views
concerning the deficiencies of southern culture, they probably agreed
with him.

Ransom, Davidson, Tate, and Warren each discovered "the South"
in different ways and for different reasons. They might have tried to
pass as cosmopolitans with no particular regional loyalty. Or they
might have become New South reformers. Instead, they decided to
construct an ideal of what the South might become from an image of
what they imagined it to have been. (In the case of Ransom, Tate,
and Warren, part of the motivation might have been a reaction against
the trendy progressivism of Vanderbilt chancellor James Kirkland
and English Department chairman Edwin Mims.) If the *objective
conditions* for a sense of cultural disinheritance were greater in earlier periods of southern history, the writers who lived in those eras
had not been forged in the crucible of modernism. The reaction of
the Fugitive-Agrarians may not have been inevitable, but neither was
it inexplicable. O'Brien is nevertheless correct in arguing that that
reaction suffered from a serious internal contradiction.

From the outset, the Agrarians agreed that the situation they confronted required a religious solution, but they disagreed on which
church offered the truest hope of salvation. In his quirky book *God
without Thunder* (1930), Ransom praised the supernaturalism of
fundamentalist religion for largely aesthetic reasons. Nevertheless,
his attempts to be a good churchgoing Methodist were foiled by his
inability to affirm the words of the Apostles' Creed. Essentially a religious skeptic, Ransom could best be described as a High Church
Unitarian. Warren asked the big questions of faith and talked incessantly about God without ever adopting a specific creed. Early on,
Tate saw that the one major flaw in the traditional South was its
Protestant individualism. His eventual conversion to Roman Catholi-
cism in 1950 was the result of a twenty-year pilgrimage. Davidson,
who survived for decades on little more than tribal loyalty to a kind
of Old Testament South, told his wife on the night before he died that

he too intended to become a Catholic.[5] To the extent that the Agrarians gave doctrinal content to their generic sense of piety, they moved as far as possible from the evangelical religion that prevailed in the literal South.

The other major problem with the Agrarian thesis is that it does not adequately account for the variety of literature produced in the South during the Renascence. One wonders what the orderly world of Agrarian myth would have to say about the overt Gothicism of Tennessee Williams, Carson McCullers, and the early Truman Capote. Agrarian poetics would have a difficult time accommodating itself to Richard Wright's *Black Boy*, much less *Native Son*. (Agrarianism is certainly more promising than Marxism, however, as an approach to the work of Zora Neale Hurston.) The fact that Faulkner could be read through an Agrarian prism probably says more about his universality than it does about the adequacy of the Agrarian thesis. Writers as intractable as Erskine Caldwell and Thomas Wolfe were explicitly condemned to the realm of outer darkness. When we move beyond literature to the other arts, the situation is even more hopeless. O'Brien argues convincingly that "we would distort less to write cultural histories of the South by including [Louis] Armstrong and excluding even Faulkner than to do the reverse."[6] But Agrarianism has virtually nothing to say about jazz.

O'Brien's implicit thesis seems to be that southern culture is too varied to admit a single definition of the Southern Renascence. And if the phenomenon cannot be defined, perhaps it did not exist. For that matter, the cultural and geographical diversity that exists within the remnants of the Old Confederacy may mean that the South itself does not exist. (But then, one might just as well argue that, because no two snowflakes are exactly identical, there is no such thing as snow.) If 675,000 people died in the War between the States believing in the existence of the South, that should be sufficient evidence even for a modern-day nominalist. What Tate and his fellow Agrarians did was to make regional consciousness a formative element in American modernism. Their task was made immeasurably easier by the unique history of the South during war and Reconstruction. The fact

5. I learned this from a conversation with Davidson's granddaughter, Molly Kirkpatrick, in October 2000.
6. O'Brien, *Rethinking the South*, 169.

that the Southern Renascence was invented rather than discovered does not make it any less real.

Richard Gray is another British critic who has thought long and hard about the role of the Agrarians in creating the Southern Renascence. Although much of what he says in *Writing the South* (1986) is both accurate and reasonable, his argument is undercut by a patronizing tone that is common to much left-wing commentary on conservative thought. Gray begins by confronting the problem of pluralism within the Agrarian ranks. Virtually everyone who has written on *I'll Take My Stand* has noted how haphazardly the book came together. The organizing "Statement of Principles" was drafted after more than half the essays were completed. Several of the contributors had never met each other (some never would). Three of the twelve authors (Tate, Warren, and Lytle) almost dropped out because of their dislike for the sectional title of the symposium. Perhaps more important, different essays advanced markedly different views of the South and the Agrarian tradition. Stark Young celebrated the planter class of his native Mississippi, whereas Andrew Lytle believed that the region was best represented, both past and present, by the small yeoman farmer. John Crowe Ransom looked to British rural life for his inspiration even as Allen Tate was mesmerized by continental European models. Forget about the unity of the Renascence, did Agrarianism itself have a common denominator?

Like Michael O'Brien, Richard Gray believes that the Agrarian movement was united by the shared romanticism of its members. In this context, however, romanticism is seen not as the dynamic revolutionary force that it had been in England a century earlier. Instead, it is a pathological reluctance to accept social change. The South of Agrarian myth finally becomes a kind of never-never land that is meant to recapture the lost youth of the Agrarians themselves. "They were recalling a lost land," Gray remarks, "lost in part, certainly, because of history but also for the simple reason that they had grown up and shades of the prison house had gathered around them."[7] (The allusion to Wordsworth suggests that the Agrarian South is an imagined realm of primal innocence.) Thus, social conservatism is reduced to

7. Gray, *Writing the South: Ideas of an American Region* (Cambridge: Cambridge University Press, 1986), 142.

a diagnosis of arrested development. Such an explanation is a way of defining the situation without having to take it seriously.

Gray makes some fascinating comparisons between the argumentative style of the Agrarians and that of the southern intellectuals who denounced abolitionism in the 1850s. The point is not that the two groups shared similar views on race relations (with the exception of Robert Penn Warren's "The Briar Patch," *I'll Take My Stand* makes little explicit reference to race), but that both were defending what they saw as an embattled culture. The defenders of slavery soon saw their cause lost on the altar of Emancipation. The Agrarian cause was lost before it had begun. Consequently, the major Agrarians turned to New Criticism, where they could freeze the meaning of a literary text in a way they could not freeze the order of society. The one notable exception to this development was Donald Davidson, whose continuing political activism served only to isolate him from his former cohorts. Agrarianism can thus be understood (and dismissed) as a phase through which Ransom, Tate, Warren, and even Lytle passed on their way to adulthood. Davidson becomes the one remaining Lost Boy—doomed by his own intransigence.

Michael Kreyling, who has taught southern literature at Vanderbilt since 1985, is a revisionist scholar more interested in theories of literary politics than in amateur psychoanalysis. For him, the Fugitive-Agrarians were but the first wave of individuals responsible for creating a kind of conventional wisdom or party line about southern literature. It was the second- and third-generation neo-Agrarians who closed the deal. If Kreyling is not exactly alleging conspiracy, he does suggest a remarkable coincidence of interest. Because he begins with the a priori assumption that social reality is constructed, it is not necessary to evaluate the truth of the Agrarian philosophy. "I propose," he states, "that the Agrarians produced the South in the same way that all historically indigenous social elites produce ideological realities: out of strategies for seizing and retaining power (cultural, political, sexual, economic, and so on) that are then reproduced as 'natural.'"[8] As the paradigmatic figure in this process, Kreyling cites Faulkner's Quentin Compson. The revisionist scholars are cast as Quentin's roommate, Shreve—the Canadian interlocutor,

8. Kreyling, *Inventing Southern Literature* (Jackson: University Press of Mississippi, 1998), 6.

who is always urging Quentin to "tell about the South" without believing a word that he says.

Kreyling correctly identifies Richard Weaver as the missing link between the original Agrarians of the thirties and the neo-Agrarians of the sixties and later. A native of Weaverville, North Carolina (which is on the outskirts of Thomas Wolfe's Asheville), Weaver entered the master's program in English at Vanderbilt in 1932. Although the first wave of controversy over Agrarianism had subsided, Weaver wrote a thesis under John Crowe Ransom. If this experience was not sufficient to turn Weaver into a conservative, it did disabuse him of the socialist beliefs he had acquired as an undergraduate at the University of Kentucky. After finishing his master's degree, he saw mass culture up close during a stint as an instructor at Texas A&M University. By 1939, he was in the doctoral program in English at Louisiana State University, where he wrote his dissertation under Cleanth Brooks. At the time of his death in 1963, Weaver was a widely respected scholar of rhetoric and a widely acknowledged influence on American conservative thought.

Those familiar with Weaver's background and with the southern essays he wrote in the forties and fifties recognized his kinship with the Agrarians under whom he had studied. In the minds of his fellow academics, however, he was probably best known for his not particularly southern book *Ideas Have Consequences* (1948). It was not until the posthumous publication of his dissertation in 1968 that Weaver's southernness was fully appreciated. Brought out under the title *The Southern Tradition at Bay*, this book appeared shortly after Stewart and Karanikas had published their initial revisionary accounts of the Agrarians but before the wealth of neo-Agrarian scholarship that would appear in the seventies.

In a sense, Weaver is a perfect foil for Kreyling because his view of traditional southern culture is based more on ideology than empirical analysis. (The same could be said of W. J. Cash at the other end of the political and philosophical spectrum.) Kreyling asserts that Weaver "was, according to Hayden White's definition, a metahistorian. . . . The South was not and never had been, for Weaver, 'the present world of social praxis.' The South was rather the legitimate successor to the ontological and moral authority husbanded in the 'Platonic-Christian tradition,' the enhanced but essential South in which Weaver took his stand."[9] If such a description is meant to fault Weaver's skills as a sociologist, then the proper response is that Weaver was not trying to function as a sociologist. He was a philosopher trying to identify certain virtues that were exemplified by traditional societies throughout the history of Western civilization. For all its imperfections, Weaver believed that the Old South was the nearest paradigm of those virtues. The point was not to turn the clock back to the past *as it was* but to use an ideal image of the past as a touchstone against which to measure the present and chart the future.

The most spurious claim by some recent critics of Agrarianism is that the movement was protofascist. This accusation seems to be based on everything from a seriously tendentious reading of history to outright paranoid fantasy. As I have mentioned elsewhere in this volume, during the midthirties, the Agrarians found a welcome outlet for their writing in Seward Collins's *American Review*. When they began writing for the *American Review*, Collins seemed to be nothing more than an eccentric dilettante looking for traditionalist solutions to the political and economic crisis gripping the United States and Europe. It was not until the winter of 1936, however, that the ultimate direction of Collins's sympathies became clear. In February, a small procommunist publication called *Fight against War and Fascism* published an interview in which Collins revealed the extremity of his current beliefs.

He told his interviewer, Grace Lumpkin, that he wanted to destroy factories. He also expressed his longing for a king, his disdain for Negroes, and his contempt for Jews. He praised Hitler, declared himself a fascist, and seemed to imply that all the contributors to the *American Review* were of the same persuasion. In a letter to the *New Republic*, Allen Tate immediately and vociferously dissociated himself and the Agrarians from these sentiments. He pronounced himself so deeply opposed to fascism that "I would choose communism if it were the alternative to it." He also rejected Collins's romantic medievalism. "I do not want to restore anything whatsoever," Tate wrote. "It is our task to create something."[10]

9. Ibid., 31.
10. Albert E. Stone Jr., "Seward Collins and the *American Review:* An Experiment in Proto-Fascism, 1933–37," *American Quarterly* 12 (Spring 1960): 17.

Given the history of their relationship with the *American Review*, one might assume that even those who disagreed with the Agrarians might give them a kind of grudging credit for their principled opposition to totalitarianism of both the Left and the Right. Guess again. There has been a concerted effort in recent years to link the Agrarians with the most outrageous sentiments of Seward Collins, despite what they actually thought and said about those sentiments. For example, in the May 24, 2001, issue of the *London Review of Books*, Ian Hamilton sneeringly observes: "Tate was more than ready to overlook the antisemitism and pro-Hitlerism of the *American Review* in order to promote his 'spiritual' defence of the Deep South's traditions." Hamilton makes no mention of Tate's letter to the *New Republic* or to an equally strong statement he made a year later. In the Winter 1937 issue of the *Marxist Quarterly*, Tate is quoted as saying: "I would not, now that its policies have become unmistakably clear, write a piece for the *American Review* if it were the last publication left in America—as it might become if America goes fascist." Both of these statements are recorded in Thomas A. Underwood's biography of Tate, the book Hamilton was ostensibly reviewing.[11]

Five years earlier, Walter Kalaidjian, writing in a collection of essays called *Marketing Modernisms*, had offered a more detailed but equally distorted denunciation of the supposedly fascist-loving Agrarians. After citing some of the more scurrilous statements made in the *American Review* (none of them by Agrarians), Kalaidjian concludes that "by publishing their writing in the same venue as such anti-Semitic and pro-fascist ideologues . . . , the Southern Agrarians arguably aligned themselves with these troubling cultural politics." This is, of course, guilt by association, a favorite tactic of right-wing demagogues trying to brand liberal dupes as communists. The use of the weasel word *arguably* adds nothing to Kalaidjian's case. One could just as easily argue the opposite position and say that one is not responsible for what other people write in the same publication that also carries one's own work.

Not content to trash the combative polemicist Tate, Kalaidjian goes after the seemingly apolitical Cleanth Brooks. Although Brooks

11. Underwood, *Allen Tate: Orphan of the South* (Princeton, NJ: Princeton University Press, 2000), 242; Hamilton, "I Intend to Support White Rule," *London Review of Books*, May 24, 2001, 30–31.

was neither a Fugitive poet nor a contributor to *I'll Take My Stand*, he was sympathetic to both movements and eventually wrote an essay on religion for *Who Owns America?* What is even more damning in Kalaidjian's eyes is the fact that Brooks also published in the *American Review*. This fact alone "reveals a certain positioning of his work within, not beyond, the political debates of the moment."[12]

One wonders what Kalaidjian might make of the fact that, in 1937, Brooks's own magazine, the *Southern Review*, published a spirited defense of Joseph Stalin. To confuse matters even more, the following issue of the *Southern Review* contained a flood of rebuttals to that article, most of them written by contributors to the Trotskyite *Partisan Review*. One not infected with the disease of political correctness might conclude that Brooks favored the exposure of a wide variety of conflicting views in the marketplace of ideas.

At the very least, Brooks's intellectual openness should make it more difficult to accept Kalaidjian's absurd notion that the New Criticism was a more genteel (and hence more insidious) version of the fascist threat posed by Agrarianism. But alas, Brooks not only made the mistake of publishing in the *American Review* but also compounded his error by championing modernist poetry without regard to the politics of the poet. In Kalaidjian's judgment, this seemingly disinterested approach to literature was little more than a Trojan horse: "The New Critical agenda had wider cultural implications that—tied as they were to the social elitism and outright fascism of high modernists like Eliot, Pound, and Yeats—sought to intervene in the shaping of everyday life in twentieth-century America."[13] It seems to me that the plain meaning, underlying assumptions, and broader implications of this statement are all questionable.

It does not follow that one must endorse the views of the poet in order to admire the poetry. (If that were the case, no one could ap-

---

12. Kalaidjian, "Marketing Modern Poetry and the Southern Public Sphere," in *Marketing Modernisms: Self-Promotion, Canonization, Rereading*, edited by Kevin J. H. Dettmar and Stephen Watt (Ann Arbor: University of Michigan Press, 1996), 303, 304. In 2004, Kalaidjian was the main author of a textbook called *Understanding Literature*. It is more than a bit ironic that he should profit from such an obvious allusion to a critical tradition that he has been trashing for most of his career. See Kalaidjian, Judith Roof, and Stephen Watt, *Understanding Literature: An Introduction to Reading and Writing* (Boston: Houghton Mifflin, 2004).

13. Kalaidjian, "Marketing Modern Poetry," 311.

preciate both Dante and Milton.) Nor is it clear that the New Critics promoted only right-wing poets. W. H. Auden, even in his leftist phase, was one of their favorites, just as T. S. Eliot was a frequent contributor to the left-leaning *Partisan Review*. Moreover, to tar the Irish nationalist W. B. Yeats and the patriotic Englishman Eliot with the brush of fascism borders on slander.

The prime evidence that Kalaidjian cites of New Critical fascism in action is the fact that "of the 94 poets anthologized in the 1938 edition of [Brooks and Warren's] *Understanding Poetry* not one is black; less than a handful are female; and not a single poet of the American left is preserved." If this means that some worthy poet was excluded (and some may have been), we cannot tell—because Kalaidjian cites no names, only numbers. If he were to do a similar survey of *American Literature: The Makers and the Making*, the textbook that Brooks, Warren, and R. W. B. Lewis published in 1973, Kalaidjian would find plenty of blacks, women, and leftists. If he were to examine the membership of the Fellowship of Southern Writers, an organization that Brooks founded in 1987, he would find all three categories amply represented.[14] For that matter, the only time the supposedly fascist Brooks failed to vote for the Democratic candidate for president was in 1948, when he cast his ballot for the socialist Norman Thomas.

Writing in the *Mississippi Quarterly* in 1998, Karen O'Kane was even more blatant than Kalaidjian had been in alleging sinister connections between the political associations of the Agrarians and the subsequent program of the New Critics. "Although it would certainly be a mistake to argue that the Agrarians were literally fascists," O'Kane admits, "their social views were in some sense just less extreme versions of Collins's. In other words, the politics of the *American Review* were where the views of the Agrarians *led*."[15] Of course, where Collins's politics *led* the Agrarians was right out of the *American Review*.

The only real evidence O'Kane offers that Agrarianism was

14. Ibid. In referring to Brooks's lifelong friend and collaborator Robert Penn Warren, John Parish Peede notes that "Ralph Ellison was not in the habit of reading eulogies at the funerals of paternalistic white Southerners" ("Mr. Tate in the Emperor's Clothes," *Modern Age* 43 [Fall 2001]: 334).

15. O'Kane, "Before the New Criticism: Modernism and the Nashville Group," *Mississippi Quarterly* 51 (Fall 1998): 694.

"amenable to a fascistic interpretation" is that communism is repeatedly criticized in *I'll Take My Stand* and three of the contributors had wanted to call the book *Tracts against Communism.* The fact that the New Critics were later too cozy with the anti-Soviet *Partisan Review* is then offered as proof of continuing fascistic tendencies. How quaint that a would-be intellectual, writing at the end of the twentieth century (and in the self-styled "Journal of Southern Culture," at that), could imagine no "third way" between Joseph Stalin and Adolph Hitler!

To date, the most ambitious revisionist account of the Agrarian legacy is Paul V. Murphy's *The Rebuke of History: The Southern Agrarians and American Conservative Thought* (2001). If nothing else, this book is a definitive refutation of the notion that nobody any longer pays attention to the Agrarians. Murphy clearly shows the influence of Agrarian ideas upon a particular variety of contemporary American conservatism. Although Agrarianism itself achieved no *political* victories, the efforts of its followers (particularly Richard Weaver and M. E. Bradford) have secured its continuing presence in the world of ideas. Whereas earlier scholars have examined the Agrarianism of Weaver (who died in 1963) and Bradford (who died in 1993), Murphy is the first commentator to show how the ideas of the Nashville Twelve continue to inform traditionalist conservatism at the dawn of the twenty-first century.

Because of the fragmentation of the conservative movement (which became impossible to deny by the end of the 1980s), Agrarianism now has at least as many enemies on the Right as on the Left. One will find reverence for the southern conservative tradition (which was best exemplified in the twentieth century by the Agrarians and their heirs) in such magazines as *Chronicles* and *Southern Partisan* and in neo-Confederate organizations such as the League of the South. The position of the conservative establishment, however, was most forcefully articulated by Norman Podhoretz when he denounced T. S. Eliot, Russell Kirk, the Agrarians, and present-day paleoconservatives for "being ranged on the wrong side of the culture wars."[16] Whatever failings he might have, Podhoretz does know an enemy when he sees one. Had he read Paul V. Murphy, he would

16. Podhoretz, "Letters from Readers" *Commentary* (June 1996): 16.

have realized that his worst enemies were the intellectual children of Donald Davidson.

By the 1940s, Davidson was just about the lone defender of the Agrarian faith. Unlike Ransom, Tate, and Warren, he had not left the South. According to Murphy, Davidson's poetic muse had dried up. Having no great reputation as a literary critic to maintain, he increasingly turned his attention to social issues. His two-volume history of the Tennessee River, published in the late forties, ended with a savage indictment of the Tennessee Valley Authority (TVA). By the 1950s, Davidson was devoting the lion's share of his energy to segregationist politics. For this reason, Murphy argues, he made alliances with the sort of industrialists he had previously condemned and sought to accommodate his version of southern traditionalism to the emerging conservative coalition being forged by William Buckley at the *National Review*. In essence, Murphy believes that Davidson sold out the most original and valuable aspects of Agrarianism in order to keep his seat in the front of the bus. The truth, however, is a bit more complex.

Donald Davidson is easy to caricature, especially if one has no qualms about presenting a partial and tendentious version of his life and work. Murphy quotes extensively from Davidson's book-length poem *The Tall Men* to prove that its author was little more than a southern chauvinist, unlike his more sophisticated and ironic brethren Tate and Ransom. Murphy goes on to cite correspondence between Ransom and Tate from the 1930s to demonstrate that they too held a low opinion of Davidson's development as a poet and thinker. (Michael O'Brien had used these same letters in an earlier hatchet job on Davidson.) From there we move to Davidson's career as a segregationist and all-around southern bigot. If he wrote any poetry other than *The Tall Men* or any social criticism that was not tainted by either white supremacy or the most simplistic regional nostalgia, one would not glean those facts from Paul V. Murphy.

It is true that Davidson did not join Tate in following the poetic example of Eliot. But southern chauvinism hardly seems to be the reason. Before he began work on *The Tall Men*, Davidson had had very little to say about the cause of the South. If anything, he seemed moderately liberal in the tradition of James Kirkland and Edwin Mims. It was clear, however, that Davidson as poet was chafing against the strictures of high modernism. His earliest verse (like Faulkner's) reflected the influence of A. E. Housman and the British decadents. After writing a few blatantly modernist poems in the vein recommended by Tate, Davidson was looking for a new, more vernacular idiom. The myth of Tennessee's frontier past, which is the subject of *The Tall Men*, gave him material suited to such an idiom. I suspect that it was his imaginative involvement with this poem that helped to crystallize Davidson's views about the South. In short, he came to social activism through poetry rather than the other way around.

If Davidson did not find Eliot to be a useful model, he wrote in the equally honorable tradition of Thomas Hardy and Robert Frost. (Davidson regarded Hardy as a southern writer who had simply failed to emigrate, and he maintained a friendship with Frost that lasted for more than three decades at the Bread Loaf School of English.) Several of the poems Davidson published in *Lee in the Mountains* (his next volume after *The Tall Men*) were probably too declamatory; however, at least half a dozen others reflect a mastery of voice and technique far beyond that of *The Tall Men*. Even as Ransom and Tate were privately ridiculing *Lee in the Mountains* after its publication in 1938, both of these poets had ceased writing verse altogether. For Ransom, the silence would prove permanent.

In order to maintain that polemicism had destroyed Davidson as artist, Murphy must ignore the publication of *The Long Street* in 1961. This book appeared after Davidson had spent the 1940s battling the TVA and the 1950s fighting the civil rights movement. Surely, those struggles should have destroyed whatever youthful talent he possessed as a poet. Instead, *The Long Street* (which was written mostly in the late fifties, after the crusade for segregation had been lost) established Davidson as second only to Warren among the Fugitive poets writing after World War II. If politics did not improve his poetry, it had not hurt it, either. (In all likelihood, Davidson's work on the libretto for Charles Faulkner Bryan's folk opera *Singin' Billy*—first produced in 1952—enabled him to return to poetry better than ever after a silence of nearly two decades.) With the publication of *The Long Street*, Ransom and Tate both admitted that they had been too quick to write Davidson off so many years earlier. But don't expect Murphy to tell you that.

Davidson's achievement as a poet might seem largely irrelevant to his influence on Agrarian and neo-Agrarian political thought. Nevertheless, the best of his poetry, along with his most enduring essays on regionalism, simply could not have been written by the sentimental racist buffoon that Murphy depicts. Anyone who believes (as Murphy does) that Allen Tate had a firmer grasp of history and politics should compare Tate's pedestrian and derivative biographies of Stonewall Jackson and Jefferson Davis with Davidson's magnificent account of the Tennessee River. Even if Davidson said some silly things about race in the fifties, those views are almost totally absent from his poetry and more peripheral than one might imagine to the main body of his social thought. (White supremacy is far less prominent in his writing than anti-Semitism is in the work of Pound and Eliot.) Davidson's pleas for political devolution and for genuine cultural diversity (before that term had become a shibboleth in the lexicon of political correctness) seem more pertinent today than when he was making them at the height—or depth—of the New Deal.

However much Davidson might have courted mainstream conservatives, those whom Murphy correctly identifies as his heirs are, in their own way, as radical as the original Agrarians themselves. While *Commentary, National Review,* and the *Weekly Standard* were beating the war drums, *Chronicles* consistently aligned itself with the noninterventionist Right. In championing the populism of Pat Buchanan, Davidson's followers separated themselves from those who wanted to make the free market into a secular religion.[17] Nor would anyone mistake the neo-Davidsonian League of the South for an accommodationist think tank grooming cabinet members for some future Bush administration.

In acknowledging the centrality of Davidson's influence on today's neo-Agrarians, one would seem to be playing into the hands of those revisionists who see southern traditionalism as invincibly racist. Yet Davidson was a more complicated man than his detractors might suspect. Although he opposed the civil rights movement in the forties and fifties, he had met socially with black professors from Fisk University in the twenties. When he edited the book page of the *Nashville Tennessean* from 1924 to 1930, he had included several of them as reviewers and had himself written with insight and sensitivity about black literature. In particular, he was very much taken with James Weldon Johnson's *Autobiography of an Ex-Coloured Man,*

17. See, for example, the January 2002 issue of *Chronicles: A Magazine of American Culture.*

which he found to be "astonishingly impressive."[18] If Brooks and Warren did nothing to promote African American literature in the 1938 edition of *Understanding Poetry*, the same could not be said of Donald Davidson writing in his hometown newspaper a decade earlier.

Consider also the correspondence between Davidson and Seward Collins regarding Collins's most egregious prejudice—his anti-Semitism. Apparently, Collins wrote to Davidson sometime in the fall of 1934 to chide him for not launching a more explicit attack on Jewish activists in an essay he had written for the *American Review*. Davidson responded in a letter dated October 10, 1934. Although he concedes a high incidence of Jews in the enemy camp, Davidson argues that ethnicity is an essentially bogus issue. "The new Jewish influence seems only a part of the larger problem," he contends, "and a part which, under the circumstances, would only serve to muddle the issues if it were stressed. Besides, I can't really believe that [Ludwig] Lewisohn, much as I dislike his views, or [V. F.] Calverton, or any one of a number of prominent Jewish writers, does any more damage than a number of altogether Gentile writers, editors, critics, philosophers, educationalists, etc. who can easily be named."[19]

Later in the same letter, Davidson consults his personal experience to argue against a blanket condemnation of the Jewish people. Perhaps remembering his friendships with the founding Fugitive Sidney Hirsch and other members of the tribe, Davidson remarks: "The Jews themselves are not all of the same school. Like the 'New Negroes,' they are divided. In the South there has never been any real anti-Semitic feeling—at least until the Scottsboro case. We have in this city, for example, a number of old Jewish families who are all but assimilated. To all intents, they are as much Southern as Jewish. They have little in common with the new element among the N. Y. Jews. I know some of these people well and like them." If Tate's sentiments against fascism might have been prompted in part by a desire to protect his public image, Davidson could have had no such motivation in a private letter to a man he considered a friend and benefactor.

18. Davidson, review of *Autobiography of an Ex-Coloured Man*, by Johnson, *Nashville Tennessean*, May 23, 1926, 6.
19. This letter is housed in the Fugitive Collection of the Jean and Alexander Heard Library at Vanderbilt University.

It is important that the band of anti-Davidsonians represented by Paul Murphy not be allowed to have the final word on the Agrarian movement and its legacy. (Mark G. Malvasi's *Unregenerate South* [1997] is a far more evenhanded treatment of many of the same issues Murphy discusses.) Nevertheless, Murphy is correct in seeing the Davidsonian tradition as the contemporary face of the Agrarian movement. In doing so, he might do well to remember the experience of a scalawag professor who spoke in Edgefield County, South Carolina, a few years ago. In an apparent effort to break the ice after his talk, the scalawag asked, "Do you folks still lynch as many people as you used to?" To this, the resident Davidsonian replied, "It depends on who they are and what they have to say about us."

Part Two

The Lower South

7

The Faulkner Wars

More than a half century after he won the Nobel Prize, William Faulkner's stature in world literature looms so large that any group that can claim him as a kindred spirit can also claim to be on the side of the titans, if not necessarily the angels. In the fall of 1992, Lance Lyday reported that "William Faulkner and his writings have now been the subject of more than 6,000 essays and reviews, more than 300 books, and about 500 dissertations—more than the total amount of critical attention devoted to any other writer in English except Shakespeare."[1] More than a decade later, Faulkner is still a blue-chip stock in the literary marketplace.

If this attention to the laureate of Yoknapatawpha has not been entirely posthumous, it would have been unimaginable during the time that he was producing the novels on which his reputation now rests. During that time, Faulkner's praises were sung by a few fellow writers and literary intellectuals, while the general public and the literary establishment regarded him as a grotesque curiosity—when they were not ignoring him altogether. Although the reversal in Faulkner's critical reputation was the better part of a decade in coming, the process began in 1939. In January of that year, Robert Cantwell wrote a cover article on the Mississippi novelist for *Time* magazine. In the summer issue of the *Kenyon Review*, George Marion O'Donnell published an influential essay that saw the world of Yoknapatawpha as being divided between the Sartorises and the Snopeses. (Although this simplistic dichotomy would later become a cliché of Faulkner criticism, O'Donnell was the first serious literary scholar to

1. Lyday, "Faulkner Criticism: Will It Ever End?" *South Carolina Review* 25 (Fall 1992): 183.

argue that Faulkner had a coherent vision of the world.) Finally, in November, the *Atlantic Monthly* carried Conrad Aiken's brilliant defense of Faulkner's much maligned prose style.

This initial burst of critical appreciation gathered momentum in the early forties with an essay by Delmore Schwartz in the *Southern Review* (Summer 1941) and influential articles by Warren Beck—in the *Antioch Review* (Spring 1941), *College English* (May 1941), and the *Rocky Mountain Review* (Spring–Summer 1942). Unfortunately, Faulkner published no books between *Go Down, Moses* in 1942 and *Intruder in the Dust* in 1948. At the same time, his earlier works were going out of print, and, in some cases, the very plates on which they were printed were melted down for war material. Students excited by the new wave of critical interest in Faulkner were forced to seek their primary texts in the remainder bins of secondhand bookstores.

The rehabilitation (indeed the creation) of Faulkner's literary reputation can be traced to the publication of Malcolm Cowley's *The Portable Faulkner* in 1946. In editing this volume, Cowley paid scant attention to the formal distinction between novels and stories. Believing Faulkner to be less the careful craftsman than the grand mythmaker, Cowley arranged his contents chronologically, giving us a history of Yoknapatawpha County over a period of two centuries. To a large extent, Cowley's argument was an extension of the one that O'Donnell had made in the *Kenyon Review* seven years earlier. The main difference was that Cowley was reaching a much larger audience and had the accompanying texts to back him up. Four years after the appearance of Cowley's volume, Faulkner won the Nobel Prize, and two professors from Ole Miss, Harry M. Campbell and Ruel E. Foster, published the first of the hundreds of books devoted to his work.

In 1952, Irving Howe became the first nationally known critic to attempt a book-length assessment of Faulkner's fiction. (Although Campbell and Foster had preceded him, they were unknown academics whose work was published by a university press; Howe, a distinguished contributor to *Partisan Review*, was writing under the imprimatur of Random House.) For one who has read little or no other Faulkner criticism, there is much to admire in Howe's *William Faulkner: A Critical Study*. In addition to appreciating Faulkner's stylistic gifts, Howe recognizes that he is dealing with a serious moralist whose work compares favorably with the most fully engaged fiction being written in Europe. Howe even bends over backward to be fair to a southern tradition for which he obviously has little sympathy. Unfortunately, he can't quite bring it off.

Part of the problem is structural. In the first half of the study, Howe deals with the general themes in Faulkner's work; in the second half, he analyzes specific texts. In his general commentary, however, Howe is forced to refer to the very works he will later discuss in depth. This creates a divided focus, with Howe's discussion of a particular novel often split between the two sections of his book. For example, his chapter on *The Sound and the Fury* says virtually nothing about Dilsey's role in the novel—apparently because he has already discussed her in an earlier chapter, "Faulkner and the Negroes." (In general, disjointed narrative works better for Faulkner than for his would-be explicator.) Because he finds Dilsey too servile to merit his unqualified admiration, Howe chooses to see Benjy as the hero of the novel—if not a moral norm, at least an embodiment of amoral purity. In Howe's reckoning, *The Sound and the Fury* is great precisely because it is "a tale told by an idiot."

Although Howe's book had gone into a fourth edition by 1991, he did no more than add commentary on the novels Faulkner published after 1952. Because he had not changed his opinion in four decades, Howe saw no need to acknowledge the considerable body of Faulkner criticism that had been published in that time. In the process, he spared himself the bother of defending positions that other critics had challenged. It might have seemed reasonable enough in 1952 to say that *The Unvanquished* was "the least serious of the Yoknapatawpha novels" and to write it off as drivel composed for the slick magazines. To render the same dogmatic judgment in 1991 is to act as if Andrew Lytle, Cleanth Brooks, and M. E. Bradford had never defended the book against those very charges.[2]

The most anachronistic chapter in Howe's study is his discussion of "The Bear." Although he was certainly not alone, Howe helped to perpetuate what James B. Meriwether considers "perhaps the most

---

2. Howe, *William Faulkner: A Critical Study*, 4th ed. (1975; reprint, Chicago: Ivan R. Dee, 1991), 42. See Lytle, "The Son of Man: He Will Prevail," *Sewanee Review* 63 (1955): 114–37; Brooks, *William Faulkner: The Yoknapatawpha Country* (Baton Rouge: Louisiana State University Press, 1963), 75–99; and Bradford, *Generations of the Faithful Heart: On the Literature of the South* (La Salle, IL: Sherwood Sugden, 1983), 29–39.

disgraceful situation in the Faulkner field"—the tendency to treat "The Bear" as a separate novella, rather than as the fifth chapter of *Go Down, Moses*. Such a reading encourages us to see Ike McCaslin as a secular saint, doing penance for the sins of his family and his region. Howe remarks: "Given what Isaac McCaslin has been trained to be in the first three sections [of "The Bear"], a youth who will prove worthy of Sam Fathers and Old Ben, it follows that his moral gesture in Section 4 should seem right and inevitable."[3] If other parts of *Go Down, Moses* might call that judgment into question, one simply ignores them. Otherwise, the effort to make Faulkner into a cornpone version of Henry David Thoreau would be seriously jeopardized.

Although the cosmopolitan critics had Faulkner much to themselves from the late forties on, the situation changed dramatically in the early 1960s. Almost from the time he was laid his grave in 1963, the author's fellow southerners launched an effort to claim him for their own. As Thomas H. Landess describes the conflict, "Faulkner was no longer a head mounted on the wall of Malcolm Cowley. Like Hector, his body was being fought for by his own people." If the battle was a long time brewing, the publication of Cleanth Brooks's *William Faulkner: The Yoknapatawpha Country* in 1963 constituted the assault on Fort Sumter. Recognizing the challenge for what it was, Marvin Mudrick fired back with a review called "The Over-Wrought Urn" in the January 9, 1964, issue of the *New York Review of Books*. "After decades of the bowler-hat and furled umbrella litcrit that made his academic reputation," Mudrick states, "Cleanth Brooks has reverted with a rebel whoop to the Confederacy. His Faulkner book is a Southern blend of vitriol, tart courtliness, regional piety, genealogies back to Adam, the stupefying trivia of life in a small town, and uninhibited hero worship."[4] The battle had been joined.

Brooks had had the effrontery to argue that, far from being an inhibiting force that needed to be overcome, Faulkner's "provincialism" was itself an essential component of his genius. By this, Brooks

3. Meriwether, "William Faulkner," in *Sixteen Modern American Writers*, edited by Jackson R. Bryer (Durham, NC: Duke University Press, 1974), 250; Howe, *William Faulkner*, 256.

4. Landess, "Mel Bradford as Literary Critic," paper delivered before the Philadelphia Society, North Charleston, SC, October 28, 1994, 4; Mudrick, "The Over-Wrought Urn," *New York Review of Books*, January 90, 1964, 8.

does not mean that Faulkner was a country bumpkin who was limited in his knowledge of the world away from home. Instead, like William Butler Yeats and Robert Frost, Faulkner was so rooted in a particular region that he was able to expose the shortcomings of the larger urban and commercial culture. (In other words, the South was more his touchstone than his whipping boy.) The advantages of this perspective are evident throughout the Yoknapatawpha saga. Consider, for example, Faulkner's first great novel—*The Sound and the Fury.*

On the surface, *The Sound and the Fury* would appear to be a case study of a single southern family. Because the Compsons are so emphatically southern, some readers have erroneously interpreted their plight as symbolizing that of the region as a whole. That is to say at once too much and too little. Brooks argues that

> the real significance of the Southern setting in *The Sound and the Fury* resides, as so often elsewhere in Faulkner, in the fact that the breakdown of a family can be exhibited more poignantly and significantly in a society which is old-fashioned and in which the family is still the center. . . . What happens to the Compsons might make less noise and cause less comment, and even bring less pain to the individuals concerned, if the Compsons lived in a more progressive and liberal environment.[5]

In addition to giving his work a thematic richness, Faulkner's sense of community also helps to unify what might otherwise seem disparate and episodic tales. *Light in August* is a case in point. Readers who ignore the importance of community in that novel are apt to find it a pastiche of brilliant writing that lacks the unity and coherence we demand of novels. Brooks elaborates on this point: "One way to gauge the importance of the community in this novel is by imagining the action to have taken place in Chicago or Manhattan Island, where the community—at least in Faulkner's sense—does not exist."[6]

To his credit, Howe has dimly perceived this quality in *Light in August.* In it, he notes, "a new voice is heard, partly Faulkner's own and partly, as it were, an over-voice speaking for the memories and

5. Brooks, *William Faulkner: The Yoknapatawpha Country*, 341.
6. Ibid., 312.

conscience of a people. Sounding again and again a characteristic note of anguish, lingering over the spectacle of heroism and failure, this voice records the entire Yoknapatawpha story."[7] Unfortunately, this isolated observation comes at the end of Howe's chapter on *Light in August*. In contrast, Brooks makes the role of the community in this novel the central focus of his discussion.

Whether giving a rebel yell or wearing a bowler hat, Cleanth Brooks made his reputation by reading texts so closely that he often found meanings different from those assumed to be there. For example, in place of the beatified Ike McCaslin who dominates "The Bear," he finds a far more equivocal figure moving through the pages of *Go Down, Moses*. The novel's first chapter, "Was," begins with Ike as an old man ("uncle to half the county and father to no one") but quickly flashes back to a story involving his father and mother, two uncles, and a second cousin, eight years before his own birth. Ike does not appear in his own right until the fourth chapter, an elegiac tale called "The Old People." Taken together with sections 1–3 and 5 of "The Bear," "The Old People" depicts Ike's initiation into manhood in the context of a disappearing wilderness. When read against his renunciation of his tainted patrimony in section 4 of "The Bear," this hunting idyll has convinced many readers (Irving Howe included) that Ike is the unambiguous conscience of Yoknapatawpha County.

By placing "The Bear" back in the context of *Go Down, Moses*, Brooks demonstrates that Ike's desire is more to evade than to embrace moral responsibility. In "Delta Autumn" (the chapter that immediately follows "The Bear"), Uncle Ike is depicted as an ineffectual old man whose lonely stance against civilization has failed to preserve the wilderness. Even his refusal of his inheritance has done more harm than good. Not only has it failed to atone for the central sin of his grandfather (the continual denial of love and its obligations), but this grand gesture may actually have helped bring about a repetition of that same callousness generations later. Whatever one makes of this argument (which is made by Roth Edmonds's mixed-blood mistress), Brooks contends that its very presence in *Go Down, Moses* "effectively undercuts any notion that Faulkner is asking the reader to accept Isaac's action as the ideal solution of the race problem or even to regard his motivation as obviously saintlike."[8]

7. Howe, *William Faulkner*, 214.
8. Brooks, *Yoknapatawpha Country*, 274.

Although Brooks is invariably polite in disagreeing with other critics, the extensive notes to his book are filled with challenges to the conventional wisdom. (He devotes two pages to Irving Howe's discussion of Faulkner's treatment of the Negro.) One name that appears frequently in those notes is that of Olga W. Vickery. If nothing else, this is a tribute to the importance of Professor Vickery's *The Novels of William Faulkner: A Critical Interpretation.* Published originally in 1959, her study quickly superseded the more general introductory works of Howe and others. More than any previous critic, Vickery read Faulkner's novels as carefully constructed artifacts rather than as fragments of some mythic saga perceived in divine madness. In other words, Vickery's approach is one that Cleanth Brooks must certainly have endorsed in principle. The problem lay in the detail of some of her readings.

The recurring weakness that Brooks finds in Vickery's book (other than occasionally getting her facts wrong) is an antisouthern bias. Because this bias is neither polemical nor obviously tendentious, we may overlook it. Still, it distorts Vickery's understanding of several of Faulkner's major works—among them *Light in August, Go Down, Moses,* and *Absalom, Absalom!* To begin with, Vickery is one of several critics (William Van O'Connor and Irving Howe are also mentioned) who assert imprecisely that Joe Christmas is "lynched" by Percy Grimm. As Brooks points out, lynching is, by definition, a collective action, whereas Grimm's brutality is strictly personal. To characterize him as the head of a lynch mob is to miss the fact that Percy is nearly as much of an outcast in the community of Jefferson as Christmas himself. Brooks accuses Vickery, in particular, of being so "bemused by the Negro-white question . . . she errs in trying to interpret the whole of *Light in August* as a study of 'myths' got out of hand."[9]

Unlike those critics who turn Isaac McCaslin into a primitivist saint on the basis of a simplistic and noncontextual reading of "The Bear," Vickery realizes that Ike is a flawed character in other parts of *Go Down, Moses.* She simply misperceives the nature of his flaws. Contrary to Vickery's assertions, Uncle Ike does not condone Roth Edmonds's misbehavior in "Delta Autumn": he is simply unable to do anything about it. Ike's problem was never an inability to discern

9. Ibid., 377. See also Vickery, *Novels of Faulkner* (Baton Rouge: Louisiana State University Press, 1959).

good from evil, but rather the naive belief that his own purity of will could make the world a better place in which to live. If anything, his resignation in "Delta Autumn" bespeaks a greater self-knowledge.

The most fundamental disagreement between Brooks and Vickery concerns the southernness of Thomas Sutpen. In an essay on *Absalom, Absalom!* published in the *Sewanee Review* in 1951, Brooks had argued that the quality of Sutpen's "innocence" is more typically American than southern. Although Vickery makes no explicit reference to this essay in her book, Brooks notes that "she devotes a good deal of space to arguing that Sutpen's 'design' is really 'a microcosm of the South.'" In *The Yoknapatawpha Country*, Brooks devotes at least as much space to showing how Sutpen is a regional anomaly. (Some fifteen years later, he would pursue this argument at even greater length in an appendix to his second book on Faulkner, *Toward Yoknapatawpha and Beyond* [1978], citing authorities as diverse as C. Vann Woodward and Eugene Genovese.) Although Vickery never responded directly to this or any other of Brooks's objections, she did review *The Yoknapatawpha Country* in *American Literature*. Though agreeing that Brooks "has many astute things to say," Vickery contends that "the general impression is one of very uneven critical performance, one whose dominant trait seems that of nervousness. . . . One is led to conclude that Mr. Brooks has no critical rationale for his study of fiction."[10]

One might be tempted to see the Faulkner wars as a regional skirmish, a bloodless refighting of the War between the States. The truth, however, is more complicated. Just as a sizable number of southern scholars have resisted the attempt to make Faulkner into a kind of neo-Agrarian, some critics whose provenance is far from the Old Confederacy are in surprising agreement with Brooks and company. The most notable figure in the latter category is Michael Millgate, a native of Southampton, England, and chairman of the English Department at York University when his landmark study *The Achievement of William Faulkner* was published in 1966.[11] Although the appearance of Brooks's *The Yoknapatawpha Country* three years earlier had anticipated some of his revisionary readings, Millgate's book nevertheless represented a watershed in Faulkner studies. Previously,

10. Vickery, review of *William Faulkner: The Yoknapatawpha Country*, by Brooks, *American Literature* 36 (March 1964–January 1965): 379–81.
11. Millgate, *The Achievement of William Faulkner* (New York: Random House, 1966).

no Faulkner scholar had combined criticism with biographical and textual research to the extent that Millgate did. Not only were his interpretations of the novels plausible, but they were also supported by an as yet unmatched knowledge of Faulkner as a man and practicing writer. From this point on, it would be difficult to disagree with Millgate without knowing as much about Faulkner as he did.

In the nearly four decades since the appearance of Millgate's book, the best work on Faulkner has tended to combine textual and biographical scholarship with critical reading. (One thinks immediately of the work of James B. Meriwether, Noel Polk, and Thomas L. McHaney.) Such an eclectic approach is certainly apparent in Cleanth Brooks's second book on Faulkner, *Toward Yoknapatawpha and Beyond.* Although *The Yoknapatawpha Country* was an incredibly detailed book (filled with notes, appendixes, and references to previous criticism), there is little discussion of Faulkner's life or much investigation of his manuscripts. Only Brooks's richly informed observations on southern culture would call into question his strawman image as an essentially intrinsic reader. In *Toward Yoknapatawpha and Beyond,* however, we see some of the skills Brooks employed over more than a half century in editing Bishop Thomas Percy's correspondence. Whether or not Millgate's example influenced his methodology in this book, it seems just the right approach for Faulkner's minor work.

If the focus of *The Yoknapatawpha Country* might be described as "the Faulkner everybody knows," *Toward Yoknapatawpha and Beyond* deals with the unknown Faulkner. It examines what Faulkner was doing when he was not laying claim to his "little postage stamp of soil." Where Brooks's earlier book made a strong positive case for the importance of the Yoknapatawpha fiction, this later volume makes a strong negative case for the same judgment. Even if Brooks is correct in saying that "nothing that the mature Faulkner ever wrote is without interest," the non-Yoknapatawpha material commands our interest largely because of the light it sheds on Faulkner's major work. (Can anyone imagine Cleanth Brooks writing or the Yale University Press publishing, in the last quarter of the twentieth century, a 430-page study of James Branch Cabell, the southern romantic whom the early Faulkner most resembles?)[12]

12. Brooks, *Toward Yoknapatawpha and Beyond* (New Haven, CT: Yale University Press, 1978).

The Yoknapatawpha Country will always be the more appealing book, because it deals with superior material and argues a provocative thesis; however, in its own way, *Toward Yoknapatawpha and Beyond* is an equally valuable work.

Much had occurred in Faulkner studies in the fifteen years between the publication of Brooks's two books. The single most important event was the publication, in 1974, of Joseph Blotner's two-volume biography of Faulkner. If Millgate had demonstrated the importance of bringing extrinsic information to the critical reading of Faulkner's work, Blotner provided a veritable encyclopedia of such information. And, like an encyclopedia, his book was more a work of reference than an arresting narrative. The criticism many reviewers leveled against his two-volume tome was that Blotner considered nothing that Faulkner did too insignificant to record. (The book seemed weighted down with biographical trivia, as well as tedious summaries of just about everything Faulkner ever wrote and far too much of what was written about him.) At the same time, other readers detected a squeamishness when it deals with the less flattering aspects of Faulkner's life.

We have no explanation of why Faulkner's wife Estelle tried to drown herself on the couple's honeymoon. (A less reticent Faulknerian told me it was owing to her husband's inadequacies as a lover.) Although Faulkner's longtime affair with Howard Hawks's secretary, Meta Carpenter, was widely known, it played no role in the two-volume *Faulkner*. Was this simply because Meta Carpenter declined to be interviewed (Blotner's explanation) or because—as many believe—the biographer was loath to embarrass Estelle Faulkner, who was still alive and had been of immense help to him in his labors?

A decade later, in 1984, Blotner redeemed himself with a revised one-volume version of *Faulkner: A Biography*. In paring 1,846 pages of text down to 718 pages, Blotner cut much of the prolixity that had made his earlier book unreadable for many nonspecialists.[13] At the same time, Blotner was much more candid about Faulkner's personal life (particularly his affair with Meta Carpenter) and far more willing to venture critical and analytical judgments. Any student of

13. Blotner, *Faulkner: A Biography*, one-volume ed. (New York: Vintage Books, 1984).

the craft of biography would be well advised to study the differences between Blotner's two accounts of Faulkner's life. If the man is buried under a mountain of information in the first edition, he emerges as a formidable historical and literary figure in the revised version.

One comes away from Blotner's *Faulkner* convinced that William Faulkner was his own most impressive creation. If someone of Faulkner's own talents (a tall order, indeed) were to write a novel about him, the product would probably be more compelling than either *The Sound and the Fury* or *Absalom, Absalom!* Under the best of circumstances, the body of work that Faulkner produced would have been breathtaking in its range and power. Given the actual circumstances of his life, Faulkner seems a virtual impossibility. With little formal education and limited contact with fellow writers, he made sophisticated literary techniques accomplish things they had never done earlier and have not done since. In the midst of genteel poverty, crushing financial and familial obligations, and a Dionysian thirst for booze, he created the most powerful fictional community of the twentieth century out of one of the most backward settings imaginable. While awaiting the critical and popular attention that was being lavished on his less talented contemporaries, he dutifully cranked out scripts for Hollywood and potboilers for the *Saturday Evening Post*. Then, when recognition belatedly came his way, he was too bashful and introspective to enjoy it. Faulkner seemed entitled to a lot more self-pity than he allowed himself to feel.

Does the student of Faulkner's life find the southern gentleman of Agrarian myth or the iconoclast so revered by alienated modernists? There is enough in Blotner to suggest that he was a little bit of both. But the point that Brooks makes in discussing the Yoknapatawpha fiction applies to Faulkner's life as well. Even if he was a misfit and an eccentric, it is different to be such things in a traditional community than in a totally deracinated culture. Although it might be difficult to envision Faulkner contributing to *I'll Take My Stand*, he felt a real sense of obligation to his region, his community, and his extended family. Can anyone imagine Ernest Hemingway or Norman Mailer remaining in an unhappy marriage for the sake of his child? (Far too many people know of his telling his daughter Jill that no one remembered Shakespeare's children, but how many know that the only reason Faulkner traveled to Sweden to receive the Nobel Prize in person was that he was convinced that Jill wanted to make the trip?) Faulkner was a man of many vices, God knows, but his virtues were characteristic of the traditional South.

The Shreve McCannons of the critical establishment have assumed a bit too glibly that Faulkner hated the South (how could a man of his intellect and sensibility not hate it?). But the available literary and biographical evidence suggests that they are no more than partially correct. Back in the early fifties, Faulkner told Leslie Fiedler that "to write about a place well, you *must* hate it . . . , the way a man hates his wife."[14] In our own time of serial monogamy, that hardly seems a strong enough comparison. But, for the squire of Rowan Oak, it was all that needed to be said.

14. Fiedler, *The Collected Essays of Leslie Fiedler* (New York: Stein and Day, 1971), 2:333.

8

Family Values in *Go Down, Moses*

More than six decades after its publication, *Go Down, Moses* (1942) remains the most controversial and problematical of William Faulkner's major novels. Even to call this book a novel is to beg a question that has long been a point of critical debate. The first printing of the first edition contained the title *Go Down, Moses and Other Stories*, and at least until the publication of seminal critical studies by Cleanth Brooks and Michael Millgate in the early 1960s, most of the attention lavished on *Go Down, Moses* focused on its fifth chapter, "The Bear," to the exclusion of the rest of the book. In the opinion of James B. Meriwether, such selectivity constituted "perhaps the most disgraceful situation" in the field of Faulkner criticism.[1]

I suspect that the failure of so many critics to view *Go Down, Moses* as a unified work is due, at least in part, to the notion that Faulkner's entire Yoknapatawpha saga is a single ongoing narrative, which has been rather arbitrarily divided into individual "novels" and "stories." (This is, of course, the underlying premise of Malcolm Cowley's *The Portable Faulkner.*) Even if we concede that Faulkner intended *Go Down, Moses* to be a novel consisting of seven chapters, rather than a collection of seven related stories, we must still determine whether this volume "possesses the organic unity we are accustomed to require of books we agree to call novels."[2] Those who argue that *Go Down, Moses* does possess such unity usually contend

1. Meriwether, "William Faulkner," in *Sixteen Modern American Writers*, edited by Jackson R. Bryer (Durham, NC: Duke University Press, 1974), 250.
2. Millgate, *The Achievement of William Faulkner* (New York: Random House, 1966), 203.

that its seven narratives are variations on a common theme. This position, however, raises additional problems.

The most obvious unifying focus of this "novel" is the issue of race relations. Three of the narratives concentrate on black characters, whereas the other four deal in varying degrees with the interaction between the white McCaslin family and various blacks. Yet in "The Old People" and four of the five sections of "The Bear," the race question is clearly a less prominent concern than the destruction of the wilderness. Unless these two themes are essential parts of a larger dialectic, those readers who pick and choose among the various parts of *Go Down, Moses* would appear to be justified. One might argue that the impulse to subjugate nature and to enslave one's fellow man constitutes an indivisible violation of the ideal that united precivilized races in what Faulkner calls "the communal anonymity of brotherhood." Such an argument, however, is predicated on the illusion of the noble savage and trivializes slavery as simply the most egregious example of property-as-theft. This is essentially the position that Ike McCaslin adopts and the one that those who see Ike as Faulkner's spokesman are forced to accept. Consequently, those readers who find *Go Down, Moses* to be a unified work but who reject Ike as a moral norm must discover some other common denominator to link the disparate elements of this book.[3]

I am convinced that, contrary to appearances, *Go Down, Moses* is not primarily concerned with race relations as such but with that age-old American dilemma—the conflict between the wilderness and the hearth. On the one hand, we have the primitive asexual allure of the forest, on the other the settled familial bonds of home. For Faulkner, Indian men seem to be the primary exemplars of the wilderness life, whereas black women are the primary guardians of the hearth. The white characters in *Go Down, Moses*, particularly the McCaslins and preeminently Ike, stand between these two ideals—

3. One of the best early discussions of Ike McCaslin as a primitivist can be found in Harry M. Campbell and Ruel E. Foster, *William Faulkner: A Critical Appraisal* (Norman: University of Oklahoma Press, 1951), 140–58. Commenting on the possible connection among the various motifs running through this novel, Millgate states: "In *Go Down, Moses* the linking of the wilderness material with the themes of white-Negro relationships and of the ownership of land is sometimes thought to be rather forced; but the tenuousness of the connection between the hunting episodes and the rest of the novel may be in some measure a direct and deliberate reflection of Faulkner's conception of Ike and Ike's idealism" (*Achievement of Faulkner*, 210).

almost never doing justice to either. Although I believe that Faulkner finally endorses the domestic over the wilderness myth, he presents each as containing both charms and liabilities.[4]

In the opening chapter of *Go Down, Moses*, an antebellum narrative called "Was," the theme of domesticity is developed through the behavior of three brothers—Theophilus and Amodeus McCaslin (Uncle Buck and Uncle Buddy) and their colored (that is, half-black) sibling, Tomey's Turl. Buck and Buddy have turned their father's plantation over to their slaves and have moved into a modest shack on the property. They are a sort of fraternal odd couple, living in a misogynist utopia, free of petticoat government. The only disruption in their routine occurs when Tomey's Turl (still a slave despite his McCaslin blood) periodically runs off to visit his inamorata Tennie on the Beauchamp plantation and Uncle Buck is sent to bring him back.

Tomey's Turl is a slave in name only. Buck and Buddy are indulgent masters who would free any slave who wanted to leave. Paradoxically, then, Tomey's Turl is fleeing from the relatively unrestricted environment of the McCaslin place (which resembles a wilderness camp more than a civilized plantation) to the more regimented ambience of the Beauchamp estate (rather pretentiously dubbed Warwick by the haughty Sophonsiba Beauchamp). Whereas Tomey's Turl actively seeks the domestic bliss of life with Tennie, Buck and Buddy are on guard against predatory females. As Weldon Thornton has demonstrated, however, Buck is at least subconsciously receptive to the matrimonial designs of Miss Sophonsiba Beauchamp.[5] Not only is it he who always goes to retrieve Tomey's Turl, but he also makes a point of wearing a necktie (something Buddy does not own) and of delaying his departure long enough to ensure that there will be no chance of apprehending his prey short of Warwick. Thus,

---

4. Karl Zender argues, with considerable plausibility, that the tension between personal freedom and domestic responsibility was the dominant concern of Faulkner's private life at the time he was writing *Go Down, Moses* ("Faulkner at Forty: The Artist at Home," *Southern Review*, n.s., 17 [Spring 1981]: 288–302).

5. Lewis M. Dabney contends: "Miss Sophonsiba is the necessary scapegoat of the piece, the threat that enhances the male Eden of the sixty-year-old Buck and Buddy and the nine-year-old Cass, which Mr. Hubert so envies. . . . Like *Huckleberry Finn* 'Was' is a classic protest against growing up insofar as this means 'settling down'" ("'Was': Faulkner's Classic Comedy of the Frontier," *Southern Review*, n.s., 8 [Autumn 1972]: 743). See also Weldon Thornton, "Structure and Theme in Faulkner's *Go Down, Moses*," in *William Faulkner Critical Collection*, edited by Leland H. Cox (Detroit: Gale, 1982), 338–39.

Tomey's Turl actively pursues a woman, and Buck allows himself to be trapped by one, while Buddy remains an impotent old bachelor uncle.

In creating Sophonsiba Beauchamp, Faulkner fully justifies the contention that he has little regard for white women of childbearing age.[6] Sophonsiba is a belle who possesses the ruthlessness of Scarlett O'Hara with none of Scarlett's redeeming charm. Her brother Hubert plays cards with both of the McCaslin twins on the understanding that the *loser* gets "Sibbey." Later, when she does marry Buck, they move into the mansion and throw the blacks out. Although some readers may be inclined to find humor in her vanity and deviousness, Sophonsiba's pursuit of Buck contrasts markedly with Turl's more straightforward wooing of Tennie. Nor is it insignificant that, in the courtship of the blacks, traditional sex roles are maintained.

Faulkner's narration of "Was" is several levels removed from the primary action of the story. The author has created a third-person narrator who tells us what the aging Ike McCaslin remembers of a tale that his cousin McCaslin Edmonds has told him about an incident that took place prior to Ike's birth. (Uncle Buck and Miss Sophonsiba are Ike's future parents.) Consequently, this tale can be placed in the oral tradition of the McCaslin family. This gives Faulkner greater license for comic distortion than he would otherwise have had. Moreover, our response to the colloquy between Ike and Cass in section 4 of "The Bear" is affected to some degree by our already having read this earlier story that Cass has told to Ike.[7]

*   *   *

6. This generalization goes back at least as far as Leslie Fiedler's *Love and Death in the American Novel*. For a more recent feminist articulation of the same notion, see Ellen Douglas, "Faulkner's Women," in *A Cosmos of My Own: Faulkner and Yoknapatawpha*, edited by Doreen Fowler and Ann J. Abadie (Jackson: University Press of Mississippi, 1981), 149–67.

7. In commenting on the different perspectives of these two cousins, David Walker states: "For Ike, born after the Civil War, brought up in a fiercely individualistic way, and forced to confront his responsibility to the environment, it is clear that he cannot accept the land and the legacy of injustice it conveys. But to Cass, who has seen a comic and idealized social world overturned and devastated without any apparent benefit to anyone, the moral alternatives are far less clear-cut" ("Out of the Old Time: 'Was' and *Go Down, Moses*," *Journal of Narrative Technique* 9 [Winter 1979]: 6–7).

At the heart of *Go Down, Moses* is a three-chapter sequence, which follows Ike McCaslin from childhood to old age. The initial narrative in this sequence, "The Old People," focuses on Ike's forest mentor, Sam Fathers. In many ways an enormously appealing character who exemplifies the wilderness heritage of the Indian, Sam is essentially an anachronism in the modern world. He is not the last in a long line of noble savages so much as a cultural reactionary. His father, Ikkemotubbe, was a hideous assimilationist who aped the white man's vices. Ikkemotubbe ran away to New Orleans in his youth and returned seven years later with a French companion and a quadroon slave woman. When Ikkemotubbe impregnated the quadroon, he married her to another slave and sold them both to Carothers McCaslin. (Old Carothers had himself arranged a similar marriage between slaves to disguise his own dalliance with a slave woman.) Significantly, Cass Edmonds believes that Sam blames his mother for having bequeathed him Negro blood rather than his father for having sold mistress and child.

In the forest, Sam is a magnificent hunter and woodsman, but he is out of his element back in town, where he tries to uphold an image of Indian culture that had become passé even before he was born. His pride in being the son of a chief is seriously undercut by our knowledge that Ikkemotubbe's lineage is on the distaff side (he is the nephew of the old chief Issetibbeha) and that Ikkemotubbe has ascended to his position by tricking and intimidating the rightful heir into abdication. Like other Faulkner characters of mixed blood, particularly Joe Christmas, Sam suffers from a severe crisis of identity. As Cass observes, "His cage ain't McCaslins."[8]

If Sam Fathers is Faulkner's most impressive exemplar of the wilderness myth, then we must seriously question the efficacy of that myth for our own time. As Weldon Thornton notes, Sam's influence on young Ike "is not wholly benign":

> Faulkner rather explicitly suggests some troublesome currents beneath the surface in Sam when he describes him as "barren" and says that he "had no children" . . . , and later when he describes the hermit Jobaker as "even more incredibly lost than Sam Fathers." . . . Though he gives Isaac woodslore and orients

---

8. Faulkner, *Go Down, Moses* (New York: Random House, 1942), 67.

him reverently toward Nature and the Old People, Sam is incapable of providing him with an example of how to live through changing times into the future. Isaac's later failure comes in part from his following the pattern Sam Fathers set for him.[9]

In "The Old People," Sam baptizes Ike with the blood of the first deer the boy has killed. Symbolically, then, Ike is initiated into the mysteries of the wilderness. He becomes one of the "old people"—an honorary Indian. Of course, the story of the white boy who is adopted by the Indians has been a staple of our literature from the earliest captivity narratives through Thomas Berger's *Little Big Man* (1964). What makes Ike's situation different is that there is no tribe for him to be taken into.[10] Instead, he and Sam form the kind of interethnic male bond that Leslie Fiedler celebrates in "Come Back to the Raft Ag'in, Huck Honey!" We do not, however, appreciate the full consequences of this bonding until later in the novel (particularly in section 4 of "The Bear" and in "Delta Autumn"). At the end of "The Old People," there is even a hint that Ike's infatuation with the forest and with Sam Fathers is something he might eventually outgrow. After all, the thoroughly domesticated Cass Edmonds tells Ike that he too had a mystical vision when, under Sam's tutelage, he killed his first deer.

When we get to the hunting episodes of "The Bear," we move into a kind of wilderness men's club whose members have more in common with the animals they hunt than with the females of their own species. "There was always a bottle present," Faulkner tells us, "so that it would seem to [Ike] that those fine fierce instants of heart and brain and courage and wiliness and speed were concentrated and distilled into that brown liquor which not women, not boys and children, but only hunters drank." Then, when Old Ben, principal object

9. Thornton, "Structure and Theme," 350.
10. As Paul S. Stein notes: "It is an initiation which runs directly counter to that mythic rite's supposed purpose, which is, as Mircea Eliade declares, to render the initiate 'fit to be integrated into the community of adults'—but one which fits well within an American tradition of initiations: rites from which novices emerge profoundly *un*fit for life within their communities, unable to accept their values, share their beliefs or live their lifestyles—initiations that are deeply traumatizing and isolating, rather than liberating or reassuring" ("Ike McCaslin: Traumatized in a Hawthornian Wilderness," *Southern Literary Journal* 12 [Spring 1980]: 70).

of the hunt, is introduced, Faulkner makes a point of stressing his celibate isolation. The bear is described as "widowered childless and absolved of mortality—old Priam reft of his old wife and outlived all his sons."[11]

The hunt for Old Ben is not necessary for survival. The men who participate in that hunt all live in civilization and derive their sustenance from activities other than shooting bear. To use John Crowe Ransom's terminology, they are engaged in play forms rather than work forms. There is such little urgency about consummating the hunt that, on at least two occasions, Ike passes up the opportunity to shoot Old Ben. To kill the incarnate spirit of the wilderness would be to bring down the curtain on a drama that none of them wants to see end. By wishing to continue the hunt indefinitely, Ike (and to a lesser extent the other men—particularly Sam Fathers) is in the paradoxical position of denying the ostensible rationale for his presence in the wilderness. The only way that he could truly fulfill his deepest longings would be to leave the world of mutability and enter a timeless realm where hunting was pure ritual, not the *deadly* game it actually is. James Dickey would later imagine such a realm in his poem "The Heaven of Animals." Here, in a poetic never-never land, animals continue to hunt and to be hunted; they just never die:

> They tremble, they walk
> Under the tree,
> They fall, they are torn,
> They rise, they walk again.

Such a world, however, can be entered only in the imagination. And, even then, it is a heaven only for animals.[12]

In a sense, Old Ben is the one who is in control of things. Sam realizes that the ritual will end only when the bear wants it to. Old Ben

11. Faulkner, *Go Down, Moses*, 192, 194.

12. Dickey, *Poems, 1957–1967* (New York: Collier, 1968), 60. In "Antique Harvesters," Ransom was willing to admit southern gentlemen to the happy hunting ground: "Here come the hunters, keepers of a rite; / The horn, the hounds, the lank mares coursing by / Straddled with archetypes of chivalry; / And the fox, lovely ritualist, in flight / Offering his unearthly ghost to quarry; / And the fields themselves to harry" (*Selected Poems* [New York: Knopf, 1963], 71). See also Cleanth Brooks, *William Faulkner: The Yoknapatawpha Country* (New Haven, CT: Yale University Press, 1963), 260.

finally indicates that that time has come when he invades Major de Spain's property and kills one of the major's colts. By breaking the rules of the game, Old Ben brings the game to a close. At that point Sam finds Lion, a dog who can be made fearless enough and ferocious enough to pursue the legendary bear. What had been an idyllic pastime becomes a grim necessity. In the torture training of Lion, a regimen that consists of starving the dog into obedience, Sam reveals one of the least attractive sides of his personality. (But then his father, Ikkemotubbe, had killed little puppies in his quest for political power within the Indian tribe.) We find a contrast to the cold single-mindedness of Sam, the wilderness aristocrat, in the instinctive humanity of the plebeian Boon Hogganback. Boon cares for the dogs and develops a particular fondness for Lion. It is one of the crowning ironies of "The Bear" that Old Ben is not killed in some obviously sacramental way by Ike or Sam but falls prey to Boon, who is simply trying to keep his beloved Lion from being clawed to pieces.

Considered solely as a hunting narrative, "The Bear" is a postfrontier story. For all of its primal mystery, the forest in which the men hunt is something of a benign landscape. ("In a complete reversal of the mythic cosmology of traditional initiations," notes Paul S. Stein, "it is civilization which for Ike becomes the Realm of Shades, the land of dissolution, sterility and death, while the wilderness which would normally contain those terrors becomes a completely idyllic, non-threatening Realm of Eternal Life.")[13] Old Ben is himself more of a nature symbol than a ferocious beast: for years, he had observed the "rules" of the game, and he seems more potent as a legend than as an actual presence. In the two most extensive descriptions we have of him, he comes across primarily as an object of aesthetic contemplation.

Had this simply been a hunt for a marauding beast who had been destroying crops and farm animals, the hunters would have been glad to accomplish their mission and return to more important business—a position that the practical Cass Edmonds does adopt. Sam Fathers, however, chooses to lie down and die when the killing of Old Ben destroys the fairy-tale world in which he has always managed to live.[14] Because Ike has not spent as many years devoted to

13. Stein, "Ike McCaslin," 81.
14. For all intents and purposes, Sam's life does end at this point; however, the literal consummation of his death comes sometime later and is shrouded in

the wilderness, he does not give up the ghost, but he is faced with an agonizing dilemma: does he return to the workaday world of the white man, or does he try to find some way of practicing the primitive values of the free fathers in an age when no one else remembers what those values are?

Toward the end of section 3 of "The Bear," this dilemma causes a clash between Ike and Cass. Here, the boy insists on being allowed to stay with the dying Sam Fathers while the other hunters return to town. Siding with Ike, General Compson rebukes Cass:

> You've got one foot straddled into a farm and the other foot straddled into a bank; you aint even got a good hand-hold where this boy was already an old man long before you damned Sartorises and Edmondses invented farms and banks to keep yourselves from having to find out what this boy was born knowing and fearing too maybe but without being afraid, that can go ten miles on a compass because he wanted to look at a bear none of us had ever got near enough to put a bullet in and looked at the bear and came the ten miles back on the compass in the dark; maybe by God that's the why and wherefore of farms and banks.[15]

What should be stressed here is that General Compson is not rejecting civilization in favor of the wilderness. Rather, he is arguing that *both* have a place in the world (nature is "the why and wherefore of farms and banks"). Moreover, the question at issue is simply whether Ike should depart immediately from the forest or wait three days before doing so. To argue that General Compson, or Faulkner, is endorsing Ike's future lifestyle would be a serious misreading of this scene.

Perhaps the most compelling reason for reading *Go Down, Moses* as a unified novel is section 4 of "The Bear." (Faulkner himself contends that, when "The Bear" is printed separately, section 4 ought to be deleted because its primary relevance is to the entire novel rather than to the hunting narrative in which it is embedded.)[16] Although

---

mystery. When a student at the University of Virginia asked Faulkner to clarify the circumstances of Sam's death, the author replied: "I think Boon murdered him, because Sam told him to" (Frederick L. Gwynn and Joseph Blotner, eds., *Faulkner in the University* [New York: Vintage, 1965], 10).

15. Faulkner, *Go Down, Moses*, 250, 251.

16. See Gwynn and Blotner, *Faulkner in the University*, 4, 273.

this section is devoted to a colloquy between Ike and Cass, it makes relatively few references to the wilderness theme that dominates the rest of "The Bear" and seems primarily concerned with the demands of domestic life. Structurally and thematically, Faulkner made a wise choice in placing this colloquy where he did; however, it would have made almost as much narrative sense had it appeared elsewhere in *Go Down, Moses.*

The colloquy occurs when Ike, at age twenty-one, relinquishes his claim to the McCaslin inheritance. Through his examination of the commissary ledgers, Ike has discovered that his grandfather Carothers McCaslin had had sexual relations with two slave women, the second of whom was his daughter by the first. Among other things, this means that the three surviving children of Tomey's Turl and Tennie Beauchamp are Ike's half cousins. Ostensibly, his renunciation of his inheritance is an act of atonement for his grandfather's transgressions. Yet when Ike and Cass turn their attention from the issue of landownership to Ike's earlier failure to shoot Old Ben, this explanation is called into question. Weldon Thornton argues persuasively that "Isaac's refusal of the land and his failure to kill Old Ben are two expressions of a single flaw." Thornton also reminds us that "Isaac's failure to kill Ben occurred several years before he learned of the miscegenation and incest which he claims are significant sources of his decision to relinquish the land. This implies that Isaac's relinquishing the land is not so much the result of an outraged moral sensibility, prompted by his learning specific facts, as of a general failure of will and courage."[17]

Although I thoroughly agree with Thornton, I think that we can go one step further and interpret Ike's flaw in terms of the conflict between the wilderness and domestic myths. Because he has committed himself to the primitivist lifestyle exemplified by Sam Fathers, Ike is reluctant to kill Old Ben; to do so would be to conclude the hunt whose very meaning for Ike and Sam lies in the prospect of its continuing forever. Cass sees an analogy between this attitude and the posture of the lovers on Keats's Grecian urn. The moment frozen on the urn is one of pursuit. Keats's lovers will never know disillusionment because they will never experience consummation. (It was no accident that the Elizabethans referred to the sex act as "dying.")

17. Thornton, "Structure and Theme," 357.

For Ike, the end of the hunt would be the consummation of a very different pursuit. Like so many romantics, he prefers to freeze time at the moment of anticipation.

The responsibilities and rewards of domestic life are fundamentally incompatible with a romantic sensibility. Marriage and family impose limitations on one's freedom, whereas the mythic allure of the wilderness lies in its absence of restraint. Ike may honestly believe that in renouncing his birthright he is simply trying to expiate the evil that his grandfather has done; however, at a subconscious level, he is probably fleeing from the social demands that property ownership would place on him. The domestic life commences only *after* consummation has occurred. At one point, Ike harbors the illusion that he can enjoy the pleasures of hearth and home while maintaining his personal eccentricities. This experiment proves a failure when his wife stops sleeping with him after his refusal to claim possession of his property. Thomas Merton comments on this situation: "Poverty without chastity remains in some sense ambiguous and ineffective, as Ike's wife intuitively senses in the scene where she tries to bind him again, by erotic ecstasy and the generation of a child, to the earth he has tried to renounce."[18]

Although many readers are inclined to agree with Faulkner's quip that Mrs. Ike possesses the ethics of a prostitute, I suspect that at the worst she is no more than a vulgar embodiment of essentially positive domestic values. Andrew Lytle, for example, speaks of her desperation in offering "her naked body, a renunciation of her modesty, . . . for the sake of a communion of real marriage . . . , [which] is certainly strengthened by the physical location in property, as the personal communion is fixed in the sensible joining of flesh."[19] If Ike's wife has the ethics of a prostitute, then her husband more nearly resembles a client who takes his pleasure and refuses to pay.

Chronologically, the events in section 5 of "The Bear" follow those in section 3. Here, we see Ike as he returns to the hunting camp for one final visit before the lumber company moves in. With Old Ben and Sam Fathers dead, an era has ended, and the tone of this section

18. Merton, "'Baptism in the Forest': Wisdom and Initiation in William Faulkner," in *Mansions of the Spirit: Essays in Literature and Religion*, edited by George A. Panichas (New York: Hawthorn, 1967), 29.

19. Gwynn and Blotner, *Faulkner in the University*, 275–76; Lytle, *The Hero with the Private Parts* (Baton Rouge: Louisiana State University Press, 1966), 118.

is appropriately elegiac. If we move directly from section 3 to section 5, then "The Bear" becomes a simple evocation of the destruction of the wilderness (disregarding, of course, the fact that this "wilderness" is more of a vacation resort than a menacing jungle). Once we include section 4, however, the thematic implications of the rest of "The Bear," as well as of *Go Down, Moses* itself, become much more complex.

In a sense, section 4 of "The Bear" is simply the most extended of several dialogues between Ike and Cass. "Was," we will recall, is presented as the paraphrase of a tale that Cass has told to Ike so frequently that he remembers it even in old age. Then, "The Old People" concludes with the cousins discussing the phantom deer that Ike has seen after his first kill. Finally, in section 3 of "The Bear," Cass and Ike are twice at odds. First, we have the debate over whether Ike can spend the weekend with the dying Sam. And later, when Cass returns to the woods and interrogates Boon about the circumstances of Sam's death, Ike intervenes, his entire face soaked with tears: "'Leave him alone!' he cried. 'Goddam it!'"[20] These various confrontations between the two cousins (the last of which concludes section 3) set the stage for the much longer conversation that transpires in section 4.

Each of the encounters between Ike and Cass involves a variation on the conflict between wilderness and domestic values. In "Was," Tomey's Turl is the character who is most deeply committed to the domestic life, while his white half brother (and half uncle), Buddy McCaslin, is just as dedicated to the rustic freedom of bachelorhood. (Buck McCaslin and Sophonsiba and Hubert Beauchamp fall somewhere between these two extremes.) At the end of "The Old People," the ostensible issue in question is the objective existence of the deer that Ike has seen. Ike accepts his vision with childlike faith, whereas Cass attempts to find a rational explanation for it. But when he finally concedes that he too had such an experience after he killed his first deer, Cass shifts the terms of the debate. He is not so much buying the wilderness mystique as suggesting that it is a phase some boys go through and eventually outgrow on the path to a more conventional life. At the end of section 3 of "The Bear," Cass's intellectual curiosity once again emerges when he seeks to probe the

20. Faulkner, *Go Down, Moses*, 254.

mystery of Sam's death. Characteristically, Ike opposes such a probe.

When we get to section 4 of "The Bear," then, it should come as no surprise that Ike argues for the primitive simplicity of the isolated wilderness life, while Cass advocates assuming responsibility within the existing structures of society. In a sense, the race issue is simply a touchstone against which these two differing philosophies can measure themselves. Cass argues for the conservative approach of doing the best one can within the circumstances in which one finds himself. Ike, however, is a radical who admires the direct action of John Brown. What he seems not to realize is that mere renunciation and passivity are a far cry from direct action. Ike resembles John Brown much less than he does Brown's most eloquent defender—Henry David Thoreau.

As I have suggested elsewhere in this volume, those critics who see Faulkner as a social iconoclast (for example, Irving Howe) are quick to canonize Ike, whereas those who regard the author as essentially a southern traditionalist are more apt to side with Cass. Although Olga W. Vickery, Cleanth Brooks, and Michael Millgate are the best-known expositors of the latter view, it was perhaps stated most forcefully by M. E. Bradford in a paper delivered at a meeting of the South Central Modern Language Association in 1962. Bradford argued that Ike misunderstands the nature of true brotherhood. Rather than use his position, however tainted its origins, to minister to his actual kin, he retreats from the community to serve an ideal that Ike describes as "the communal anonymity of brotherhood." Against this abstract commitment (which is really an abnegation), Faulkner posits the ideal of pragmatic stewardship represented by Cass Edmonds. Bradford put the matter as follows:

> A brother is one whose place is defined by either his dependence upon or his responsibility for another. Cain's question, "Am I my brother's keeper?" is implicitly egalitarian. It posits the "communal anonymity of brotherhood." But Ike's horror at his grandfather's sins, at the events recorded in the old ledgers of the McCaslin plantation commissary, has meaning only in terms of an ideal of brotherhood, of family and community relationships that insists (to use a phrase from Albert Schweitzer) that all brothers in the family of man are either "younger brothers or elder brothers," that some men are inevitably responsible for

others and cannot "abandon them" to an equality that does not (and cannot) exist.[21]

The end of section 4 depicts Ike's domestic failures, as we see his wife laughing at him. (The lack of terminal punctuation implies that the laughter will continue indefinitely.) The ultimate reason for this failure is suggested about two-thirds of the way into section 5. In a description of events that occurred several years before Ike's marriage, we read: "The woods would be his mistress and his wife." Because Ike never really renounces this commitment (that is, never "divorces" the woods), his subsequent marriage is symbolically an act of infidelity—or even bigamy. Thomas Merton suspects that, once this act has been performed, Ike cannot simply return to the status quo ante. Speaking of Mrs. Ike's striptease, Merton notes: "It is almost as if she has instinctively sensed the power of a counter-mysticism, another more elemental 'wisdom,' to cancel out the spiritual vision in the wilderness. And perhaps she succeeds, for after this Ike McCaslin remains an ambiguous personage."[22]

Approximately half a century elapses between the final events in "The Bear" and those of "Delta Autumn." In this time, Ike McCaslin has become an old man, "uncle to half the county and father to no one," and the wilderness has shrunk to the point where it is now necessary to drive two hundred miles from Jefferson to find an adequate hunting ground. What has happened to the land is clearly foreshadowed in two complementary scenes at the end of "The Bear." In the first of these, Ike remembers the story of the train's first trip into the woods. At that time, the locomotive had scared a bear into a tree, and six hunters (Boon, Ash, Major de Spain, General Compson, Walter Ewell, and Cass) had stayed up all night to keep anyone from shooting it. Now, twenty years later, Ike comes across the solitary figure of Boon hammering the breech of his dismembered gun, while trying to keep a bunch of squirrels captive in a gum tree. Without even looking up to see who is approaching, Boon shouts: "Get out of here! Don't touch them! Don't touch a one of them! They're mine!" These scenes are obviously instances of the machine in the garden; however, the

21. Bradford, *The Reactionary Imperative: Essays Literary and Political* (Peru, IL: Open Court, 1990), 41.

22. Faulkner, *Go Down, Moses*, 326; Merton, "'Baptism in the Forest,'" 29–30.

reduction in scale is significant.[23] In the first scene, we had a train, a bear, and six men. In the second, we have only a broken gun, a tree full of squirrels, and the buffoonish Boon Hogganback. What had once been a mythic conquest has now become a pathetic farce.

As many readers of "Delta Autumn" have noted and as a cursory glance at the McCaslin genealogy indicates, Carothers Edmonds duplicates the miscegenation and incest committed by his great-grandfather Carothers McCaslin. However, miscegenation is itself no more than a cultural taboo, and Roth Edmonds and his colored mistress are too distantly related for their coupling to pose any genetic danger to their offspring. (I suspect that the miscegenation and incest motifs have been so frequently employed because of their symbolic richness in representing what might be regarded as opposite violations of the natural order.) The real crime of both Roth and his ancestor is in using women and then discarding them for the sake of appearance. This is not just a failing of the McCaslin and Edmonds families, however. In section 4 of "The Bear," Ike's maternal uncle Hubert Beauchamp is forced to send his high-yaller concubine packing when "Sibbey" claims that the woman's presence has defiled his mother's home.

Ike comes across as such an ineffectual character in "Delta Autumn" that even those who have admired his behavior in "The Old People" and the hunting sections of "The Bear" are forced to wonder what went wrong. If we buy the argument of Roth's mistress, then Ike's renunciation of his land has helped to spoil three generations of Edmondses and, thus, has led—however indirectly—to Roth's repetition of Old Carothers McCaslin's crime. Such an interpretation would lend a kind of Sophoclean irony to Ike's story because his renunciation was motivated by a desire to expiate that ancestral crime. There are a few hints in "Delta Autumn" that Ike may even realize the error of his ways.

In remembering the wife who had been depicted so grotesquely in "The Bear," he concludes that he lost her "because she loved him."

23. Faulkner, *Go Down, Moses*, 331. Boon's language here echoes Ike's protest to Cass at the end of section 3. Perhaps Faulkner wants us to reflect on the vast difference between protecting the secret of Sam's death and burial and merely guarding a treeful of squirrels. For a fuller discussion of the entrance of technology in the pastoral landscape in American literature, see Leo Marx, *The Machine in the Garden* (New York: Oxford University Press, 1964).

Then, later in the same paragraph, he confesses to himself that the uncomfortable tent in which he is lying "was his home and these men, some of whom he saw only during these two November weeks and not one of whom even bore any name he used to know . . . were more his kin than any."[24] When one considers that these men tolerate Ike only to have him as the butt of their jokes, one wonders whether he was too hasty in giving up a farm, a home, and a wife who loved him. This is especially true if, by so doing, he accomplished the opposite of what he had intended.

As an old man, Ike is alienated from both the home that he has forsaken and the wilderness that has forsaken him. His most intense experience of nature is now confined to his dreams. Rather than participating in the hunt as the aging Sam Fathers had done, he lies around the tent all day and has difficulty getting to sleep at night. What is even more remarkable is that this childhood admirer of John Brown now urges a light-skinned young Negress to stay among her own kind and to wait a couple thousand years for the racial situation in the United States to improve. He seems almost to have adopted the cautious outlook of his cousin Cass Edmonds. This transformation is subtly suggested by the fact that Faulkner's narrator now refers to Ike as "McCaslin." Previously in *Go Down, Moses*, that name had been used only to refer to McCaslin Edmonds—a man who was always able to articulate conservative, domestic values without really *doing* much to promote them.

If Ike McCaslin exemplifies the fallacy of the wilderness myth and his various relatives either violate or fail adequately to embody the domestic ideal, then we must look elsewhere for the moral norm in *Go Down, Moses*. It seems to me that such a norm is represented by black women in general and by Aunt Molly Beauchamp in particular.[25] This novel can be interpreted at one level as depicting a conflict between the example of white uncles and that of black aunts. On the one hand, we have Buck and Buddy McCaslin, Hubert Beauchamp, and Uncle Ike. (If we stretch the bonds of consanguinity, it

24. Faulkner, *Go Down, Moses*, 352.
25. In "The Fire and the Hearth," this woman's name is spelled "Molly." By the time we get to "Go Down, Moses," however, the spelling has been inexplicably changed to "Mollie." This is apparently another example of Faulkner's notorious carelessness concerning matters of textual consistency.

might be argued that Cass Edmonds is also an essentially avuncular figure.) On the other, we have Molly Beauchamp, who plays a prominent role in "The Fire and the Hearth" and "Go Down, Moses," and Rider's aunt in "Pantaloon in Black."

In the arrangement of *Go Down, Moses*, "The Fire and the Hearth" immediately follows "Was." Because these two narratives are spaced more than eighty years apart (1859 and 1941), they define the time spectrum encompassed by the novel. The second narrative points back to the first, in that the principal white character in "The Fire and the Hearth" (Roth Edmonds) is the grandson of Cass Edmonds, whereas the principal black character (Lucas Beauchamp) is the son of Tomey's Turl and Tennie Beauchamp. "The Fire and the Hearth" also foreshadows events in at least three subsequent narratives: it makes reference to Ike's troubled marriage and his repudiation of his inheritance (both important themes in section 4 of "The Bear"), it anticipates Roth's rejection of his black kinsmen in "Delta Autumn" and "Go Down, Moses," and it establishes Molly as the strong maternal figure she will once again prove to be in "Go Down, Moses."

In section 4 of "The Bear," Ike's renunciation of his land is presented as a grand—if misguided—gesture, so firmly rooted in idealism that one could never imagine his having second thoughts about it. In contrast, his marriage is depicted as a brief and unpleasant interlude in an otherwise hermetic existence. "The Fire and the Hearth," however, gives us a somewhat different picture of Ike's moral certitude and of his marriage.

> He could ask her forgiveness as loudly thus as if he had shouted, express his pity and grief; husband and wife did not need to speak words to one another, not just from the old habit of living together but because in that one long-ago instant at least out of the long and shabby stretch of their human lives, even though they knew at the time it wouldn't and couldn't last, they had touched and become as God when they voluntarily and in advance forgave one another for all that each knew the other could never be.[26]

26. Faulkner, *Go Down, Moses*, 107–8. Years later, in "Delta Autumn," Ike says: "I think that every man and woman, at the instant when it dont even matter whether they marry then or afterward or dont never, at that instant the two of them together were God" (348).

Because Roth plays such an important role in "Delta Autumn" and is a strong implicit presence in "Go Down, Moses," it is only fitting that we get an early look at him in "The Fire and the Hearth." For the most part, he appears to be a gruff but paternalistic landlord; however, beneath that benign exterior are less admirable character traits. In a crucial flashback, we are told that he and Lucas's son Henry had been virtually inseparable as children. Then, at age seven, Roth had refused to share his bed with Henry and had made the black boy sleep on a pallet on the floor. The consciousness of race has caused Roth to violate a human bond solely for the sake of appearances. This is essentially what Carothers McCaslin had done with his black mistresses and what Roth will later do with his (not to mention Hubert Beauchamp's similar transgression). The fact that both his mistress and Henry are Roth's distant cousins makes his racial condescension ludicrous as well as sad. Moreover, these two acts of repudiation prefigure the expulsion of another black cousin, Butch Beauchamp, from his plantation. That expulsion is, of course, an important catalyst to the action of "Go Down, Moses."

In terms of Faulkner's moral vision, however, the most significant character in "The Fire and the Hearth" is Molly Beauchamp. She has generously bestowed her maternal love on her own son Henry and the white boy Roth (nursing them both when Roth's mother dies in childbirth). Even as a grown man, Roth thinks of her as the person "who had given him the motherless, without stint or expectation of reward that constant and abiding devotion and love which existed nowhere else in the world for him."[27] (This dedication echoes Faulkner's dedication of *Go Down, Moses* to Mammy Caroline Barr, "who was born in slavery and who gave to my family a fidelity without stint or calculation of recompense and to my childhood an immeasurable devotion and love.") When Lucas's obsession with finding gold threatens the stability of their marriage (symbolized by the perpetual fire in the hearth), Molly shocks Lucas back to his sanity by seeking a divorce. Thus, she ironically saves the marriage by coming close to terminating it.

Certainly, the chapter that does least to enhance the narrative unity of *Go Down, Moses* is "Pantaloon in Black." Its major character, a young black man named Rider, is connected to the McCaslins

27. Ibid., 117.

only by virtue of renting a cabin from Roth Edmonds and knowing Lucas and Molly. Faulkner's inclusion of such a chapter in his novel can be justified only on thematic grounds. Thus, the emphasis that "Pantaloon in Black" places on domestic values suggests the importance of those values to the total message of *Go Down, Moses*. In telling Rider's story, Faulkner employs one of his most effective technical devices: he presents some of the same events from two different perspectives. First, an impersonal narrator tells us of Rider's agonizing efforts to come to terms with the death of his young wife, Mannie. Unable to find solace in either work or drink, he enters a crooked dice game and kills the white man who runs it. (One suspects that Rider is playing out a secret death wish so that he can join Mannie in the hereafter.) In the short second section of "Pantaloon in Black," a white deputy sheriff gives his interpretation of these incidents in a conversation with his wife. The "conversation," however, is more like a dramatic monologue, in that the deputy—who does almost all of the talking—reveals himself to be grotesquely insensitive.[28] Faulkner's clear implication is that, in order to justify their behavior, white racists find it psychologically necessary to view blacks as comic and subhuman creatures—as pantaloons.

We are obviously meant to contrast the deputy's cold relationship with his wife to the loving one that existed between Rider and Mannie. Yet, as Weldon Thornton has correctly noted, Faulkner also depicts Rider as a man of tragic limitations. It is right that he should grieve for his wife, but his self-destructive refusal to accept the consolation offered by his friends and family is not entirely admirable. His aunt, who has raised him from childhood, tries to get him to return to her home for a time and urges him to pray for strength and comfort.[29] In rejecting the support of both family and religion, Rider is forced to deal with his misfortune as an isolated individual. It is that isolation

28. If anything, the deputy's wife is even worse. She is impatient for her husband to finish his story so that she can clear the table and get to the movies. As Warren Akin IV notes, "It is ironic that she should be seeking drama where she has remained unresponsive to a situation far more moving than any she will see at the picture show" ("'The Normal Human Feelings': An Interpretation of Faulkner's 'A Pantaloon in Black,'" *Studies in Short Fiction* 4 [Fall 1978]: 404).

29. In the opinion of Donald R. Noble, Rider's aunt "is articulating the theme of much of *Go Down, Moses:* the theme of family, of community as opposed to isolation" ("Faulkner's 'Pantaloon in Black': An Aristotelian Reading," *Ball State University Forum* 14 [Summer 1973]: 18).

that proves to be his downfall. When his aunt finally accompanies him to jail, hoping to serve as a buffer against the lynch mob, her presence comes too late to save him.

Although Cleanth Brooks believes that Faulkner should have ended his novel with "Delta Autumn," I am convinced that the title chapter is indeed the proper conclusion for *Go Down, Moses*. "Delta Autumn" brings the wilderness and racial themes to an end and gives us our final glimpse of Ike McCaslin. If, however, there is a more abiding motif than either the destruction of the wilderness or the oppression of one race by another, it is the unselfish and unstinting sense of family love that Faulkner finds exemplified in black women. In "Go Down, Moses," as in "The Fire and the Hearth," the particular exemplar of this love is Mollie Beauchamp. Mollie's feelings toward her wayward grandson, the executed murderer Butch Beauchamp, can best be understood in relation to the behavior and attitudes of three white characters: Roth Edmonds, Gavin Stevens, and Miss Belle Worsham. To begin with, Roth has sent Butch away from the plantation when the latter was caught breaking into the commissary. On the surface, this would seem to be a moderate response to the crime of breaking and entering, and Mollie would appear to be irrational in blaming Roth for Butch's subsequent fate. "Roth Edmonds sold my Benjamin [into Egypt]," she moans. Yet in her own way Mollie is right. Because her grandson is, in effect, the child of her old age, he is her Benjamin. For Roth Edmonds, however, Butch more nearly resembles the biblical Joseph.

It was Joseph, not Benjamin, who was sold into Egypt. This deed was performed by Joseph's half brothers, men who felt they had ample provocation for their action. In sending Butch away from the plantation, Roth also exiles a relative (in this case, a black distant cousin) from the only home he has ever known. When seen in the light of Roth's previous conduct toward his mistress and child and toward Henry Beauchamp, the exile of Butch appears less the isolated act of a wronged property owner than the latest in a series of brutal rejections. By this point, Faulkner does not need to depict the act itself, only to show its consequences. In stark contrast to Roth Edmonds, Gavin Stevens represents the possibility of genuine compassion between the races. (Gavin arranges for Butch's body to be returned to Jefferson and collects money from the townspeople to help defray the expense.) Arthur Mizener contends that "Go Down,

Moses" "shows us the grandeur and pathos, the innocence and the incongruity of the community's solidarity."[30]

Nevertheless, for all his good intentions, Gavin indulges the elitist notion that he knows what is best for the family and is decidedly uncomfortable in the presence of Mollie's overt emotionalism. At the end of the chapter (and, hence, the novel), he is eager to get back to town, as he tells the newspaper editor: "I haven't seen my desk in two days." (How nicely this parallels Uncle Buck's statement at the end of "Was": "It seems to me I've been away from home a whole damn month.")[31] In the character of Gavin Stevens, Faulkner seems to be suggesting that even the sincerest compassion is all too often accompanied by incomplete understanding.

Significantly, something very close to complete interracial understanding does exist between Mollie and Miss Worsham. If an interethnic male bonding has joined Sam Fathers and Ike McCaslin as wilderness brothers, a similar sort of female bonding has joined Mollie Beauchamp and Belle Worsham as domestic sisters.

In the penultimate paragraph of chapter and novel, we learn that Mollie has insisted that the news of Butch's funeral be put in the paper because, even though she is unable to read, "Miss Belle will show me whar to look and I can look at hit." (Interestingly enough, all seven chapters of *Go Down, Moses* end with direct statements: the first three refer to domestic situations and the next three to wilderness and hunting themes; finally the two concluding paragraphs of the last chapter consist of the newspaper editor's quoting Mollie's lamentations and then of Gavin Stevens's inadequate response to the situation.)[32] Although black women may be Faulkner's primary moral exemplars, it is encouraging that a white person such as Miss Worsham can occasionally achieve an empathy that crosses racial lines.

At the most fundamental level, the wilderness and domestic myths

30. Mizener, "The Thin, Intelligent Face of American Fiction," *Kenyon Review* 17 (1955): 517.

31. Faulkner, *Go Down, Moses*, 30.

32. Mollie's statement tells us a good deal about her own sensibility and about her own relationship with "Miss Belle." However, Faulkner avoids ending his novel with an affirmation that is too simple and too sentimental. By filtering Mollie's words through the perceptions of Gavin Stevens and the newspaper editor and then sending these three men back to their daily routines, the author preserves an aura of mystery about Mollie and maintains an aesthetic distance between her and the reader.

embody contradictory approaches to salvation. As Lewis P. Simpson argues, the nature mystique of postindustrial man ultimately derives from a Rousseauesque desire to return to an imagined primal innocence. Put another way, the attempt to reverse or simply ignore the first fall of man inevitably leads to a second fall—what Simpson calls "the Fall of New World Man." Unlike the original Adamic Fall, the second one contains few redemptive possibilities. According to Olga W. Vickery:

> In rejecting sin, Isaac also rejects humanity. Significantly, he holds himself aloof from close human ties; though he is uncle to half the county, he is father to no-one and husband solely to the wilderness. Having confused the wilderness with the Garden of Eden, he not only dedicates but sacrifices his life to it. Man must leave the garden in order to discover his humanity and whatever the reason, Isaac does not do so; his knowledge stops just short of the paradox of the fortunate fall.[33]

If the wilderness life represents an attempt to return to prefallen individualism, the domestic vision recognizes that in an irreversibly fallen world we are dependent on each other for our salvation.[34] In theory, the free fathers may have endorsed a communal ethic, but that community no longer exists in the modern world. To pretend that it does is to retreat into romantic solipsism. In contrast to such a stance, we have the simple humanity and maternal love of women such as Aunt Molly Beauchamp and Mammy Caroline Barr. (If Uncle Ike is father to none, Aunt Molly and Mammy Caroline are mothers to all.) Long after the wilderness has vanished and those who destroyed it are forgotten, these women and the values they embody will continue, not only to endure but to prevail.

33. Simpson, "Isaac McCaslin and Temple Drake: The Fall of New World Man," *Nine Essays in Modern Literature*, ed. Donald E. Stanford (Baton Rouge: Louisiana State University Press, 1965), 88–106; Vickery, *The Novels of William Faulkner: A Critical Interpretation* (Baton Rouge: Louisiana State University Press, 1959), 133. For a more affirmative view of Ike as a New World figure, see R. W. B. Lewis, *The Picaresque Saint* (Philadelphia: J. B. Lippincott, 1959), 193–209.

34. James Ellis suggests that marriage and the family serve important functions within the Christian theme of redemption when he argues that "the marriage relationship itself, properly understood, becomes a metaphor for the Paradox of the Fortunate Fall" ("Human Sexuality, the Sacrament of Matrimony, and the Paradox of the Fortunate Fall in *The Scarlet Letter*," *Christianity and Literature* 29 [Summer 1980]: 53).

9

Why *Streetcar* Keeps Running

With remarkably few exceptions, sophisticated literary critics mistrust works that have touched a mass audience. Particularly since the rise of modernism, the gap between elite and popular culture has become an article of faith. As a result, the literary clerisy spends its time analyzing and deconstructing texts, while the majority culture continues to enjoy songs and stories. (As Dwight Eisenhower is reputed to have said, " I may not know what's art, but I know what I like.") Of course, in times past, Shakespeare appealed to both the aristocracy and the groundlings, the serialized fiction of Dickens and Thackeray was read as avidly as soap operas are now watched, and Longfellow, prior to reading before Queen Victoria, signed autographs in the servants' quarters.

Among twentieth-century American poets, only Robert Frost bridged the gap between serious and popular literature. In the realm of fiction, the trick was turned (but only in selected novels) by Ernest Hemingway, John Steinbeck, F. Scott Fitzgerald, and Robert Penn Warren. In drama, where performance enables a writer to reach an audience beyond the confines of the printed page, the record is no better. Eugene O'Neill never seized the popular imagination, and Edward Albee came close only in *Who's Afraid of Virginia Woolf?* For Arthur Miller, *Death of a Salesman* enjoyed a popular and critical success never duplicated elsewhere in his career.

The one American playwright who is a conspicuous exception to this dichotomy between "high" and "low" culture is Tennessee Williams. Williams's South—with its sexual ambivalence, self-delusion, and irrational violence—has become part of our popular mythos, the ambience of countless B movies and television melodramas. With only slight exaggeration, Marion Magid states:

> A European whose knowledge of America was gained entirely
> from the collected works of Tennessee Williams might garner a
> composite image of the U.S.: it is a tropical country whose vege-
> tation is largely man-eating; it has an excessive annual rainfall
> and subsequent storms which coincide with its mating periods;
> it has not yet been converted to Christianity, but continues to
> observe the myth of the annual death and resurrection of the
> sun-god, for which purpose it keeps on hand a constant supply
> of young men to sacrifice. . . . [T]he sexual embrace . . . is as
> often as not followed by the direst consequences: cannibalism,
> castration, burning alive, madness, surgery in various forms
> ranging from lobotomy to hysterectomy, depending on the na-
> ture of the offending organ.[1]

Beyond this, particular Williams plays—such as *The Glass Menagerie* and *Cat on a Hot Tin Roof*—have entered American popular
culture to a degree unmatched by the work of any other critically ac-
claimed dramatist. But even those achievements pale to insignificance
in comparison to what Williams wrought in *A Streetcar Named Desire*. Surely, no play of the American theater, perhaps no play in
English since the time of Shakespeare, has won such praise from
both the critics and the populace. When they agree on so little in the
realm of literature, one wonders why the critics and the people are
of a single mind on this one play.

In seeking to answer this question, I have found myself repeatedly
borrowing concepts from the criticism of Leslie Fiedler. Although
Fiedler's massive bibliography includes commentary on most major
works of American literature (as well as many minor ones), I am not
aware of his having written on *A Streetcar Named Desire*. Nevertheless, *Streetcar* seems particularly suited for a Fiedlerian treatment
(if such a pompous phrase does not violate the populist spirit of
Fiedler's muse). At least after his seminal essay "Cross the Border—
Close the Gap" (1969), Fiedler plumbed the universal sources of literary response by treating popular culture with the same reverence
critics automatically extend to canonical texts. Moreover, *Streetcar*
raises many of the same issues that Fiedler continually found to be
at the heart of our storytelling tradition.

1. Magid, "The Innocence of Tennessee Williams," in *Essays in the Modern
Drama*, edited by Morris Freedman (Boston: D. C. Heath, 1966), 290.

A Fiedlerian approach to *Streetcar* would identify those elements in the play that transcend the distinction between elite and popular culture. What is needed is an understanding of the play's mythopoeic power. This is something quite different from a cataloging of allusions to ancient legends, which may or may not be known to a mass audience.[2] *Streetcar* is a play that raises disturbing questions about hearth and home, sex roles, family loyalty, and the power of eros. Because this is done within the context of a drama, the aesthetic distance between audience and artifact is much less than it would be with a sociological essay or even a novel. We respond to issues of universal concern at a visceral level long before that response is articulated, or "rationalized," in the form of criticism. I suspect that *Streetcar* remains such a riveting play in the country of its origin precisely because its particular treatment of universal themes—myth as opposed to mere mythology—is deeply rooted in American culture and literature.

For more than a half century, Fiedler argued that we can pretty well divide the canon of American literature between works that view home as heaven and those that see it as hell. The texts celebrated in *Love and Death in the American Novel* (1960) (and, before that, in D. H. Lawrence's *Studies in Classic American Literature* [1923]) belong to the latter category. Beginning with Washington Irving's Rip Van Winkle, "The uniquely American hero/anti-hero . . . rescues no maiden, like Perseus, kills no dragon, like Saint George, discovers no treasure like Beowulf or Siegfried; he does not even manage at long last to get back to his wife, like Odysseus. He is, in fact, an anti-Odysseus who finds his identity by *running away from home.*"[3] The reason for this is quite simple. At home, he is subject to a loathsome form of tyranny known as "petticoat government." The tyrant may be a henpecking wife, such as Rip's Dame Van Winkle, or a nitpicking guardian, such as Huck Finn's Miss Watson (we have seen endless variations of these two in TV situation comedies and the funny pages of the daily newspaper). In either case, the only escape is into the wilderness and the society of fellow males.

2. See, for example, Judith J. Thompson, *Tennessee Williams's Plays: Memory, Myth, and Symbol* (New York: Lang, 1987), 25–51.
3. Fiedler, *What Was Literature? Class Culture and Mass Society* (New York: Simon and Schuster, 1982), 152.

Against this basically misogynistic canon is a countertradition of domestic literature. From the popular women novelists whom Hawthorne dismissed as that "damned tribe of scribbling females" to the writers of today's soap operas, laureates of the domestic tradition posit a stable home life, complete with heterosexual bonding and close family ties, as the greatest human good. Even when it is thwarted by the conflicts necessary to literature and endemic to life, it is still the ideal. As antithetical as they might seem, the domestic paradigm and the misogynist tradition both agree that the woman rules the home. The only disagreement is whether she is a benevolent despot or a hideous shrew. The patriarchal insistence that the man is king of his castle is generally understood as mere male bluster.

To say the least, Stanley Kowalski does not conform to the matriarchal conventions of our literature. Stanley is unquestionably the king of his castle. As a traveling salesman, he enjoys the freedom of the road. As captain of his bowling team, he is at no loss for male camaraderie. These experiences, however, are not an evasion of domestic unhappiness. Stanley's loving and *obedient* wife is always waiting for him, eager to gratify and be gratified. Even in the home, she accommodates him and his friends. Rip Van Winkle might have to meet his buddies at Nicholas Vedder's tavern. Dagwood Bumstead might have to hold his card games in the garage. Stanley plays poker in the middle of his apartment. Only in the person of Eunice, who threatens to pour boiling water through the floorboards of the upstairs apartment, do we see even a vestige of the henpecking wife. As politically incorrect as it may be, the Kowalski household embodies a patriarchal vision of Home as Heaven. There is not enough potential conflict here for tragedy or farce. At least, not until Blanche enters the scene.

From the moment of her first entrance, Blanche brings with her an ideal of home that varies sharply from what she encounters in Elysian Fields. Even before she utters a word, her expression of "shocked disbelief" speaks volumes. In first identifying Stella by her maiden name, Blanche instinctively places her sister back in her old home rather than in the one where she is "Mrs. Stanley Kowalski." Later in the scene, Blanche verbalizes her displeasure with Stella's current living arrangements, suggesting that she has somehow betrayed the memory of Belle Reve. Only a little scrutiny is required to show how problematic Blanche's air of superiority actually is.

To begin with, she has come to Elysian Fields not from Belle Reve but from Tarantula Arms. It is doubtful that accommodations there were any more aristocratic than in the French Quarter. Moreover, reliable information about "Belle Reve" itself is quite sparse. Clearly, the family home in Laurel has been lost on a mortgage. But how grand was it? With the exception of Stella, the closest that anyone in Elysian Fields has come to the place is a photograph of a mansion with columns. That photograph has been enough to impress Eunice and Stanley; however, Stella, who has actually lived in Belle Reve, seems unconcerned about its loss. Blanche, who at the very least is a pathological liar, remembers the place as a plantation. But there are no plantations in Laurel, Mississippi, which is in the heart of the piney woods. If there were even servants at Belle Reve, we hear nothing of them. In fact, Stella says that when *she* waits on Blanche, it seems more like home. There are enough hints in the play to suggest that the grandeur of Belle Reve is as suspect as the value of Blanche's rhinestone tiara and summer furs. (The supposedly hardheaded Stanley is taken in by all three.)

Even if we see Belle Reve as a latter-day Tara, it is lost in a way that Tara never was. Margaret Mitchell's image of the Old South as a matriarchal Eden had captured the public imagination by the time *Streetcar* premiered on Broadway in 1947. In 1950, moviegoers would have been reminded of this image by the mere fact that Vivien Leigh, who had played Scarlett O'Hara on the screen, was cast as Blanche in the film version of Williams's play. In Mitchell's antebellum South, women ruled the home while men fought duels and argued over secession. These same men mortgaged the matriarchal paradise by leading the South into a war it could not win. After the war, Scarlett adapted to changing circumstances to do whatever was necessary to regain Tara and hold off the carpetbaggers. This Darwinian feat, however, was beyond the capabilities of the leading men of the old order (anachronistic cavaliers such as Ashley Wilkes), who were reduced to riding in white sheets at night to prove their manhood. The only exception was the social outcast Rhett Butler.

Belle Reve was not destroyed by war or Reconstruction, but like Margaret Mitchell's South, it was victimized by a failed patriarchy. Over a period of centuries, to hear Blanche tell it, Belle Reve was lost as her "improvident grandfathers and father and uncles and brothers exchanged the land for their epic fornications."[4] (In fact, only a *female* cousin left enough insurance money to provide for her own burial.) Unlike Scarlett, the women of Belle Reve are incapable of filling the void left by these inadequate men. Stella escapes from this doomed home, and except for Blanche, all the other women die. Blanche herself is denied a normal family life when she discovers her husband's homosexuality, and the guilt she experiences from driving him to suicide leads to a series of debaucheries that render her incapable of even pursuing the modest career of a high school English teacher.

Although Blanche is less than an admirable character, she strikes some audiences as at least an object of pity when she falls into Stanley's brutish clutches. Yet if we look at the situation objectively, Stanley's motives—if not his methods—are superior to Blanche's. His patriarchal authority is never challenged by Stella; however, Blanche does little else from the moment of her arrival at Elysian Fields. When she tells Stella in scene 1 that she will not be put up in a hotel because she wants to be close to her sister, her need for companionship is apparent (not to mention her lack of funds). But this residency also gives her a strategic position from which to undermine Stanley and to entice Stella with fantasies of life among the aristocracy. Not only does she install herself as an indefinite squatter in a two-room apartment, she does everything within her power to wreck the contented home life that had existed in that apartment. One can hardly blame Stanley for fighting back.

Throughout much of the play, the conflict between Stanley and Blanche would seem to be between a crude member of the underclass and the quintessential schoolmarm. The standards of etiquette and decorum that Blanche purports to represent have been the scourge of every red-blooded American male since Miss Watson tried to force Huck to mind his manners (while she was preparing to sell Nigger Jim down the river). What Mark Twain plays for farce is deadly serious in the world of *Streetcar*. Blanche is not trying to "sivilize" an urchin who is living in her home. She is trying to wreck the home she has invaded. Although never really hidden, this intention is made unmistakably clear in Blanche's speech to Stella toward the

4. Williams, *A Streetcar Named Desire*, in *The Theatre of Tennessee Williams* (New York: New Directions, 1971), 1:284.

end of scene Four (a speech that Stanley overhears). What she has just finished proposing to Stella is a kind of feminist variation on the anti-Odysseus theme. In this scenario, Stella will run away from home to join Blanche (who has already fled Laurel) in a chaste female bonding—not in the forest or on the river, but in a shop of some sort endowed by a sexually unthreatening Shep Huntleigh.

When Stanley's boorish behavior proves insufficient to drive Blanche away, he discovers something that must be the realization of every rebellious schoolboy's fantasy—that the schoolmarm is not what she pretends to be. As Henry Fielding observes in his preface to *Joseph Andrews*, the exposure of hypocrisy is the source of endless delight. When Stanley reveals the sordid details of Blanche's recent conduct to Stella in scene 7, it is with a kind of righteous gloating. "That girl calls *me* common!" he says.[5] The only reservation that might prevent the audience from sharing Stanley's glee is the hope that a reformed Blanche will find happiness as Mitch's wife, a solution that would also remove her from the Kowalski household. Stella is convinced that this would happen if Stanley would only keep his mouth shut.

Unfortunately, all available evidence suggests otherwise. Blanche's newfound circumspection is only a ruse to lure Mitch to the altar. If there is any doubt of this, consider the end of scene 5, where Blanche's attempted seduction of the newsboy is followed immediately by the arrival of Mitch, with a bunch of roses in his hand. As Blanche's husband, Mitch would probably arrive home one afternoon to find his wife in the sack with a less hesitant newsboy (just as Blanche found her former husband in bed with a man). She sees Mitch not as a spouse to love (even in the exclusively physical way that Stella loves Stanley) but as a sexually timid benefactor—a poor girl's Shep Huntleigh. It is hardly dishonorable for Stanley to want to protect his naive friend from such a fate. In the world of male camaraderie, his bond with Mitch is just as compelling as the blood ties that unite Stella and Blanche.

If Stanley is justified in wising Mitch up about Blanche's past, he clearly crosses the line of acceptable behavior when he attacks her sexually in scene 10. Yet even this inexcusable act must be analyzed within the context of the play. There is little evidence to suggest that

5. Ibid., 358.

Stanley returned home that night with the intention of raping Blanche.[6] He is in a good mood because of the impending birth of his child and even offers to "bury the hatchet" and drink "a loving cup" with Blanche.

It is only after she speaks of casting her pearls before swine that his mood changes. This reference cannot help reminding Stanley of the tirade he overheard in scene 4. (That speech, with its Darwinian imagery, was more than a little ironic, as it is Blanche—not the ata- vistic Stanley—who is in danger of becoming extinct because of an inability to adapt to the environment.) Although he has not over- heard her references to Shep Huntleigh in that earlier scene, a woman as talkative as Blanche might well have tipped her hand to him at some point during her interminable stay in the Kowalski apartment. In any event, *the audience* is reminded of Blanche's plot to "rescue" Stella by breaking up her marriage to Stanley. As Stanley has yet to lay a hand on Blanche, their sympathies must still be with him.[7]

Because the consummation of what happens between Stanley and Blanche occurs offstage, we are left to imagine the details. On the basis of what we do know, it is reasonable to assume that Stanley be- lieves he is simply doing what Mitch was unable to do in the preced- ing scene—enjoy the favors of a notoriously promiscuous woman. Blanche held Mitch off by screaming "Fire," something she does not do when Stanley approaches her. When he says, "So you want some roughhouse! All right, let's have some roughhouse," his assumption is that she enjoys violent foreplay. It is possible to interpret Stanley's next statement—"We've had this date with each other from the be- ginning"—as a confession that he was plotting to destroy her. But it is at least as plausible that he is referring to Blanche's flirtatious ad-

6. Bert Cardullo argues convincingly that "Williams carefully structures Act Three, Scene Four, so as to make the rape seem incidental, the result more of Stanley's sudden and uncontrollable drunken lust than of his calculation and deliberate cruelty" ("Drama of Intimacy and Tragedy of Incomprehension: *A Streetcar Named Desire*," in *Tennessee Williams: A Tribute*, edited by Jac Tharpe [Jackson: University Press of Mississippi, 1977], 138).

7. Harold Clurman notes that during the original Broadway production, the audience sided with Stanley for the bulk of the play (*Lies Like Truth* [New York: Macmillan, 1958], 78). Emily Mann goes even further in contending that, con- trary to Williams's intentions, Stanley (as played by Marlon Brando) eventually "became a folk hero" for American audiences (Philip C. Kolin, ed., "*A Streetcar Named Desire*: A Playwright's Forum," *Michigan Quarterly Review* 29 [Spring 1990]: 19).

vances, which began as early as scene 2. Whatever happens offstage, Stanley can hardly be said to have driven Blanche insane. She may think that she is waiting for Shep Huntleigh when the doctor and the matron come to cart her off to the insane asylum in scene 11, but she also thought that in scene 10 before Stanley even came home. If anyone drives Blanche crazy, it is Mitch by foiling her wedding plans.[8]

Despite all of these mitigating factors (which seem far more disingenuous in the postfeminist era than they would have in 1947), the rape so diminishes Stanley morally that we are deprived of any easy satisfaction we might have felt in his triumph over Blanche. If Williams personally empathized with Blanche more than with Stanley, the rape may be his desperate attempt to win audience sympathy for a victimized woman. But that is about all he is able to do. It is beyond even Williams's considerable art to convince us that Blanche is a genuinely tragic figure—she has too many flaws, too little stature, and almost no self-knowledge. Blanche can excite pity in the truly sensitive, but fear only in the most defeated and self-loathing among us.[9]

Although critics have never been entirely comfortable with the confused feelings Williams's two antagonists evoke, some balance is necessary to maintain dramatic tension. The rape creates that balance. It does not elevate Blanche to the level of tragic heroine, but it does prevent the audience from siding too enthusiastically with

8. Roger Boxill notes that Stanley "is quite right in telling [Blanche] that she accepted the date with him a long time ago" (*Tennessee Williams* [New York: St. Martin's, 1987], 82). Also, a director who so chooses can accentuate Blanche's sexual attraction to Stanley and her complicity in her own ravishment. For a discussion of how John Erman did this in his television production of *Streetcar*, see June Schlueter, "Imitating an Icon: John Erman's Remake of Tennessee Williams's *A Streetcar Named Desire*," *Modern Drama* 28 (March 1985): 5–6. The question of when, and even whether, Blanche goes mad is controlled to some extent by the actress playing the role. For a discussion of the different interpretations of Blanche's mental state in the performances of Jessica Tandy and Uta Hagan, see Eric Bentley, *In Search of Theater* (New York: Knopf, 1953), 88–89.

9. Blanche has had her critical defenders. Their arguments, however, tend to focus on Williams's own sympathies or on philosophical elements in the play rather than on audience reaction. See, for example, Benjamin Nelson, *Tennessee Williams: The Man and His World* (New York: Obolensky, 1961), 149; and Nancy Tischler, *Tennessee Williams: Rebellious Puritan* (New York: Citadel, 1961), 138. I think that Roger Boxill has it about right when he says that "audiences favor Stanley, at least in the beginning, while readers favor Blanche" (*Tennessee Williams*, 80).

Stanley. Remove the rape, and *Streetcar* is reduced to a sexist melodrama, in which the gaudy seed bearer regains patriarchal control over a household threatened by a hypocritical and self-serving matriarchy. Of course, the circumstances of the rape are so ambiguous that what the mass audience loses in melodrama it gains in sadomasochistic titillation.[10]

In a sense, Williams's audience can have it both ways: it can censure Stanley and pity Blanche (the "proper" moral response, to be sure), while guiltily enjoying his triumph over her. At least, this would seem to be true for the men in the audience. As males, we have secretly cheered the bad boy on as he proves something we have always wanted to believe—that the sententious schoolmarm is really a secret nympho. There is even a sense in which the male who has allowed himself to identify with Stanley can see *Streetcar* as having a fairy-tale ending. The witch has been dispatched (if not to the hereafter, at least to the loony bin), the home is safe, and the prince and princess of Elysian Fields live happily ever after—seeing colored lights unsubdued by magic lanterns. But what of the woman spectator? In what way is she able to experience the mythic power (as opposed to merely admiring the artistry) of Williams's play? It is certainly not through a macho identification with Stanley.

One can imagine a woman who believes herself wronged by men feeling an affinity with Blanche. If we read *Streetcar* as a feminist fable, Stanley's rape of Blanche might be a paradigm for how men deal with women in a patriarchal society. (Stanley and Mitch would both seem to be purveyors of the double standard, whereas Stella is nothing more than a sex object and childbearer.) Not surprisingly, Sandra M. Gilbert and Susan Gubar see the play as an indictment of "the law of the phallus and the streetcar named heterosexual desire." In an even more detailed feminist analysis, Anca Vlasopolos reminds us

10. For a plausible defense of the balance that Williams has struck in his characterization of Stanley and Blanche, see Normand Berlin, "Complementarity in *A Streetcar Named Desire*," in *Tennessee Williams: A Tribute*, edited by Tharpe, 97–103. Roger Boxill notes: "If Blanche is portrayed as a neurotic and pretentious woman of whom history is well rid, and Stanley as a healthy animal whose brutishness is a symptom of his 'acute sensitivity,' then *Streetcar* becomes a melodrama" (*Tennessee Williams*, 90). According to Signi Falk, the opening-night theatergoers sided with Stanley to the point that during the rape scene, "waves of titillated laughter swept over the audience" ("The Profitable World of Tennessee Williams," *Modern Drama* 1 [December 1958]: 175).

that it is not just Stanley but the entire cast of the play that expels Blanche at the end.[11] Stanley and Mitch may have been the catalysts of Blanche's downfall, but Stella—with the encouragement of Eunice—seals her sister's fate by choosing to believe Stanley, so that her marriage might be preserved. The poker buddies simply stand around in awkward bovine acquiescence.

The problem with these interpretations is not that they are untrue but that they are inadequate. For much of her life, Blanche's difficulties stemmed from the lack of a forceful patriarchy. As we have seen, her male forebears abdicated their role as providers and saddled her with mortgage and debt. Her behavior toward her husband may have had terrible consequences, but it was not without provocation. Allan Gray wronged Blanche by marrying her, knowing that she loved him in a way that could bring only traumatic pain when she discovered the truth about his sexual orientation. He then allowed her to believe that the fiasco of their wedding night was her fault. Finally, when she quite understandably tells him that he is disgusting (which he is), he takes the coward's way out by killing himself—apparently not caring what effect this will have on Blanche or anyone else he leaves behind. It is the absence of assertive men, not their chauvinistic presence, that has been Blanche's undoing. In fact, Blanche even admits to Stella that Stanley may be "what we need to mix with our blood now that we've lost Belle Reve."[12]

For women, the emotional power of *Streetcar* may come from an identification with Stella. Unlike Stanley and Blanche, who (depending on your perspective) are either demigods or demons, Stella appears to be a fairly ordinary person. In purely Darwinian terms, however, she is clearly the heroine of the play. She has survived because she has successfully adapted herself to changing circumstances. (Blanche is doomed by her inability to adapt, whereas Stanley seems bent on adapting the environment to himself.) Although Blanche blames Stella for betraying Belle Reve by leaving, there is no reason to believe that she could have saved the place by staying. Unlike Lot's wife, she does not even cast a regretful glance back. Stella has no illusions about the desirability of a world in which

11. Gilbert and Gubar, *No Man's Land: The Place of the Woman Writer in the Twentieth Century*, vol. 1, *The War of the Words* (New Haven, CT: Yale University Press, 1988), 52; Vlasopolos, "Authorizing History: Victimization in *A Streetcar Named Desire*," *Theatre Journal* 38 (October 1986): 322–38.

12. Williams, *A Streetcar Named Desire*, 285.

women are worshiped but not supported. Stanley spells out the difference between these two worlds in his typically blunt manner. He reminds Stella: "When we first met, me and you, you thought I was common. How right you was, baby. I was common as dirt. You showed me the snapshot of the place with the columns. I pulled you down off them columns. I pulled you down off them columns and how you loved it, having them colored lights going!"[13]

In pulling her "down off them columns," Stanley brings Stella into a world of male dominance. At least symbolically, it is an act of brute force, and one that Stella "loves." As Gore Vidal noted nearly forty years after the Broadway premiere of *Streetcar:* "When Tennessee produced *A Streetcar Named Desire*, he inadvertently smashed one of our society's most powerful taboos (no wonder Henry Luce loathed him): he showed the male not only sexually attractive in the flesh but as an object of something never before entirely acknowledged by the good team, the lust of women."[14] Moreover, the fact that Stanley, as a "Polack," is considered socially inferior to the Dubois sisters makes his sexual assaults on them what Fiedler calls "rape from below." For Stella, this simply adds to the fun; for Blanche, it presumably adds to the horror.

We know that Stella was "thrilled" when Stanley broke the lightbulbs with her slipper on their wedding night and that she nearly goes crazy when he is away on the road. The notion that women enjoy this kind of brute sexuality has long been a commonplace in popular literature. After all, an entire genre of romance novels, which are purchased almost exclusively by women, are called "bodice rippers." In one of the most memorable scenes in the greatest romance novel of all time—*Gone with the Wind*—Rhett Butler takes Scarlett by force in what is quite literally an act of marital rape. After quoting this scene in the novel, Fiedler contends: "Finally, however, [Scarlett] *likes* it (as perhaps only a female writer would dare to confess, though there are echoes of D. H. Lawrence in the passage), likes being mastered by the dark power of the male, likes being raped."[15]

We have a similar phenomenon in the relationship of Stanley and Stella, except that Stella does not put up even token resistance. In the scene from *Gone with the Wind*, Rhett carries a protesting

13. Ibid., 377.
14. Vidal, *United States: Essays, 1952–1992* (New York: Random House, 1993), 448.
15. Fiedler, *What Was Literature?* 208.

Scarlett up the staircase of their mansion. In *Streetcar*, we have a scene that is almost the mirror opposite. After Stanley has gone ape on his poker night and hit the pregnant Stella, she and Blanche flee upstairs to Eunice's apartment. When he realizes what has happened, Stanley proceeds to scream (with heaven-splitting violence): "STELL-LAHHHHH." According to the stage directions:

> *The low-tone clarinet moans. The door upstairs opens again. Stella slips down the rickety stairs in her robe. Her eyes are glistening with tears and her hair loose around her throat and shoulders. They stare at each other. Then they come together with low, animal moans. He falls to his knees on the steps and presses his face to her belly, curving a little with maternity. Her eyes go blind with tenderness as she catches his head and raises him level with her. He snatches the screen door open and lifts her off her feet and bears her into the dark flat.*[16]

(Like Scarlett, Stella wears a look of serene contentment on the morning after.)

If there is a single scene in *Streetcar* that remains in the memory, it is this one. The film version has been endlessly replayed as a kind of touchstone in the history of the cinema. It has been parodied and spoofed by countless impressionists and nightclub comedians. Now a permanent part of our popular culture, this scene can be said to sum up iconographically what *Streetcar* is all about: for men, it is a fantasy of complete domination, for women one of complete submission.

Like other works that have entered the realm of popular myth, *Streetcar* loses none of its power when transferred to another medium. This fact is particularly astonishing when one considers that, in bringing this play to the screen, Williams and director Elia Kazan faced not only the normal aesthetic challenges of such an undertaking but a battle with the censors as well. The story has been frequently told of the many lines of vulgar or suggestive dialogue that had to be bowdlerized.[17] Then, there was the insistence that any hint of Allan Gray's homosexuality be removed. Finally, the censors

16. Williams, *A Streetcar Named Desire*.

17. For discussion of the film version of *Streetcar*, including the issue of censorship, see Gene D. Phillips, *The Films of Tennessee Williams* (Philadelphia: Arts Alliance, 1980); and Maurice Yacowar, *Tennessee Williams and Film* (New York: Ungar, 1977).

would allow Stanley's rape of Blanche to remain only if Stella would punish Stanley by leaving him (on the assumption that only the break-up of this home could preserve traditional family values.) Nevertheless, the subversive appeal of the play manages to survive.

The sanitizing of Williams's language (which is not all that shocking when judged by today's standards) is about as effective as the bleeping of profanity on television. Adult theatergoers know how people such as Stanley Kowalski talk without having to hear the actual words. Besides, more than enough sexual energy is conveyed by Marlon Brando's body language and magnetic screen presence. The issue of Allan's homosexuality is not crucial, either. In talking about her husband's weakness, Blanche at least implies a deviancy that dare not speak its name. It is perhaps even more in character for her to withhold the sordid details from Mitch.

Finally, when Stella leaves Stanley in the movie (just after Blanche has been escorted out of the apartment by the psychiatrist and the matron), it is not for the first time. She has left him many times before, most recently in the aftermath of the poker game. As Maurice Yacowar points out, "Stella's last speech is undercut by several ironies. She expresses her resolve to leave to the baby, not to the rather more dangerous Stanley. And she does not leave the quarter, but just goes upstairs to Eunice's apartment; and Stanley's call had been enough to bring her back from Eunice's before."[18] When the movie closes with Stanley screaming for Stella, it is difficult to visualize her not returning much as she had in that earlier unforgettable scene.

It is more than a little ironic that Tennessee Williams, the homosexual misfit, should have written such an aggressively heterosexual play. As a man who shared many of Blanche's faults (promiscuity, self-hatred, and paranoia, though never hypocrisy), he must have felt closer to her than most of his audiences do, pity being the greatest kindness that most of these strangers are willing to extend to her. Certainly, it takes a jaundiced view of home and family to present the Kowalski household as their embodiment. But that is exactly what *Streetcar* does. For nearly sixty years, there has been a place in the American imagination where it is always three a.m., and a man in a torn T-shirt screams for his wife with "heaven-splitting violence."

18. Yacowar, *Tennessee Williams and Film*, 23.

Despite the protests of film censors and outraged feminists, she will always slip down the rickety stairs and into his arms. This is because "there are things that happen between a man and a woman in the dark—that sort of make everything else seem unimportant" and because "life has got to go on."[19] As long as people continue to believe such things, *A Streetcar Named Desire* will keep running.

19. Williams, *A Streetcar Named Desire*, 321, 406. John Gassner argues that "Williams . . . seems to have succumbed to a generally jaundiced view of normality by giving the impression that the common world is brutish, as if life in a poor neighborhood and Stan and Stella's sexually gratifying marriage were brutish" ("*A Streetcar Named Desire:* A Study in Ambiguity," in *Modern Drama: Essays in Criticism,* edited by Travis Bogard and William I. Oliver [New York: Oxford University Press, 1965], 377).

10

Come Back to the Locker Room Ag'in, Brick Honey!

he ideal of male companionship is one of the most enduring myths in American literature. As Leslie Fiedler argues in "Come Back to the Raft Ag'in, Huck Honey!" the works that we most revere tend to be boys' books. These narratives "proffer a chaste male love as the ultimate emotional experience. . . . In Dana, it is the narrator's melancholy love for the *kanaka* Hope; in Cooper, the lifelong affection of Natty Bumppo and Chingachgook; in Melville, Ishmael's love for Queequeg; in Twain, Huck's feeling for Nigger Jim." These books and others like them celebrate "an essential aspect of American sentimental life: the camaraderie of the locker room and ball park, the good fellowship of the poker game and fishing trip, a kind of passionless passion, at once gross and delicate, homoerotic in the boy's sense, possessing an innocence above suspicion." Fiedler insists that "to doubt for a moment this innocence . . . would destroy our stubborn belief in a relationship simple, utterly satisfying, yet immune to lust; physical as the handshake is physical, this side of copulation."[1] Tennessee Williams's *Cat on a Hot Tin Roof* is a scandalous, and ultimately subversive, play precisely because it does doubt the "innocence" of such a relationship.

1. Fiedler, *The Collected Essays of Leslie Fiedler* (New York: Stein and Day, 1971), 1:144–45, 143. The one essential aspect of Fiedler's paradigm that is totally absent from *Cat on a Hot Tin Roof* is the interethnicity of the male bond. The wilderness couples whom Fiedler identified in 1948, as well as the additional pairings that he and others kept citing in American literature and popular culture, inevitably consisted of a white and a dark-skinned male. Brick and Skipper are, of course, both Caucasian. For the situation to have been otherwise in 1955, Williams would have to have sent Brick to an integrated northern school. Perhaps sexuality was an explosive enough issue to deal with in the midfifties without adding race to the mix.

Williams's treatment of homosexuality in *Cat on a Hot Tin Roof* represents an advance over the clichés of *A Streetcar Named Desire*. In *Streetcar*, Blanche's homosexual husband, Allan Gray, conforms to stereotype ("There was something different about the boy, a nervousness, a softness and tenderness which wasn't like a man's"), even to the point of killing himself by shoving a phallic revolver into his mouth. In *Cat*, Brick and Skipper inhabit the macho world of big-time athletics. To all outward appearances, their friendship conforms to the sentimental myth that Fiedler describes. The thought that it might be anything more than that is enough to kill Skipper. It also drives Brick to drink, threatens to destroy his marriage to Maggie, and endangers his inheritance of the plantation upon Big Daddy's demise. In the hands of a less gifted, or less conflicted, playwright, this situation might have lent itself to an angry polemic against homophobia. In Williams's play, however, homoeroticism is more a personal than a political or social problem.

Because Skipper has died before the play begins, his relationship with Brick is never dramatized. Instead, Williams gives us at least five different interpretations of that relationship. These different interpretations serve a theatrical function similar to multiple points of view in a novel. Just as we get a more rounded picture of Thomas Sutpen by seeing him from a variety of perspectives in Faulkner's *Absalom, Absalom!* we understand more about Brick and Skipper by seeing the impact of their friendship on an entire cast of characters. What remains uncertain is the view of Williams himself. In the alternative third acts that he wrote for the play and the various contradictory comments he has made about his intentions, Williams has reflected an ambivalence that finally makes *Cat* a problematic, if undeniably powerful, work of art.

The most conventional interpretation of Brick's relationship with Skipper is rendered by Mae and Gooper. They see these two gridiron heroes as examples of arrested development. In the original version of the third act, Mae says: "Brick kept living in his past glory at college! Still a football player at twenty-seven!"[2] In the Broadway version of the play, these observations are split between Mae and Gooper. In both versions, the brother and sister-in-law try to convince Big Daddy and Big Mama that Brick is a sexual deviate. It would be in-

2. Williams, *Cat on a Hot Tin Roof*, in *The Theatre of Tennessee Williams* (New York: New Directions, 1971), 3:150.

exact, however, to characterize Mae and Gooper as homophobic. They undoubtedly support the official taboos against homosexuality, but there is no evidence that they are viscerally offended by the thought that Brick is a "pervert." The only emotions that seem to move them are avarice and envy. If anything, they are probably delighted by the thought that Brick is the antithesis of the all-American male everyone has believed him to be. That notion would vindicate the less gifted and less favored Gooper, while giving him his most plausible claim to Big Daddy's inheritance.

In his characterization of Mae and Gooper, Williams seems downright heterophobic. By making the only monogamous heterosexuals in the play his two most ridiculous and loathsome characters, he invites us to deplore the traditional family. Big Daddy compares Mae's fertility to that of a farm animal, and Maggie refers to her nieces and nephews as "no-neck monsters." A more evenhanded playwright might have generated some small degree of sympathy for the slighted older brother, but Williams is unrelentingly contemptuous in his portrayal of the entire Gooper clan.[3] If this is what the nuclear family looks like, then perhaps the embittered celibacy of Brick or the primal lecheries of Big Daddy represent more authentic responses to life. The male bonding of two football teammates or even the same-sex marriage of Jack Straw and Peter Ochello may be even better.

To see Brick and Skipper as only cases of arrested development, with no sexual overtones, is still to evoke the ideal of male companionship that Fiedler argues is at the heart of our classic literature. The heroes of our boys' books (Huck and Jim, Natty and Chingachgook, Ishmael and Queequeg) are themselves boys who never grew up. Whatever else they may have been, Brick and Skipper were certainly of this company. When Richard Brooks adapted *Cat* for the screen in 1958, he was forced to purge any allusions to homosexuality. The theme of prolonged adolescence was stressed instead. Brick could not be a husband to Maggie or an heir to Big Daddy because

3. Charles Brooks describes Gooper's children as follows: "Everyone is supposed to adjust his life to these monstrous children: no matter how they slobber and drool over the tablecloth and the guest's clothing, the children must eat at the family table; everyone must applaud their gawkish, unwanted, and extended singing performance; the sister-in-law must calmly accept their precocious and vulgar insults; all belongings must be toys for the children, and no one should have possessions which might be dangerous for those grasping young ones" ("The Comic Tennessee Williams," *Quarterly Journal of Speech* 44 [October 1958]: 278).

those roles would have forced him to assume adult responsibility. (Skipper fell apart because his athletic inadequacies were graphically exposed when he was forced to play in a televised game without the injured Brick at his side.) By enabling Brick finally to assume those responsibilities, Brooks's film manufactures an upbeat ending that violates the spirit of Williams's play. Nevertheless, by making the issue of maturation the crux of this film, Brooks remains in the tradition of the classic American myth and reminds us how much of that myth can survive even the bowdlerizing efforts of the censors.[4]

Brick's own view of his friendship with Skipper is both complex and defensive. If Mae and Gooper are only casually homophobic, Brick is profoundly disturbed by the thought of unconventional sexuality. In act 2, he tells Big Daddy that "at Ole Miss when it was discovered a pledge to our fraternity, Skipper's and mine, did a, *attempted* to do a, unnatural thing with—We not only dropped him like a hot rock!—We told him to get off the campus, and he did, he got!" At no point in the play does Brick ever entertain the notion that he and Skipper are anything more than good locker-room buddies. He protests (perhaps too much) that, unlike Straw and Ochello, he and Skipper were not "ducking sissies . . . queers." He asks Big Daddy: "Why can't exceptional friendship, *real, real, deep, deep friendship!* between two men be respected as something clean and decent?"[5]

Then, he goes on to give his version of that friendship:

> Skipper and me had a clean true thing between us!—had a clean friendship, practically all our lives, till Maggie got the idea you're talking about. Normal? No!—It was too rare to be normal, any true thing between two people is too rare to be normal. Oh, once in a while he put his hand on my shoulder or I'd put mine on his, oh, maybe even when we were touring the country in pro football an' shared hotel-rooms we'd reach across the space between the two beds and shake hands to say goodnight.[6]

What Brick has described is "a relationship simple, utterly satisfying, yet immune to lust; physical as the handshake is physical."

---

4. For discussions of Brooks's film, see Gene D. Philips, *The Films of Tennessee Williams* (Philadelphia: Arts Alliance, 1980), 133–54; Maurice Yacowar, *Tennessee Williams and Film* (New York: Ungar, 1977), 38–48; and William Sacksteder, "The Three Cats: A Study in Dramatic Structure," *Drama Survey* 5 (Winter 1966–1967): 252–66.

5. Williams, *Cat on a Hot Tin Roof*, 119, 118, 120.

6. Ibid., 120–21.

Brick is quite right is saying that Maggie destroyed this idyllic relationship by suggesting that it was not entirely innocent. To speak of "innocence" in this context is not to imply that fully realized homosexual lust is "guilty" (although Brick obviously thinks that it is). Innocence simply means a lack of knowledge. A closeness that might seem suspect in grown men is accepted between boys. As long as Brick and Skipper are able to foster the illusion that they are still boys (with a barnstorming football team that is nearly as much of a fantasy as Tom Sawyer's Gang), they are safe in their homoerotic Eden. The fall from innocence occurs with the knowledge that Maggie forces Skipper to consider. She may see herself as a cat on a hot tin roof, but in this particular situation she more closely resembles the snake in the Garden. Brick blames himself for Skipper's death because he failed to help his friend face the truth when Skipper called him to make a tearful and drunken confession. If Skipper is undone by too much knowledge, Brick suffers from a desperately *willed* innocence. Like the doomed naifs in Nathaniel Hawthorne's fiction, he will not face his fallen condition. Instead, he waits for the alcoholic "click" that will allow him to evade responsibility. For most of the play (and perhaps even at the end), he is unwilling to accept Maggie's belief that "life has got to be allowed to continue even after the *dream* of life is—all—over."[7]

As Arthur Ganz argues, Brick bears a remarkable resemblance to the more obviously delusional Blanche Dubois. Like Blanche, Brick drives a homosexual to self-destruction by withholding love and understanding. (In response, both Blanche and Brick seem intent on righting the balance by destroying themselves.) The audience reaction to their situations is different, however, especially since the plays were produced in an age when homosexuality was thought to be a curable affliction. "The audience, although it sympathizes with Blanche, can accept her as guilty," Ganz believes. "She is a woman, and had she been able to give her husband love instead of contempt, she might have led him back to a normal life. Brick, however, confronted with Skipper's telephoned confession of a homosexual attachment, is hardly in a position to do the same—short of admitting a similar inclination."[8]

7. Ibid., 57.
8. Ganz, "The Desperate Morality of Tennessee Williams," *American Scholar* 31 (Spring 1962): 286.

Whether Brick has experienced a similar inclination is not entirely clear. In an interview with Arthur B. Waters, which occurred while *Cat* was still playing on Broadway in 1955, Williams asserts:

> Brick is definitely not a homosexual. . . . Brick's self-pity and recourse to the bottle are not the result of a guilty conscience in that regard. . . . It is his bitterness at Skipper's tragedy that has caused Brick to turn against his wife and find solace in drink, rather than any personal involvement, although I do suggest that, at least at some time in his life, there have been unrealized abnormal tendencies.

Many playgoers, particularly in 1955, would have thought it strange for such tendencies to manifest themselves in the insistently masculine world of college and professional sports. (In ballet or interior decoration, yes, but not in football!) However, Williams may be doing something here beyond a mere playful shattering of stereotypes. Whether we admit it or not, the all-male world has always had the potential for more than chaste camaraderie. As Fiedler notes, "The buggery of sailors is taken for granted everywhere, yet it is usually thought of as an inversion forced on men by their isolation from women; though the opposite may well be true: the isolation sought more or less consciously as an occasion for male encounters."[9]

Another perspective on this issue was suggested by David Gelman in an article in *Newsweek* when President Clinton was trying to ease the ban on homosexuals in the military. "There is . . . an undercurrent of homoerotic tension in the shared latrines, shower rooms and sleeping quarters of barracks life," Gelman suggests.

> G.I.s get used to the loss of privacy soon enough, but not, perhaps, to the enforced physical intimacy. "If I'm in the shower," says Mike Tuttle, a specialist at Ft. Bragg, N.C., "I'd like to know I'm not being ogled over by some guy." It's an unaccustomed worry for men. By imagining themselves as objects of homosexual lust, they unwittingly place themselves in the feminine role—which may explain the vehemence of their objections.[10]

9. Waters, "Tennessee Williams: Ten Years Later," *Theatre Arts* (July 1958): 73; Fiedler, *Collected Essays of Fiedler*, 1:149.
10. Gelman, "Homoeroticism in the Ranks," *Newsweek*, July 26, 1983, 28.

Even if Brick possesses no "abnormal tendencies" himself, the thought that he is the object of male lust raises questions of gender identity that may help to account for the vehemence of *his* objections.

Because Skipper is dead before the play opens, we know of his views only through hearsay. Apparently, the face he showed to the world was as homophobic as Brick's. He was involved in the fag bashing that went on in the fraternity at Ole Miss and responded with panicked denials when Maggie dared to mention the feelings he harbored for Brick. In a moment of drunken candor, she said: "SKIP-PER! STOP LOVING MY HUSBAND OR TELL HIM HE'S GOT TO LET YOU ADMIT IT TO HIM!" Skipper slapped her hard on the mouth and ran away. Later that night, he came to her hotel room and tried to prove his masculinity in bed. When that attempt failed, Skipper was convinced that he must be homosexual. It was then that he made his hapless confession to Brick and quickly degenerated into a frenzy of self-loathing. When Maggie recalls her sexual encounter with Skipper, she tells Brick, "We made love to each other to dream it was you, both of us!" Paradoxically, Maggie's body is the one place where Brick and Skipper can experience a blameless physical communion. It has an appeal akin to what Fiedler characterizes as the appeal of the whorehouse— "a kind of homosexuality once removed."[11]

The notion that Skipper's liaison with Maggie may actually be a repressed manifestation of his lust for Brick would seem to be supported by recent studies in gender theory. The feminist critics Gayle Rubin and Eve Kosofsky Sedgewick argue that, in a patriarchal society such as ours, the primary social bonds are the ones between men. Christopher Looby contends that because these bonds "entail degrees of libidinal investment" that might be mistaken for homoeroticism, they "are chronically under pressure to guarantee their own heterosexual status, to ward off the threatening possibility that they are not, after all, so very different from direct homosexual bonds." (The prolonged athletic camaraderie of Brick and Skipper would certainly fall into this category.) Such guarantees often take the form of "casting male same-sex bonds as relations of rivalry or competition for a female object of desire rather than as directly desirous re-

11. Williams, *Cat on a Hot Tin Roof*, 59; Fiedler, *Love and Death in the American Novel*, rev. ed. (New York: Stein and Day, 1966), 318.

lations between men."[12] Skipper's misfortune is that for him this guarantee fails to work.

One of the ironies of Williams's play is that its two most overtly heterosexual characters—Maggie and Big Daddy—are also the most tolerant of the latent erotic ties between Brick and Skipper. Brick takes the position that anything other than chaste male friendship would be literally unspeakable, while his wife and father try to show an understanding that he hysterically rejects. In act 1, Maggie describes the affection she has detected between Brick and Skipper:

> It was one of those beautiful, ideal things they tell about in Greek legends. It couldn't be anything else, you being you, and that's what made it so sad, that's what made it so awful, because it was love that could never be carried through to anything satisfying or even talked about plainly. Brick, I tell you, you got to believe me, Brick, I *do* understand all about it! I—I think it was *noble!* . . . Why I remember when we double-dated at college, Gladys Fitzgerald and I and you and Skipper, it was more like a date between you and Skipper. Gladys and I were just sort of tagging along as if it was necessary to chaperone you!—to make a good public impression—[13]

If the theme of homosexuality is closer to the center of the plot in *Cat on a Hot Tin Roof* than it is in *A Streetcar Named Desire*, the physical fact of such relations is more distant. Not only is there a lack of sexual intimacy between Brick and Skipper, but the very language with which Maggie describes the situation elevates it to a platonic status. The analogy she makes is not even to something as near as the bonding of males in the mythic American wilderness but to "those beautiful, ideal things they tell about in Greek legends." When Brick accuses her of naming his friendship with Skipper dirty, Maggie responds: "I'm naming it so damn clean that it killed poor Skipper!—you two had something that had to be kept on ice, yes, incorruptible, yes!—and death was the only icebox where you could keep it." The irony here is that literal homosexuality was very much

---

12. Looby, "Innocent Homosexuality: The Fiedler Thesis in Retrospect," in *Mark Twain['s] Adventures of Huckleberry Finn: A Case Study in Critical Controversy*, edited by Gerald Graff and James Phelan (Boston: Bedford, 1995), 547.

13. Williams, *Cat on a Hot Tin Roof*, 57.

a part of life in ancient Greece. (Myles Raymond Hurd argues that Williams, who had been familiar with classic Greek literature from the age of twelve, based the friendship of Brick and Skipper on the relationship between Achilles and his "masculine whore" Patroclus.)[14] It is clear, however, that Maggie is not being snide or disingenuous in holding up the Greeks as examples of chaste male love. Any *intentional* irony is on the part of the playwright himself.

If Arthur Ganz is correct in comparing Brick to Blanche Dubois, Maggie makes an even more instructive contrast to Blanche. Whereas Blanche expresses disgust at discovering her husband's homosexuality, Maggie offers understanding. Of course, the circumstances of the two situations are crucially different. Blanche stumbles across her husband in the act; Maggie discerns nothing more than evidence of unconsummated desire in her husband's best friend. Still, Williams could have turned Maggie into a castrating bitch rather than a seductive cat had he chosen to do so.

In "Three Players of a Summer Game," the short story from which *Cat* is derived, the original character of Brick Pollitt is driven to drink and a brief summer affair by his emasculating wife, Margaret. "At the end of the story," Roger Boxill argues, "Williams emphasizes the castration theme by comparing Margaret to an ancient conqueror as she drives about town with her amiably senseless husband like a captive in chains behind her." It would seem that in writing *Cat*, Williams deliberately made the character of Margaret more sympathetic than he had in the earlier story. (For one thing, in the story, Margaret withholds sex from her husband, whereas Maggie the Cat is intent on getting him into bed.) As he states in the "Note of Explanation" that accompanies the printed text of his play, "Maggie the Cat had become steadily more charming to me as I worked on her characterization."[15]

Had Williams not found Maggie "steadily more charming," he could have easily made her into a female Stanley Kowalski. Brick's assumption that she has driven Skipper to his death (much as Stanley helped drive Blanche insane) seems implausible only because Williams convinces us of Maggie's basic sincerity and decency. Had

14. Hurd, "Cats and Catamites: Achilles, Patroclus, and Williams's *Cat on a Hot Tin Roof*," *Notes on Mississippi Writers* 23 (June 1991): 63–66.

15. Boxill, *Tennessee Williams* (New York: St. Martin's, 1987), 116; Williams, *Cat on a Hot Tin Roof*, 168.

Williams wanted to, he could have made her lie about her pregnancy seem as avaricious as any plot hatched by Mae and Gooper. Instead, he presents it as an affirmation of life in the face of death. In separating Brick from his liquor until he satisfies her desire, Maggie commits an act that Williams might have presented as marital rape. Instead, he encourages us to think that she is acting in Brick's best interests as well as her own. (This is particularly true in the Broadway version of the third act.) Peter L. Hayes even goes so far as to say that "Maggie . . . gives Brick his life back, and from him, Williams implies, she will conceive more."[16]

The tolerance that Big Daddy extends to Brick is even greater than Maggie's forbearance. It is also more threatening because the thing that Big Daddy seems to be tolerating is what Brick has tried most aggressively to deny. When Brick protests that people have been suggesting that he and Skipper were "queer," Big Daddy's response is to stress his own worldliness. He talks about having "bummed this country. . . . Slept in hobo jungles and railroad Y's." The implication is that he has seen homosexual behavior and is not particularly shocked by it. (Unlike his son, he has not had the luxury of belonging to a queer-baiting fraternity at Ole Miss.) Even closer to home, he has inherited his plantation (twenty-eight thousand acres of the richest land this side of the Valley Nile) from the homosexual couple Jack Straw and Peter Ochello.

They took him in when he was young and poor and made him overseer of the place that he now owns. It would hardly be stretching a point to say that they became his surrogate parents. When Brick contemptuously refers to them as "a pair of old sisters," Big Daddy angrily responds: *"Now just don't go throwin' rocks at—."*[17] Whatever else one might say about Straw and Ochello, their stewardship of the land has been far more impressive than that of the degenerate heterosexuals who mortgaged Belle Reve to pay for their epic fornications.

16. Hayes, *The Limping Hero: Grotesques in Literature* (New York: New York University Press, 1971), 41. For a more detailed comparison of *Cat on a Hot Tin Roof* with "Players of a Summer Game," see Charles E. May, "Brick Pollitt as Homo Ludens: 'Three Players of a Summer Game' and *Cat on a Hot Tin Roof*, in *Tennessee Williams: A Tribute*, edited by Jac Tharpe (Jackson: University Press of Mississippi, 1977), 277–91.

17. Williams, *Cat on a Hot Tin Roof*, 115, 116.

Several times in the discursive stage directions he wrote for the published version of *Cat*, Williams emphasizes the fact that Brick and Maggie are staying in the room that had been shared by Straw and Ochello. At the most literal level, their coupling after the final curtain falls would be a triumph for heterosexual "normalcy." However, the symbolic implications of their act are not so clear-cut. As previously noted, Maggie's body is the one point of sexual contact that Brick and Skipper have shared. By sleeping with Maggie, Brick may be vicariously establishing a sexual bond with his dead friend.

Moreover, the practical consequences of resuming marital relations would be to enhance Brick's chances of inheriting the plantation that originally belonged to two overt homosexuals. David Savran comments on this symbolism:

> [Brick's] successful impregnation of his wife in the bed of Jack Straw and Peter Ochello would ironically attest less to the sudden timely triumph of a "natural" heterosexuality than to the perpetuation of a homosexual economy and to the success of Maggie's fetishistic appropriation of Skipper's sexuality. (It is in this sense that Brick's act of making the lie of Maggie's pregnancy true would also make true the "lie" about Brick and Skipper.)[18]

Although *Cat on a Hot Tin Roof* challenges the social taboos against homoeroticism, Williams's most vital and most memorable character is a heterosexual hedonist. Big Daddy elevates physical pleasure with women above all other values. He tells Brick that if he does not like Maggie, he should find another woman, even as he himself expresses physical disgust with Big Mama and dreams of a mistress he can "hump from Hell till breakfast." If Brick's homophobia is largely defensive, Big Daddy's tolerance is that of a man beyond suspicion. (As he reveals in his conversation with Brick, he draws the line only at child prostitution.) Refreshing as his honesty may be in a world of mendacity, Big Daddy nevertheless falls short of being a moral norm. In his treatment of Big Mama, he commits what Blanche Dubois considered the one unforgivable sin—deliberate cruelty. The

18. Savran, "'By Coming Suddenly into a Room That I Thought Was Empty': Mapping the Closet with Tennessee Williams," *Studies in the Literary Imagination* 24 (Fall 1991): 72.

contrast between Big Daddy's gusto and Brick's lethargy is so great that we are apt to miss the similarities of father and son. Both men have left the marital bed because of a self-indulgent revulsion with their wives. For both men, it is love itself that dare not know its name.

What distinguishes Jack Straw and Peter Ochello from Brick and Big Daddy is not their sexual orientation but their superior fidelity to each other. The fact that their relationship is never depicted but only described makes it seem all the more ideal. (When Brick protests that his friendship with Skipper was nothing like that of Straw and Ochello, he speaks with greater truth than he realizes.) Even though the "marriage" of these two men might seem to resemble the male bonding that Leslie Fiedler describes, it differs from that paradigm in two significant respects.

First, and most obviously, Straw and Ochello were not a chaste pair living in a realm of mythic innocence. (Brick's crudely homophobic language leaves no doubt about the nature of their relationship.) Perhaps just as important, Straw and Ochello did not run away from home, or try to escape petticoat government, but lived totally within the confines of civilization. The wilderness buddies Fiedler identifies in our classic literature can find freedom and fulfillment only in the tabula rasa of nature. Huck and Jim belong on a raft, not on twenty-eight thousand acres of the richest land this side of the Valley Nile. In Straw and Ochello, Williams subverts the American myth of male companionship not just by making its homoeroticism explicit but also by domesticating it. In contrast, the world of the Dixie Stars seems far closer to the never-never land of perpetual childhood.

Even though audiences have been moved by *Cat on a Hot Tin Roof* in the half century since its premiere on Broadway, critics and ordinary theatergoers alike have not always known what to make of the play. If Williams's treatment of homoeroticism seemed scandalous in 1955, more recent queer theorists have chided Williams for his reticence and evasiveness. Most observers have been troubled by the playwright's difficulty in achieving closure at the end of the play. Both the original and the Broadway versions of the third act leave questions unanswered and an uneasy sense that the answers suggested are willed and artificial.

We are not certain, for example, whether Brick returns to Maggie's bed for any reason other than a desire to repossess his liquor. If he is just thirsty for a drink, then his alcoholism suddenly becomes the central issue of the play rather than the sign of a more deep-seated malaise. The renewed admiration for Maggie that Brick expresses in the Broadway version of the play seems insufficiently motivated. Williams has asserted elsewhere that Brick "will go back to Maggie for sheer animal comfort."[19] It that is so, he is no better than the satyric Big Daddy and considerably less honest. Such an interpretation also leaves us wondering why Williams bothered to place such emphasis on Skipper's sad fate and on the seemingly noble legacy of Jack Straw and Peter Ochello.

If the ending of the play (in either version) is willed, what exactly has the playwright willed? He may simply have lost his nerve and returned Brick to the heterosexual fold to placate those in the audience who would have been shocked by any other ending. At the same time, he may be using a symbolic code to tell others in the audience that Brick is vicariously making love to Skipper when he "humps" Maggie in Straw and Ochello's bed. It is also possible that Williams grew to admire Maggie so much that he wanted to reunite her with Brick without finding a convincing way to do so. Perhaps he is saying that true love finally has nothing to do with sexual orientation. We can see it in Big Mama's affection for Big Daddy, in Skipper's attachment to Brick, and in the mutual fidelity of Straw and Ochello. Although it can come in many forms, such love is always a rare and elusive experience. Fiedler concludes his essay by quoting Jim's statement to Huck: "It's too good to be true, Honey. . . . It's too good to be true." Williams ends the original version of his play on a remarkably similar note—with Maggie declaring her undying love for her husband, while Brick responds, "with charming sadness," "Wouldn't it be funny if that was true?"[20]

19. Williams, *Selected Essays*, edited by Christine R. Day and Bob Woods (New York: New Directions, 1978), 73. See also John M. Clum, "'Something Cloudy, Something Clear': Homophobic Discourse in Tennessee Williams," *South Atlantic Quarterly* 88 (Winter 1989): 161–79.

20. Williams, *Cat on a Hot Tin Roof*, 166. Charles E. May interprets this line much less optimistically, comparing it to Jake Barnes's reply to Lady Brett at the end of Hemingway's *Sun Also Rises:* "Isn't it pretty to think so?" ("Brick Pollitt as Homo Ludens," 291).

11

The Achievement of William Humphrey

At the climactic point of his autobiographical narrative *Farther Off from Heaven*, William Humphrey comes back to his hometown of Clarksville, Texas, after many years' absence. Struck by the transformation he sees, Humphrey remarks:

> In a move that reverses Texas history, a move totally opposite to what I knew in my childhood, one which all but turns the world upside down, which makes the sun set in the East, Red River County has ceased to be Old South and become Far West. I who for years had had to set my Northern friends straight by pointing out that I was a Southerner not a Westerner, and that I had never seen a cowboy or for that matter a beefcow any more than they had, found myself in the Texas of legend and the popular image which when I was a child had seemed more romantic to me than to a boy of New England precisely because it was closer to me than to him and yet still worlds away. Gone from the square were the bib overalls of my childhood when the farmers came to town on Saturday. Ranchers now, they came in high-heeled boots and rolled-brim hats, a costume that would have provoked as much surprise, and even more derision, there, in my time, as it would on Manhattan's Madison Avenue.[1]

What is significant here is not just the town's transformation but the sense of wonder it evokes in Humphrey. His narrative depictions of East Texas—whether southern, western, or a little bit of both—are invariably refracted through the prism of memory. Young

---

1. Humphrey, *Farther Off from Heaven* (1977; reprint, New York: Laurel, 1984), 239–40.

Billy Humphrey left Clarksville at the age of thirteen, and spent nearly his entire adult life in the Northeast. From the midsixties until his death in 1997, he lived in Hudson, New York, a region more associated with Rip Van Winkle than with Quentin Compson or Pecos Bill. Although the little postage stamp of soil that William Humphrey claimed as his literary turf had ceased to exist outside his imagination, he fought the temptation to treat it elegiacally. He was at his best when he won that battle and at his worst when he succumbed to local color and sectional piety.

Although Humphrey was always a private man, *Farther Off from Heaven* recalls his childhood in Clarksville. The opening section of eleven pages is set on July 4, 1937, and the rest of the book keeps returning to that pivotal date. After a festive day in town, young Billy is awakened in the middle of the night with news that his father has been injured in a car wreck. As narrator, Humphrey withholds from us the fact that his father will die and that both his childhood and his own life in Clarksville will consequently come to an end. However, it is clearly the adult Humphrey looking back on this experience who says: "No wandering Jew ever carried with him a heavier freight of memories nor more of a sense of identification with a homeplace than I at thirteen, though unconfirmed in my faith, had already accumulated."[2]

In addition to recalling incidents from his boyhood, Humphrey tells us much about his family background. Particularly memorable is his withering portrait of his paternal grandmother. Nettie Humphrey "was about the size of a full-grown rattlesnake: four and a half feet of pure venom." This embittered shrew "had never been heard to say a kind or even an indifferent word about anybody." To her grandson, she seemed the perfect embodiment of malice. In contrast, however, is his great-aunt Suzie, a woman who "was all the lessons anyone would ever need in the deceptiveness of appearances." A woman so physically unattractive that she looked like a witch, Aunt Suzie was a surrogate mother to all who knew her. Of his father, Clarence, Humphrey says, "No matter where he and his family were staying, he always knew which way Aunt Suzie's house lay, as a Mohammedan knows in which direction to pray."[3]

2. Ibid., 14.
3. Ibid., 63, 68, 67–68.

Humphrey's maternal grandfather, Edward Varley, was a native of England who had run away from home after being ill-treated by his father and older brother. He walked to London from Leicester or Leeds—Humphrey is not sure which—and signed on as a cabin boy on a ship bound for Galveston. Once in Texas, he started breeding and did not stop until he had produced twelve children—three by his first wife and nine by Humphrey's grandmother. According to family doctrine, Ed Varley was the world's best father and husband. That his love of children did not extend beyond his own—"for his grand-children he had about as much feeling as a cucumber has for its"— did not seem to matter. More troublesome, however, was the fact of his first wife. Humphrey's grandmother was constantly vexed by the question of whether in heaven she would have to share her "Mister Varley," as she always called him, with her predecessor. But then, "her notion of an engaging conversation was whether we retained our bodily senses and appetites in the hereafter." The various nu-ances of this metaphysical question were endlessly discussed on seemingly endless summer nights. Humphrey remembers wondering "once as we sat on the porch in the dusk after supper talking about Heaven, what we would do for conversation once we were there and knew all there was to know about it."[4]

The character most vividly drawn is Clarence Humphrey. Born just as the frontier came to a close, he was a man out of his time. Unable to make a life for himself out-of-doors, Clarence fell in love with automobiles and channeled his restlessness into fast cars. At first, Nell Varley shared Clarence's spontaneity and love of adven-ture. His eagerness to fight for her she mistook for chivalry rather than natural pugnacity. She too enjoyed a good time and the power of a speeding automobile. But after several years as a wife and mother, Nell settled down and expected her husband to do so as well. Instead, he turned increasingly to drink and to the arms of other women. As an auto mechanic, he was never out of work—not even during the Depression. Unfortunately, enough of his customers were destitute that their bills often went unpaid. At the time of his death, he possessed the affection of the town and a small fortune in worthless IOUs.

About 60 percent of the way into the book, Humphrey casually

4. Ibid., 123, 125.

announces: "I had only a passing acquaintance with death. I myself had died once (1 had—or had had until it was destroyed—a document in testimony of the fact); but, aside from that one brief personal encounter, only one other time had death ever struck anywhere within my view."[5] What follows is an account of a friend who drowned during Humphrey's childhood. As affecting as that story is, the reader's attention lingers on the astonishing throwaway line—with details embedded in a parenthesis—of Humphrey's own premature "death." Not until near the end of the book do we get a full explanation of what happened.

At age seven, young Billy had been paddling around in his inner tube in the kiddy-pen, an enclosed area at a local lake. Diving head first into the lifesaver, he had become separated from it and started to go down in about five feet of water. He had been rescued and shaken back to consciousness by his cousin Ramsay Floyd, while the alcoholic doctor who also served as county coroner was filling out a death certificate. As mundane as this resurrection might seem, it is rendered even more anticlimactic by the fact that the certificate itself later burned in a house fire. After the black comic account of his near death, and a double-line break, Humphrey tells of the disposition of his father's body (the July Fourth car wreck had proved fatal) and his own refusal to attend the funeral. If July Fourth marks the independence of the American nation from its mother country, that particular July Fourth marks William Humphrey's separation from the country of his childhood. After the death of his father, he and his mother left Clarksville for Dallas. Not until thirty-two years later did he return, to buy a burial plot, and find the southern town of his youth transformed into the West of legend.

Upon that return, which Humphrey compares to the instinct of the salmon to swim back to his spawning ground, he discovers that many of his childhood memories were misconceptions. Not only does he learn that he had been born in a different house than he had thought, but the real dwelling is a hovel that his mother must have wanted to raze from her memory. The town clock, Old Red, does not really chime each quarter hour, and the statue of the Confederate soldier in the town plaza faces northeast, not southwest. "The town had shrunk, fit closer, like old clothes long outgrown. So much

5. Ibid., 147.

smaller now than when measured by my ten-, eleven-, twelve-year-old stride, and when, as Old Red told me then, I had all the time in the world."[6]

In these final pages, what might have been taken for a mere exercise in nostalgia becomes something more complex. By revealing himself to be that staple of modernist literature, the unreliable narrator, Humphrey casts doubt on the efficacy of memory itself. In fact, the eerie contrast between memory and reality resembles something out of Rod Serling's *The Twilight Zone*. This theme is reinforced by the epigraph from Thomas Hood that precedes the narrative itself:

> I remember, I remember
> The fir trees dark and high;
> I used to think their slender tops
> Were close against the sky:
> It was a childish ignorance.
> But now 'tis little joy
> To know I'm farther off from heaven
> Than when I was a boy.

After leaving Clarksville for Dallas, Humphrey attended public schools and Southern Methodist University, later transferring to the University of Texas. Although he had wanted to be a painter throughout his adolescence, he discovered in early adulthood, when he took an examination to become a naval officer, that he was color-blind. At that point, Humphrey decided to become a playwright and went to New York with a five-act comedy about Benjamin Franklin, featuring a cast of 340. It was only then that he turned to fiction and began to publish stories in such prestigious magazines as *Accent*, the *New Yorker*, *Harper's Bazaar*, and the *Sewanee Review*. His first book, *The Last Husband and Other Stories* (1953), was followed by his first and best-known novel, *Home from the Hill*, in 1958. This one book established Humphrey as an important new presence in postwar American literature.

Home from the Hill begins in 1954, when a Rolls-Royce hearse mysteriously appears in Clarksville. It is carrying the corpse of Hannah

6. Ibid., 241.

Hunnicutt, whose husband, Wade, and son, Theron, had both died fifteen years earlier. One of the townspeople, speaking in the first-person plural, then proceeds to narrate the tragedy of the Hunnicutt family. Captain Wade had been a gentleman farmer who hunted in the Sulphur Bottom when not bedding the sex-starved matrons of the town, while Hannah remained ignorant of her husband's compulsive tomcatting until after they had married and produced young Theron. From that point on, she devotes her life to her son. The product of her nurture, Theron grows up to be a more innocent version of his father.

Theron's adolescent romance with Libby Halstead is thwarted by Libby's father, Albert, who sends his daughter away to college rather than risk her ruin at the hands of Wade Hunnicutt's son. Pregnant with Theron's child, Libby returns to Clarksville, only to discover that Theron has finally learned the truth about his father and, out of spite, has taken up with a white-trash girl and her baby. In desperation, Libby averts the stigma of illegitimacy by quickly wooing Fred Shumway, the town's aspiring Babbitt, who not only marries her but also believes her child to be his premature progeny. At the infant's baptism, Albert overhears rumors that cause him to assume that Wade Hunnicutt is the child's father. Enraged, he guns down Wade and flees to Sulphur Bottom. Theron pursues and shoots his father's killer before learning the man's identity. Discovering that he had killed his girlfriend's father and realizing that his own life is in shambles, Theron commits virtual suicide by remaining in the wilderness. Although his body is never recovered and his mother outlives both him and his father by fifteen years, the deranged Hannah orders that their three tombstones indicate they all died on the same day.

When *Home from the Hill* has been discussed as a regional novel, it has invariably been seen as southern rather than western. For example, in his 1963 essay "The Difficulties of Being a Southern Writer Today; or, Getting Out from under William Faulkner," Louis D. Rubin Jr. cites *Home from the Hill* as a perfect example of the suffocating effect that Faulkner could have on those who came after him. In much the same vein, Walter Sullivan cites as examples of Faulkner's influence "the nameless narrator who refers to what 'we' thought or saw or said"; Theron's boar hunt, which is "a watered-down version of Ike McCaslin's pursuit of Old Ben in *The Bear*"; and the figure of

Captain Hunnicutt, who is "a kind of young Bayard or old John Sartoris, an oversexed man with a death wish."[7] It is only in his descriptions of the East Texas setting and his rendering of the East Texas language that Humphrey gives us any sense of a regional ambience. What we have in *Home from the Hill* is western local color and southern mythology.

On the whole, the local color is more impressive than the mythology. The boar hunt—although it is narrated in a style closer to the documentary realism of Hemingway—may be too obviously Faulknerian in its symbolism, but the eating of the boar—cooked in barbecue sauce applied with a kitchen mop—has the color and texture of reality. The same could be said of many other examples of local customs and folkways. It is only when people take significant action in this setting that the sense of reality becomes strained. Perhaps this is because it is *mythology* rather than myth with which Humphrey is dealing. He is of the generation of writers after Faulkner and the Southern Renascence. In Faulkner's generation, the myths that were necessary to maintain a traditional society were coming into conflict with the reality of cultural assimilation. At such a moment, the possibilities for song and story are particularly rich. However, those possibilities must inevitably wane in an age when assimilation is triumphant. Even if some of the old forms are left, they have been robbed of mythic vitality—death, not decomposition, being the mother of beauty. Humphrey's challenge is not simply to retell the tragedy of Captain Wade and Miss Hannah but to find a literary vision appropriate to the generation of Theron and Libby.

Although *Home from the Hill* is primarily Theron's story, most readers have a more vivid memory of Wade. I think that Gary Davenport is correct in arguing that, as the embodiment of the aristocratic hunter's code, Wade is an object of adoration not only for his son but for Humphrey as well. Consequently, Humphrey can show how the code can be destroyed by external forces without seriously considering contradictions within the code itself. Particularly troubling is

7. Rubin, *The Curious Death of the Novel* (Baton Rouge: Louisiana State University Press, 1967), 284; Sullivan, "The Continuing Renascence: Southern Fiction in the Fifties," in *South: Modern Southern Literature in Its Cultural Setting*, edited by Louis D. Rubin Jr. and Robert D. Jacobs (Garden City, NY: Doubleday, 1961), 382.

Humphrey's indulgence of Wade's philandering, "almost as if it were the *droit du seigneur* of a gentleman hunter."[8]

Treated with greater moral seriousness, this character trait could have been presented as Wade's tragic flaw. It wrecks his marriage and helps to warp his son's personality. Moreover, Wade's amply earned reputation as a satyr prompts Albert Halstead to make a series of mistakes that ultimately costs the lives of himself, Theron, and Wade and the happiness of Hannah and Libby. Then, there is the unexamined effect of Wade's behavior on the women he seduces. Had Humphrey eschewed moral considerations and simply depicted Wade as a vital Dionysian figure, who stirred new life in his conquests, that at least would have brought some complexity to his character. As it is, his inability to keep his pants zipped is a mere gimmick necessary to bring the plot to its contrived resolution.

The success of Humphrey's novel depends to a large extent on our ability to sympathize with Theron. That is hampered, however, by his general lack of credibility. I find it difficult to believe that he could reach young adulthood in a town as small as Clarksville before learning that his father was the town rake. By marrying Opal and adopting her child, Theron may be trying to atone for what he mistakenly believes to be another one of his father's amorous conquests—Opal was never one of Wade's women, nor is the baby his—but his gesture seems less an act of charity than a calculated affront to his family's aristocratic pretensions.

The irony of the situation is that Theron himself ends up exploiting Opal in a way that his father would never have dreamed of doing. By leaving her waiting on the wedding bed and refusing to consummate the marriage in the weeks that follow, Theron destroys her self-respect more than if he had simply taken his pleasure. For Humphrey, Opal seems to exist as a figure of ridicule; for Theron, she scarcely seems to exist at all. When she leaves to make her fortune in Dallas, we are invited to dismiss her on the condescending grounds that white trash always land on their feet.

Hannah, it seems to me, is a far more interesting character than either her husband or her son. By remaining married to Wade and trying to protect Theron from knowing the truth about him, she tries to

8. Davenport, "The Desertion of William Humphrey's Circus Animals," *Southern Review*, n.s., 23 (Spring 1987): 496.

fulfill her role as wife and mother as best she can. The fact that she errs in doing so makes her more human if not necessarily more endearing. When she and Wade come close to achieving some sort of mutual understanding and affection following Theron's boar hunt, we almost believe that this marriage could have worked had husband and wife been less the people that Humphrey's plot requires them to be. In any event, Hannah's perverse habit of befriending whoever happens to be Wade's current flame suggests that she is a formidable adversary rather than a dimwit or a doormat. Her efforts to make Theron a mama's boy may be ill-conceived, but her affection for her son is beyond question. One of the most touching moments in the novel occurs when she agrees to wear a gaudy flapper's dress to a sedate afternoon function simply because Theron likes it. As we have seen in the opening chapter, this is the dress in which she will later be buried.

Even admirers of *Home from the Hill* must be troubled by the number of coincidences and improbabilities that move the plot toward the end of the novel. It is easy to believe that Thomas Hardy was one of Humphrey's favorite novelists. However, even at his most preposterous, Hardy handled his material with a conviction that Humphrey lacks. When incredibility destroys empathy, as it does by the end of *Home from the Hill*, we are left with a potboiler aspiring to high art. And it is an unusually nihilistic potboiler at that.

Theron and Wade Hunnicutt and Albert Halstead all die pointless deaths, and Hannah Hunnicutt spends the last decade and a half of her life in the loony bin. Opal escapes unscathed only because her humanity has been denied, and we must assume that Libby will be emotionally scarred for the rest of her life. The only character to achieve even a partial triumph is Fred Shumway, and that triumph is entirely one of self-deception. If he really has fallen prey to Libby's duplicity, he is too much of an ignoramus to be the successful businessman he is depicted as being. It is far easier to believe that Fred is the sort of person who needs to showcase a beautiful wife and handsome child, even if the wife does not love him and the child is not his. In East Texas, it is the Fred Shumways, not the Flem Snopeses, who threaten the old aristocracy.

One technical feature that accentuates the other flaws of *Home from the Hill* is Humphrey's point of view. His shifts between the narrative "we" and omniscient narration are handled smoothly enough.

The problem is not who is telling the story but why. A communal narrator is usually used to emphasize the shallowness of conventional wisdom. Edwin Arlington Robinson's "Richard Cory" and William Faulkner's "A Rose for Emily" are brilliant examples of this. But Humphrey does little to exploit the ironic distance between what is commonly believed and what is really true.

On the other hand, the omniscient narrative simply calls attention to the heavy hand of authorial manipulation. It might have been far more effective for Humphrey to have gone all the way with the Faulkner paradigm and given us multiple points of view, such as we have in *Absalom, Absalom!* Perspectives that could have been used, in addition to that of the representative townsman, include those of Chauncey, Wade's old black retainer and hunting companion; Libby Halstead; Opal Jessup; Fred Shumway; and perhaps a dying Hannah Hunnicutt. Hearing what these characters had to say about Wade, Theron, and—to a lesser extent—Albert would have gone a long way toward bringing the novel to life by redeeming it from bathos and melodrama.

Humphrey's second novel, *The Ordways*, was published in 1965, while he was living in Europe with the money he made on *Home from the Hill*. Much more than the earlier novel, this book reveals the tension between southern and western regionalism in East Texas. The narrator is Tom Ordway, a modern man with an intense interest in the past—a kind of sane Quentin Compson. His narration begins on graveyard day, a ritual occasion we already have seen in *Home from the Hill*. As he joins the rest of the townspeople in caring for the graves of their ancestors, Tom recalls the story of his great-grandfather's migration from Tennessee just after the War between the States.

Blinded in battle, the original Thomas Ordway tried to commit suicide several times before finding new purpose in life by leading his small family from the poverty of the postwar South—at one point they are reduced to eating their mule—to the promised land of the West. In fact, their crossing of the Red River resembles the passage of the Children of Israel through the Red Sea, as they carry with them the disinterred bones of their forebears to be reburied in their new home. It is a consciously mythic story filled with baroque Faulknerian overtones. What makes it work as a set piece is the narrative presence of the young Tom Ordway, who remembers his great-grandfather as a kind of town monument, the inspiration for the statue of a Confederate soldier erected in the town square. Because the story of Thomas and Ella Ordway belongs to the oral tradition, its mythic pretensions can be more readily accepted than if it were rendered by an objective narrator.

The migration of the Ordway family to Texas, however, constitutes little more than a fourth of Humphrey's novel. Fully 40 percent of the text involves the attempt of Thomas Ordway's son—and young Tom's grandfather—Sam Ordway to recover his offspring, little Ned, stolen by neighbors who were caring for him while the rest of the family was shopping in town one Saturday. As the only son of Sam's first marriage, Ned has evoked ambivalent feelings in his step-mother, the former schoolmarm of the community. Like Humphrey's grandmother Varley, Hester Ordway is plagued all her married life by an unacknowledged jealousy of her predecessor, and she is at least half certain that little Ned's abduction is a punishment for her un-charitable thoughts. Her consciousness is convincingly rendered in a short section of the novel that serves as prelude to her husband's quest. It is in that quest, over a wide expanse of East Texas, that *The Ordways* becomes a fully western novel.

Gary Davenport contends that in this novel, we see "a penchant for comedy and for a sort of grotesque hyper-reality that often puts the reader in mind of Dickens or Kafka or perhaps García Márquez." Sam's bizarre experiences, which themselves constitute something of a picaresque novel, as if Tobias Smollett had been transported to the Wild West, "are engaging enough in themselves, but their real significance is that they show Humphrey no longer thinking in terms of categories and straining for universality: he is more interested in the radiantly aberrant than in the typical—and he has become more an observer than a spokesman."[9]

In *The Ordways*, Humphrey has expelled the manipulative autho-rial presence that so weakened *Home from the Hill*. But, on first reading, it seems that he may have gone too far in the other direction and given us brilliantly realized fragments that finally add up to less than the sum of their parts. Leaving aside for a moment the overall structure of the novel, Sam Ordway's quest itself often seems mere

9. Ibid., 498–99.

pretext for a series of memorable vignettes. His search for his son lacks the urgency necessary to make it convincing, and his abandonment of that search is a bit too arbitrary to satisfy the reader who has been accompanying him all this time.

But, on closer reading, we begin to suspect that the pointlessness of Sam's quest may itself be Humphrey's point. At best, Sam is a reluctant knight-errant. He has waited until after harvest to begin his quest and pursues the already cold trail in a haphazard manner. The Confederate pistol he takes with him seems more an absurd antique than an instrument of revenge. John M. Grammer contends that Humphrey's "burlesque tone is the only appropriate one for the subject-matter. For Sam, a hopelessly pacific man setting out on a revenge quest, is pretending, and he invites the fate which usually awaits pretenders. . . . Sam is continually regarded by others, and even by himself, as a kind of performer, a literary figure."

Of course, Don Quixote is the literary figure with whom he seems to have most in common. Like the Knight of the Woeful Countenance, Sam "is trying to put an essentially literary convention—the South's outdated code of honor—into practical application." But, in so doing, he "serves as his own Sancho, for he remains deeply skeptical of the convention even while he is enacting it." The fact that the quest ends in forfeit rather than outright defeat demonstrates the irrelevance of the southern code to the western environment. Sam "returns to Clarksville having failed where his blind, crippled father succeeded: he has been unable to preserve the traditions and unity of his family in the face of disaster. The West, in both its literal and metaphoric significance, has defeated him."[10]

In a February 1988 interview with Ashby Bland Crowder, Humphrey commented on the factual basis for much of the plot of *The Ordways*. His great-grandfather had been a Confederate veteran who migrated to Texas after being blinded and crippled in the War between the States. His grandfather Varley—apparently the son-in-law rather than the son of the Confederate veteran—had had a son stolen from him by neighbors with whom the boy was staying. Much of the rest of the novel, however, is pure invention. The details of the migration to Texas are completely fabricated, and there is no record of Edward Varley setting out on a quest for his stolen son.

10. Grammer, "Where the South Draws Up to a Stop: The Fiction of William Humphrey," *Mississippi Quarterly* 44 (Winter 1990–91): 12, 13.

What Humphrey intended was to embroider these elements of family history into a parable about the dual regionalism of his upbringing. As he told Crowder: "The Civil War is one of the truly great American tragedies. And the exploration of the West is a comedy; it's a farce. Indeed, it's how Americans forgot the Civil War, by getting away from the South and going West. So I made the adventures of my grandfather in search of his son, which after all is the stuff of many a John Wayne film, into a farcical, episodic picaresque, so that the book is quite broken-backed. The first part of it is tragic, and the second part of it is comic."[11]

Specifically, the tension that Humphrey sees between southern and western regionalism lies in the contradiction of wanting to make a new start in life, free of the dead hand of the past, while at the same time maintaining fealty to tradition. The lost cause of the South nearly killed Thomas Ordway in both body and spirit; however, he is renewed by the decision to move to Texas. "The West is the one unfixed pole of the compass," Humphrey remarks. "It has moved with man, always retreating before him. What was once the West is now the East. The West lies on the other side of that last range of hills, where the day still lingers, where there is still another hour to correct one's mistakes or begin a new project before nightfall."[12] But when Thomas goes west, he brings with him the bones of his ancestors, his own war wounds, and a code that becomes enshrined in a statue in the town square. In the next generation, that code becomes an imperative burden. Two generations after that, it is merely an object of aesthetic contemplation.

The Ordways ends not in conflict and contradiction, however, but with a resolution based more on fact than anything else in the novel. When Humphrey was four years old, a grown man showed up at Edward Varley's door and identified himself as the young son who had been stolen away so many years before. What followed was a family reunion involving a caravan from Clarksville to the long-lost relative's goat ranch near the Mexican border. This is essentially what occurs at the end of *The Ordways*, in an idyllic concluding section that constitutes around 10 percent of the novel's text.

The only license that Humphrey has taken is that he makes the

---

11. Crowder, "History, Family, and William Humphrey," *Southern Review*, n.s., 24 (Autumn 1988): 832.

12. Humphrey, *The Ordways* (1964; reprint, New York: Laurel, 1984), 55.

caravan larger and the reunion longer than it was in actual life. The farcical imitation of a revenge tragedy has been resolved in a comedy of forgiveness. The kidnapper, Will Vinson, had told his adopted son the truth on his deathbed. Sam Ordway and little Ned, and indeed the entire extended family, have been reunited without bloodshed. Because Will Vinson had been good to Ned, Sam bears no final ill will toward his enemy. In fact, Will had eluded capture by taking the name Ordway. Thus, the title of Humphrey's novel can be seen as referring not just to four generations of biological kin but also to the man who claimed the family name through an excess of something like paternal love—an act that could never be excused, only forgiven.

In his third novel, *Proud Flesh* (1973), Humphrey combines the pseudo-Faulknerian melodrama of *Home from the Hill* with the structural chaos of *The Ordways*. The back-cover blurb of the paperback edition declares that the novel is about "The Renshaws—a Texas family bound together by fierce pride and driven by prodigal appetites . . . a clan famous for its loyalty and its ruthlessness in dealing with an intruding world." If the passions of the Hunnicutt family made *Home from the Hill* a popular success, then it seemed only reasonable that a book with a larger and even more eccentric clan would be that much more marketable. In this case, the legendary parent is not the town stud but a dying matriarch. As the end draws near for Edwina "Ma" Renshaw, three generations of offspring gather for a final vigil, as if sheer strength of numbers would keep the old lady alive a bit longer.

The emphasis on family solidarity would seem to make *Proud Flesh* a prototypically southern novel. I think, however, that John M. Grammer is closer to the mark when he calls the world the Renshaws inhabit "post-southern." For one thing, the setting is apparently that of the late sixties, after the actual Clarksville has been transformed from Old South to Far West. Humphrey signals this in a number of ways, as when he has one of his minor characters observe, "We've seen some changes in our time, you and me. . . . Seen mules go, and now the nigger'll go the way of the mule. It's just a matter of time."[13]

Perhaps more important, the Renshaws are regarded by the sur-

13. Humphrey, *Proud Flesh* (1973; reprint, New York: Laurel, 1984), 69.

rounding community as not only eccentric but even downright insane. When the local doctor is summoned for a house call, he believes himself kidnapped and remains a captive in the Renshaw home until several days after Ma has died. He is expected not only to keep death at bay but also to stand guard over the corpse to make sure that Ma is not buried alive. The point is that the doctor has never been physically constrained or even threatened. It is his paranoid fear of the crazy Renshaws that imprisons him. In the traditional South, the family is defined in large part by an organic relationship to the community of which it is a part. The Renshaws, however, are defined by a profound alienation from their community.

What becomes apparent fairly early in the novel is that this alienation does not just divide the family and the community but also separates the various members of the family from each other. All that holds them together is a willed and self-conscious devotion to Ma or, more precisely, to the persona that Ma represents. As a consequence, this novel resembles *The Sound and the Fury* less than it does a TV western such as *The Big Valley*. Not surprisingly, each of the sons and daughters who remains in Ma's sphere of influence is a case study in neurosis and arrested development. Only the prodigal Kyle, who was always his mother's favorite, has escaped north. For much of the novel, the central action is the effort to keep Ma alive until Kyle can be found and returned. After she has unmistakably died, the family commandeers the local icehouse to preserve her body while the search for Kyle continues. "In a world where the Renshaws are utterly alien," Grammer notes, "the family's natural cohesiveness has become a destructive centripetal force. They are a sort of black hole, collapsing endlessly on itself."[14]

As thematically suggestive as it may be, *Proud Flesh* is not a particularly well-crafted novel. Whereas the digressions in *The Ordways* usually possess a charm or power of their own, those in the Renshaw saga too often seem inept. When Clifford Renshaw is milking the family cow, a husband-hunting widow hides in the barn and pretends to be the voice of the dying Ma, telling her son that he needs a good woman like "that Sweet Mrs. Shumlin" to look after him. This is the stuff of bad situation comedy. Also, we are never certain whose story this really is. Even if the point of view in *Home*

14. Grammer, "Where the South Draws Up to a Stop," 18.

from the Hill and *The Ordways* may have seemed problematic, it was at least handled with skill. In *Proud Flesh*, Humphrey presents Edwina Renshaw and her brood from contradictory perspectives.

There is nothing theoretically wrong with such an approach, and—as I have already suggested—it might well have improved *Home from the Hill*. Certainly, in the hands of a Joseph Conrad or a William Faulkner, it can weave an intricate narrative tapestry. *Proud Flesh* more closely resembles one of Emmeline Grangerford's unfinished masterpieces. Emmeline, in Mark Twain's *Adventures of Huckleberry Finn*, would paint a maiden in distress with one pair of arms folded over her breast, another stretched out in front, and a third raised in supplication. Emmeline's intention—thwarted by untimely death—was to rub out all but the pair she liked best. *Proud Flesh* may be a rich canvas, but it is covered with false starts and extraneous arms.

John Gregory Dunne once observed that the aspiring screenwriter should study the bad movies of good directors, because "in each there is a moment or sequence that stands out in such bold relief from the surrounding debris as to make the reasons for its effectiveness clear."[15] *Proud Flesh* suggests that there are also such moments in the bad books of good writers. After far too many pages of tawdry sensationalism and missed opportunities—such as the unfulfilled promise to deal with miscegenation as human dilemma rather than as obsession or metaphor—the novel comes alive in its closing pages.

Here the neurotically guilt-ridden daughter of the now deceased Ma Renshaw locks herself in a storm cellar in penance for her imagined sins, while pilgrims congregate to confess their real sins to her through the culvert pipe. Without seeming unduly derivative, Humphrey achieves the blend of black humor and grotesque spirituality that we associate with Flannery O'Connor. The novel concludes with two Renshaw sons searching for the errant Kyle, even though Ma has now been dispatched to the skull orchard. Because someone thought he had seen the prodigal in New York City several years earlier, his brothers are looking for him there. When a message sent through skywriting fails to produce a response, the dutiful sons continue their quest door by door. "Son of a bitch if this goddamned town is

15. Dunne, *Quintana and Friends* (New York: Dutton, 1978), 174.

going to make a monkey out of me," one says.[16] Such moments, alas, are virtually engulfed by the surrounding debris.

In 1968, five years before the publication of *Proud Flesh*, Humphrey brought out his second collection of short stories, *A Time and a Place*. Then, in 1985, a year after the appearance of his fourth novel, *Hostages to Fortune*, Delacorte issued an edition of Humphrey's collected stories. In this volume, we see many of the same virtues and shortcomings of Humphrey's early novels. The stories are best when describing a place—both geographical and social—or exploring the psychological subtleties of human relations. Too often, however, the effort to create a plot and a point of view from these materials proves unwieldy or unconvincing. Most of the stories that are not so slight as to be inconsequential elude Humphrey's technical control until they are "resolved" with a forced literary irony. Still, occasional moments of brilliance suggest the presence of a talented writer.

We find several such moments in one of Humphrey's earliest published stories, "The Hardys." The external action of this story concerns the efforts of a couple, married fifty years, to gather the accumulated rummage of a lifetime as they prepare to sell their old house. The dramatic tension is created by Humphrey's frequent shifts in point of view between the minds of Mr. and Mrs. Hardy. Early in the story, we learn that Mr. Hardy's first wife, Virgie, died in childbirth after three years of marriage. Now, he rarely thinks of her and cannot even remember what she looked like. Clara has long been a good and dutiful wife to the man she calls "Mr. Hardy." Her only regret is that, as a native of England, he is perhaps a bit too taciturn. As they begin to collect items for sale, we see that she is considerably more sentimental than he is. Knowing this, he proposes that she sort the things in the children's rooms and leave the rest of the house to him. "How nice it would have been, she sighed, to go around with him and recall old times together as they turned up things, but as he didn't want her, she agreed."[17] It is just such misunderstandings and personality differences that keep this couple emotionally separated.

What Clara finds particularly galling is the thought that after all

16. Humphrey, *Proud Flesh*, 328.
17. Humphrey, *The Collected Studies of William Humphrey* (1985; reprint, New York: Laurel, 1986), 17.

these years Mr. Hardy might still love Virgie more than he does her. This jealousy warps even her best experiences with her husband. Once, they spent an almost magical time together at a carnival. At the end of the day, Mr. Hardy made the moment complete by buying Clara a beautiful Spanish mantle, only to spoil everything by telling her that he had once bought an identical one for Virgie, who liked it so much he buried her in it. So densely well intentioned is he that Mr. Hardy thinks that this information will cause Clara to prize the mantle that much more. By the end of the story, Mr. Hardy's kindliness and his wife's jealousy of her predecessor have caused husband and wife to shift personalities. When he says to her with great nostalgia, "It takes you back a day like this, . . . makes you think. Brings back things you hadn't thought of for years. For instance—," his wife presses her fingers white against her temples and replies: "Oh, what's the use . . . of thinking over things past and done with?"[18]

Those who have read *Farther Off from Heaven* will recognize the origins of "The Hardys" in the experience of Humphrey's maternal grandparents. In both cases a man from Britain migrates to Texas, is married for a short time to one woman and a much longer time to a second one. The second wife, who calls her husband "Mister," remains jealous of the first wife for her entire married life. With the exception of the British birth, this same situation is repeated in *The Ordways*. Each treatment, however, is for a slightly different purpose. In *Farther Off from Heaven*, Humphrey tells us about his grandparents as a way of shedding light on his own background. In *The Ordways*, the second wife is necessary to establish little Ned as a stepchild. In "The Hardys," however, the narrative focus is confined to the husband and wife themselves. If Robert Frost can show us the deterioration of a marriage through carefully constructed dialogue, as he does in "Home Burial," Humphrey does something even more subtle in "The Hardys." He shows us how, even in the most outwardly successful marriage, differences in personality can impede communication. For this reason, a husband and wife can be married for fifty years without ever really understanding each other. To allow us to see this gradually through skillful manipulation of point of view is the mark of an extremely skilled craftsman.

Another of Humphrey's earliest stories, "Quail for Mr. Forester,"

18. Ibid., 22.

established his equivocal relation to the Agrarian myth of the South. The story is set in the 1930s, less than a decade after the Agrarian manifesto *I'll Take My Stand* had made an eloquent case for recovering the traditional values of the antebellum South. The title character of Humphrey's story appears to be a perfect example of what the modern world has done to the Old Southern aristocracy. Although belonging to what was once the most prominent family in Columbia, Texas, Mr. Forester is now forced to make his living by running a hardware store. To the nonaristocrats of the town, however, he is still seen as a monument to the glorious past. As a result, one of the ordinary families invites him to dinner after the man of the house shoots some choice quail one afternoon. The story is narrated by this man's young son, a boy who is even more enamored than his parents with the myth of the southern past.

As is so often the case, the nonpeasant class—in this case, the yeomanry—is more committed to maintaining the aristocratic mystique than are the aristocrats themselves. In the course of the evening, Mr. Forester reveals himself to be a thoroughly conventional member of the merchant class. Unlike the Agrarians, he enjoys such fixtures of modernity as the motion pictures. He is considering selling the ancestral home so that he can move into a more convenient dwelling, such as the one his hosts inhabit. When the narrator's mother argues that Mr. Forester's taxes should be remitted in recognition of his family's historical significance in the community, the old man is simply puzzled and embarrassed. He is even foggy on his history, at one point misidentifying Jeb Stuart as John Bell Hood. The irony of the story is that Mr. Forester, whom the community sees as a kind of living monument to the past, has adjusted to social change more readily than have the people who have mythologized him. As Mr. Forester leaves for the evening, afraid that he might fall asleep after such a fine meal, the boy remarks: "I felt that there was no hope for me in these mean times I had been born into."[19]

After the appearance of *The Last Husband and Other Stories* in 1953, Humphrey's next published work of short fiction was "The Ballad of Jesse Neighbours." Originally appearing in the September 1963 issue of *Esquire*, it became the initial selection in *A Time and a Place*, a collection of ten stories about the Southwest of the 1930s.

19. Ibid., 35.

Humphrey's protagonist is a hardworking young Oklahoman who is jilted by his fiancée, Naomi Childress, when her family strikes oil. The embittered Jesse dreams of becoming a romantic outlaw like Pretty Boy Floyd or Clyde Barrow, but in his novice attempt at bank robbery, he more closely resembles Woody Allen in *Take the Money and Run*. Because he has tried to pull the job in Texas, where armed robbery is a capital offense, Jesse dies in the electric chair. The story concludes with his parents bringing his body and his personal effects, including his guitar, home after the execution.

In this story, Humphrey moves with relative ease between humor and pathos. His descriptions of the newly oil-rich Childress family are hilarious. After their gusher comes in, Bull Childress and family pile into the cab of their pickup truck—cut down from a LaSalle sedan—and head straight for Dallas. When they pull up in front of the Adolphus Hotel, Bull simply lays into the horn until the whole contingent of bellhops and porters comes out to service them. He gives the truck away, buys a new Packard, sends Naomi off for a beauty treatment, and seems intent on buying out Neiman-Marcus. When all of the family's new purchases will not fit into the Packard, Bull simply buys a second Packard and hires one of the hotel porters—uniform and all—as a driver. When it turns out that the porter cannot drive, Bull hitches the second car to the first and has the man steer it back to Oklahoma. The remade Naomi is no longer interested in Jesse and his plaintive folksinging.

If the buffoonish Childresses never rise above local-color stereotype, Jesse's fascination with the cult of the outlaw brings us into the realm of western myth. The romance of the outlaw has always been a part of the libertarian ethos of the American West. Characters such as Billy the Kid and Jesse James became legends of the Old West because of their ability to outwit the authorities and their adherence to a private code of morality. In the 1930s, two crucial elements were added to the mystique of the western outlaw—widespread economic deprivation and the automobile as a mode of travel. For a Depression youth such as Jesse, who sees his Horatio Alger virtues counting for nothing, the quick fix of bank robbery must seem mighty tempting. Since banks had foreclosed on so many farms during that era, robbing those institutions was like striking back at the enemy. This was particularly true of a figure such as Pretty Boy Floyd, who was known to share his wealth with the poor who befriended him. In addition, travel by automobile made it possible to hit many small banks in a short time.

The moral vision of this story is deterministic, almost in the manner of Theodore Dreiser. Jesse seems freest at the beginning of the story, when he is exercising virtues that do him no good. As the story progresses, he is increasingly victimized by circumstances beyond his control. It is not his fault that the discovery of oil on the Childress land loses him his girlfriend and puts him out of the real estate market by sending property values sky-high. Although moralists would contend that Jesse's decision to commit armed robbery was a free choice, Humphrey shows him to be the dupe of the media-created gangster mythology. He is even unlucky in attempting the robbery in Texas, where the penalty is more severe than in his home state. If Sam Ordway can be said to have been defeated by the West, Jesse Neighbours is destroyed by it.

To my mind, the only major flaw in this story is the way it ends. By concluding with the perspective of Jesse's parents, Humphrey loses sight of the central contradiction on which the story has been based. Because Jesse has sacrificed himself for demented love of a girl, we need to see Naomi Childress's reaction to his fate. Such an ending also would have justified the otherwise disproportionate, if entertaining, emphasis Humphrey gives to the new fortunes of the Childress family. We are left feeling that the last verse of Jesse's ballad has yet to be sung.

One of Humphrey's best stories, and my personal favorite of the lot, employs a western theme that is not found elsewhere in his work—the dream of California. In "The Human Fly," the Depression-ridden community of New Jerusalem, Texas, gathers to see an itinerant daredevil climb the eight-story county courthouse, with the money raised divided between the daredevil and the town. Like marathon dancing, such an exhibition was a common amusement during the thirties. However, Humphrey is not interested in Depression-era sociology, any more than Horace McCoy was in his dance-marathon novel *They Shoot Horses, Don't They?*

In both cases, the author has stumbled on a found metaphor. For Humphrey, the spectacle of the human fly becomes an index of the length to which some people will go in order to escape small-town boredom. The grotesquely misnamed New Jerusalem is not unlike Bricksville in *Adventures of Huckleberry Finn*. In describing the inhabitants of the latter town, Huck observes: "There couldn't anything wake them up all over, and make them happy all over, like a dogfight—unless it might be putting turpentine on a stray dog and setting fire to him, or tying a tin pan to his tail and see him run himself to death."[20] For the townspeople of New Jerusalem, the possibility that the Great Grippo will fall and break his neck makes his climb all the more exciting. This is emphasized by the fact that every once in a while a woman in the crowd insists that she be taken home, although she herself makes no move in that direction.

The only person in New Jerusalem who seems to have enough character to stay away from this sick exhibition is the town malcontent, Stan Reynolds. Called "California Stan" because of his oft-repeated desire to move to the golden land, Reynolds has never hidden his contempt for the town and its people. The careful reader might find it surprising that this singular individual seems to have been forgotten when the focus of the story shifts to the climb of the human fly itself. The climb is described in such harrowing detail, however, that we too tend to forget about Stan Reynolds.

It is only when the Great Grippo loses both his balance and his goggles partway up the courthouse wall that we see he actually is California Stan, desperate to make the money needed to fulfill his dream of moving to that region Theodore Roosevelt called "west of the West." The risk and difficulty of the climb are measures of Stan's desperation to escape permanently from his surroundings. Unfortunately, his quest is no more successful than that of Sisyphus. He falls before reaching the top of the tower, suffers lifelong paralysis, and spends his last thirty-three years as a ward of the town he hates. During that time, he has to listen to the courthouse clock chime 10,571,358 times.

In 1992, Humphrey published a collection of twenty new stories under the title *September Song*. None of these selections merits comparison with the author's best earlier work. Humphrey's greatest strengths as a writer include his ability to create people and evoke a sense of place. Unfortunately, too many of the stories in *September Song* are too short to allow a full development of character and setting. Situations that might be compelling in a novel seem contrived

20. Twain, *Adventures of Huckleberry Finn* (1885; reprint, New York: Signet, 1959), 141.

and unconvincing when realized in three or four or even eight to ten pages. Unlike Hemingway, Humphrey is not a master of the vignette.

Perhaps the best story in what would be Humphrey's last collection is also the longest. In "Dead Weight," an itinerant antique dealer becomes responsible for a friend named Kelly, who finally accepts the dealer's long-standing invitation to join him on the road. A few days into their trip, Kelly's fragile health gives out. Prior to dying (while on the toilet in the dealer's camper), Kelly had given his friend a sealed envelope, which contains a will making the dealer his sole heir. Knowing that he would be suspected of murder if the will were ever discovered, the dealer forsakes his inheritance. He also has to drive undetected from Texas to New York in order to return Kelly's body to the family cemetery in his hometown. "Dead Weight" is a picaresque black comedy that represents William Humphrey at his best.

Perhaps because of the financial success of his first two novels, Humphrey has not had to perform the role of a kept writer in academe. He has, however, done various stints as a visiting professor at several eastern universities. While serving as Glasgow Visiting Professor at Washington and Lee in the midseventies, he delivered a lecture that was published by the Texas Western Press in 1977 under the title *Ah, Wilderness! The Frontier in American Literature*. Although this may well have been an engaging oral presentation, Humphrey says nothing that had not already been said better and more comprehensively by Leslie Fiedler in *Love and Death in the American Novel* or, for that matter, D. H. Lawrence in *Studies in Classic American Literature*. Nevertheless, by acknowledging the importance of the frontier in our literature, Humphrey pays homage to the image and dream of the West, even—perhaps especially—when it appears in the work of such geographically eastern writers as James Fenimore Cooper, Herman Melville, and William Faulkner.

If Humphrey's discursive prose is slight and derivative when striving to be scholarly, it achieves a high degree of artistry when playing hooky from school. Over the years, he has published a number of fine essays on hunting and fishing in such popular magazines as *Sports Illustrated, Esquire, True, Life,* and *Town and Country*. These pieces were gathered in 1986, a year after the collected stories, in a book called *Open Season*. Taken as a whole, this volume is part of a

venerable tradition of contemplative literature, extending back at
least to Izaak Walton's *The Compleat Angler* (1653) and including, in
Humphrey's own century, Ernest Hemingway's *Green Hills of Africa*
(1935). As Robert Benson notes, "In our casual and chaotic times
Humphrey understands that the rituals of hunting and fishing . . .
allow us to enter a stable and ordered world in which duty, responsibility, and status are clear to all participants."[21]

One of the two longest entries in this volume is titled "My Moby
Dick." The specific reference of the title is to a gigantic brown trout
that Humphrey—or his persona—tried unsuccessfully to land. The
essay itself also becomes a kind of *Moby-Dick* in the sense that it is
not only a tale of sporting adventure but also a compendium of fishing lore and philosophical reflections. In a tone of jovial parody,
Humphrey begins: "Call me Bill. Some years ago—never mind how
long precisely—I thought I would go fishing. It is a way I have of driving away the spleen, and after a winter spent in the Berkshire Mountains of Massachusetts, I had a whale of a swollen spleen."[22]

The essay is filled with mocking literary references that convey
the image of a man who genuinely loves both books and sport. He
tells us, for example, that "it is not the beauty and tranquility of its
habitat that draws fishermen to the trout. It is the *ding an sich*. To
some brothers, and sisters, of the angle, *where* trout live does not
mean a thing, so long as they live there. When I cross over the last
current of all, I confidently expect to see a certain breed of sinners,
oblivious of their burns, casting Rat-face McDougalls upon the waters of the River Styx." As Humphrey notes a bit later: "The literature
of angling falls into two genres: the instructional and the devotional.
The former is written by fishermen who write, the latter by writers
who fish."[23] Given the generally horrid style of the former, we are
fortunate that Humphrey falls in the latter category.

In one of the most memorable passages of "My Moby Dick," Humphrey describes the horribly polluted Housatonic River, called by his
fellow fishermen "Shit Creek." Here, worms used for bait are not killed
by the trout but poisoned by the river itself. The paper mills were

21. Benson, "Ritual of Mortality," *Sewanee Review* 96 (Spring 1998): xxxi–
xxxii.
22. Humphrey, *Open Season: Sporting Adventures* (New York: Delacorte,
1986), 3.
23. Ibid., 8, 24.

fouling these waters even in Melville's time; however, in "The Tartarus of Maids," which is set in this region, Melville was preoccupied less with "the acids generated in the manufacture of the paper [than with] the lifeblood of the millhands." In summarizing Melville's sketch, Humphrey notes that here the author's "strange preoccupation with and horror of whiteness makes yet another appearance."

It is a cold January day on which Melville's narrator visits the paper mill to order envelopes. Although his horse is named Black, it turns white with frozen sweat. The narrator's cheeks are frostbitten. White rags are shredded by pale white girls, forbidden to marry, who breathe airborne lint. The rags are turned into a milky mass that produces endless stacks of white paper. The many uses the narrator imagines for the paper do not include "the foolscap he himself is writing his sketch on, or the newsprint of the magazine that will publish it. Not to mention the dollar bill he bought the paper with, and those others he was hoping would be spent for that issue of *Harper's Monthly*." As Humphrey notes: "A writer—even one who is a freshwater fisherman—has got to be careful how he curses paper mills."[24]

The other major entry in *Open Season* is a narrative titled "The Spawning Run." Here, Humphrey is not pursuing a giant trout in the northeastern United States but fishing for salmon in Great Britain. In place of the tongue-in-cheek mythology of "My Moby Dick," we have an amusing meditation on human sexuality disguised as a scientifically detailed discussion of the salmon's fatal instinct to reproduce himself in the waters in which he was hatched. At times, Humphrey's comparisons between human beings and salmon are expressed in terms that ape the style of the popular nature writer. Since the salmon lives only seven years, we are told, each year in his life equals ten man years. "Suppose a man left home at twenty and was gone for forty years, wandering as far as sixteen hundred miles away, and then at sixty he walked back without a map and with nobody along the way to ask directions of, no signposts to guide him, no landmarks: this would be about comparable to the salmon's feat of finding his way back to his native river to spawn."[25]

Early in the narrative—which is rendered as a series of diary excerpts—we see natural creatures interacting with the world of men.

24. Ibid., 10, 11.
25. Ibid., 63.

One day, Humphrey pulls his VW between two new Bentleys in the parking lot of a fishing lodge in Wales. "An incensed peacock was pecking at himself in the hubcap of one of the Bentleys with brainless persistency. When he had obliterated with spittle the rival in that hubcap he spread his tail proudly and went strutting to attack another Bentley hubcap, passing up those of my VW with lordly disdain." That night and for several nights thereafter, Humphrey and his wife are both disturbed by what they take to be the screaming of a woman. When they finally inquire, they are told that this is the sound of a peahen. "My God, said my wife, what does her mate do to her to make her scream like that? Or not do to make her scream like that, said the other lady, vain, self-infatuated creature; had you thought, my dear, of that?"[26]

Like his earlier "memoir," this narrative is rich with literary allusions. Marcel Proust's *The Remembrance of Things Past*, Walton's *The Compleat Angler*, Charlotte Brontë's *Jane Eyre*, and the Bible are all referred to explicitly. Also, at the beginning of his stay in Britain, Humphrey meets a parking lot attendant in Dorchester who had been a driver for the illustrious Hardy. The attendant recalls that Hardy owned one of the first automobiles in the town, that he was in love with speed, and that he built some of the finest houses in the region. Puzzled to learn all of this new information about one of his literary heroes, Humphrey added: "What's more important, . . . he wrote some of the best novels and some of the most beautiful poems in the language."[27] It is only then that Humphrey realizes the parking lot attendant has been talking about Henry Hardy, Thomas's brother. Such is the fleeting nature of literary fame.

The real protagonist of "The Spawning Run" is Holloway, an angler of legendary ineptitude whose main sporting interest is not in fishing but in cuckoldry. While other men are landing fish, Holloway is back in the lodge or out in a field servicing their wives—the so-called salmon widows. The situation is not unlike that of the salmon themselves. Male and female, they swim back as much as fifteen hundred miles to their spawning ground. They have braved the perils of the deep. They have "eluded the trawlers' nets and the fishmonger's cold slate slab, or, more ignoble end still, the cannery." They have likely

26. Ibid., 65, 82.
27. Ibid., 58.

fought free of many fishermen's barbs, braved pestilence and disease, and leaped twelve-foot-high falls. Then, when the male is about ready to release "some of that pent-up milt which in two ripe testes fills his entire body"—salmon mate without actually touching—he is more often than not foiled by a parr, who "darts in and discharges his tuppence worth." Without braving any of the hazards the cock salmon has overcome, this "mischievous minnow" robs the old fish of his paternity—"for puny as they are, they are potent, these precocious parr." The only consolation for the cock salmon, who almost inevitably die shortly after their return to their native waters, is the memory of having behaved similarly in their own youth. A few females survive, however, and "return to the sea." There, the widowed hens "grow fat and sleek and silvery again and then return to spawn another time. Some durable old girls make it back twice more. A few old rips make it back three more times."[28]

Given Humphrey's love of the sport, it is not surprising that fishing would eventually become a crucial activity and a fishing lodge the primary setting of one of his novels. What is surprising is that the charm and whimsicality of these fishing essays are totally absent from Humphrey's 1984 novel, *Hostages to Fortune*. Nothing that its author had written previously would prepare a reader for the emotional catharsis of this extraordinarily harrowing book. For one thing, *Hostages to Fortune* is Humphrey's only novel to be set entirely outside of Texas. Because the experiences that inspired the tale occurred in the Northeast, Humphrey places it there. But its real setting is the mind of its protagonist, Ben Curtis. Focusing his narrative perspective on a single character, Humphrey achieves a unity and intensity lacking in his earlier novels. Because Ben is a believable person whom we are made to care about, the strategy works.

The author of *Home from the Hill* could not have written *Hostages to Fortune*. In the earlier novel, Humphrey's insistence on tying up loose ends produced a work in which the behavior of characters was driven by the needs of plot. Such an effect would have been disastrous in this novel, because Ben Curtis's situation is the stuff of which maudlin tearjerkers are made. Haunting Ben's past are the suicides of his goddaughter, his best friend—who is the girl's

28. Ibid., 81, 98.

father—and his own son, Anthony, as well as the breakup of his marriage. In the wake of these catastrophes, Ben tries unsuccessfully to take his own life but finds a measure of healing in the old fishing grounds. It is a tribute to Humphrey's honesty and conviction that this story produces empathy rather than derision.

Hostages to Fortune is so painfully introverted and introspective a book that Humphrey can afford to leave some questions unanswered. The reasons for the suicide of Ben's friend and for his own attempt at self-destruction are fairly obvious, but no one really knows why the two young people kill themselves. We see in Ben a man forced to confront the absurd and, in the process, to contemplate the meaning of his own life. For him or Humphrey to have dispelled the absurdity with any pat formulation, either positive or negative, would have been as inadequate as the surmise of Melville's lawyer that Bartleby is the way he is because he once worked in the dead-letter office. When Ben is revived after his suicide attempt, he is even less certain than before whether his life is worth living—or taking. "He lacked the strength of will to fight the return of his bodily strength. . . . He watched the life-giving fluid flow drop by drop from the bottle, down the tube, and into his veins with a passivity born of weakness and indifference."[29]

Humphrey's title, of course, comes from Francis Bacon's aphorism: "He that hath wife and children hath given hostages to fortune." It is therefore not surprising that this novel, like *Home from the Hill*, deals largely with a relationship of father and son. As Gary Davenport points out, however, that is where the similarity ends. "In *Home from the Hill* both Captain Wade and Theron escape from conventionality only when they veer into a kind of contrived eccentricity: they are characters cut to a pattern, and their relationship is relatively external, simple, and predictable."

Things are quite different in the later novel. Humphrey no longer needs to have the father serve as a masculine role model—although Ben is a competent angler, Anthony is the superior, or at least the more scientific, outdoorsman. Also, Ben believes that, in committing suicide, Anthony has cuckolded him by alienating his wife's affections. This belief hastens Ben's slide into alcoholism and his own botched suicide attempt. Ben Curtis is at once a weaker and more admirable

29. Humphrey, *Hostages to Fortune* (New York: Delacorte, 1984), 220.

figure than Wade Hunnicutt. "Clearly, Humphrey has learned to speak as a particular man, and in so doing, he has come to speak for mankind."[30]

Devotees of Humphrey's earlier work are likely to find *Hostages to Fortune* a somber and humorless book. What pleasures it offers are found in the language. Rather than sinking into easy sentimentality, Humphrey is constantly illuminating the plight of his characters with striking metaphors. For example, here is Ben observing the change that has come over his friend Tony Thayer following the suicide of Tony's daughter:

> It was as if Tony's conception of himself had been shattered and a new one, strange to him, substituted for it. An analogy suggested itself. Just days earlier he had heard on the radio an interview with a famous surgeon. From it he learned a new departure in heart transplants. Instead of replacing the patient's own diseased heart with the donor's they now left it in place alongside the new one. In tandem, the pair shared the work. For whatever the period of reprieve from death given him by the operation, the patient had two hearts, neither very reliable, the one defective, the other susceptible to rejection by its host. Tony's emotional infirmity was now comparable to that two-hearted person. His old shattered self coexisted with a new one alien to him.[31]

As impressive as this novel is, it is not without flaws. Some readers may find the probing of Ben's psyche too discursive, and none is likely to find the character of his wife, Cathy, particularly memorable. Moreover, inveterate nitpickers will argue that far from achieving originality, Humphrey has simply substituted the influence of Hemingway for that of Faulkner. As evidence, they will cite passages such as the following: "Over the years he had gotten to know the entire stream. During his years away from it, sometimes when he lay awake in bed, he had retraced it, sometimes from the top down, sometimes from the bottom up, recalling as closely as he could individual trees, boulders, shallows and pools, bends where the bank was undercut, fish he had caught and fish he had hooked and lost."[32]

30. Davenport, "Humphrey's Circus Animals," 503.
31. Humphrey, *Hostages to Fortune*, 58.
32. Ibid., 119.

Hostages to Fortune is Humphrey's most accomplished book because it represents the first time in his fiction that he gains control of his materials without the semblance of manipulation. Even the occasional echoes of Hemingway seem unobtrusive, if anything adding to the pattern of allusiveness established by Ben's habit of quoting from his favorite authors. A writer, according to an old saying that Ben recalls, "was somebody for whom writing was harder than it was for other people."[33] The problem with Humphrey's early work is that it seems to have been too easily, or at least too facilely, written. *Hostages to Fortune* gives us not a worldview asserted but a vision earned.

With his final novel, *No Resting Place* (1989), Humphrey returned to his regional roots. Like the first section of *The Ordways*, this book deals with a journey from the Southeast to the area around Clarksville. The differences, however, between *No Resting Place* and Humphrey's other southwestern novels are far more profound than the similarities. This latest narrative is a historical novel that depicts one of the most shameful chapters in the American past—the forced migration of the Cherokee Indians along the Trail of Tears. Although this story has been told many times in works of nonfiction, few imaginative writers have chosen to tackle it. Besides Humphrey's book, we have Kermit Hunter's durable outdoor drama *Unto These Hills*, Denton R. Bedford's novel *Isali*, and Dee Brown's novel *Creek Mary's Blood*. Given the inherent pathos of the story and Humphrey's own remarkable growth as a novelist, one brings high expectations to this work. Unfortunately, they are not met.

The third-person-limited point of view that served Humphrey so well in *Hostages to Fortune* is abandoned here for a confusing multiple perspective. The ostensible narrator is Amos Smith IV, a boy the age that Humphrey was in 1936. Amos becomes interested in Texas history during the celebration of the state's centennial. Rather than allow him to play the part of Mirabeau Buonaparte Lamar in a school pageant, Amos's father tells the boy an unsanctioned version of Texas history, one that had been passed on to him by his own grandfather, a mixed-blood Indian who had traveled the Trail of Tears. As we move back in time, young Amos's voice is supplanted by that of an omniscient narrator who moves at will from place to place and from

33. Ibid., 188.

consciousness to consciousness. Although all historical fiction that is not mere romance is also a commentary on the present, Humphrey's main story and his narrative frame fail to illuminate each other. Since Humphrey knew nothing about his paternal great-grandfather other than that he was an Indian, the author's interest in oral history is biographically understandable. It just does not work aesthetically.

The actual history in this novel, including biographical information about the perpetually fascinating Sam Houston, is handled rather perfunctorily. Although we should never lose our sense of righteous indignation at racism, genocide, and distortion of the historical record, none of this came as news in the last quarter of the twentieth century. In fact, John Ehle, who has written sympathetically about the plight of the Cherokees, faults Humphrey for his romanticized view of the Indians. He argues that the novel

> effectively lays the blame on both God and the white man's Government but spares the Cherokees, thus rendering a somewhat unrealistic view of their tragedy. Where, for example, are the hundreds of black slaves who were forced to accompany their Indian masters? And where are the medicine men, whose sweat-based treatments for cholera, diphtheria, internal bleeding and many other ailments surely increased the number of the dead?[34]

To make the story of the Cherokees come alive as poetry rather than rhetoric, Humphrey needs to give us imaginative access to it. The novel's protagonist—young Amos's great-grandfather—is unequal to the task. He is simply another literary half-breed whose adolescent identity crisis is exacerbated by racial schizophrenia. Young Amos himself is vaguely reminiscent of Jimmy Hawkins, protagonist of Humphrey's story "The Last of the Caddoes." In that character, Humphrey gives us a kind of Tom Sawyer figure who, finding life as a white boy too mundane, so exaggerates his pittance of Indian blood that he rejects his family in order to dream himself an Indian brave. Although Humphrey does not maintain sufficient ironic detachment in that story, his protagonist's relationship to the past is at least more complex and nuanced than that of young Amos.

34. Ehle, "God Was at Least Partly to Blame," *New York Times Book Review,* June 25, 1989, 19.

Humphrey might have found a way out of this impasse had he chosen a different narrative perspective for his novel. I agree with Robert E. Morsberger, who says that "perhaps the most interesting character [in *No Resting Place*] is the Rev. Mr. MacKenzie, a Scottish missionary whose wife is a casualty of the death march and who, amid sufferings like Job's, ultimately finds himself no longer able to justify the ways of God to man." The novel seems most authentic in those places where we see things through MacKenzie's eyes. In his compassion for the Cherokees, he has the makings of a genuine Christian martyr. In confronting the problem of evil on the trail, however, he loses his faith. His heresy is even deeper than that of the atheist—he continues to believe in God's existence but not his goodness. MacKenzie takes a Cherokee as a second wife and persists in preaching a creed he no longer believes. "This life of imposture and deception he defends on the ground that having seen the suffering he had seen he was not only justified but in duty bound to tell whatever harmless lies might alleviate any more."[35] What a contrast this man makes to that other disingenuous crypto-Cherokee, Sam Houston.

If writers can be said to "own" certain regions, William Humphrey has laid claim to East Texas.[36] His Clarksville lives in the imagination as surely as does Sherwood Anderson's Winesburg, Ohio, or Edgar Lee Masters's Spoon River. As John M. Grammer has noted, *The Ordways*, *Home from the Hill*, and *Proud Flesh* constitute a Clarksville trilogy that extends from the time of the War between the States to the present. The publication of *No Resting Place* enlarges the saga into a tetralogy that begins in the time of Andrew Jackson and includes the red man as well as the white. If region is defined by period as well as locale, *Home from the Hill*, *A Time and a Place*, and *Farther Off from Heaven* suggest that Humphrey's strongest claim may be not to East Texas as such, but to the East Texas of the 1930s.

35. Morsberger, review of *No Resting Place*, by Humphrey, *Western American Literature* 24 (Winter 1990): 392; Humphrey, *No Resting Place* (New York: Delacorte, 1989), 214.
36. Joan Didion contends: "Certain places seem to exist because someone has written about them. . . . A place belongs forever to whoever claims it hardest, remembers it most obsessively, wrenches it from itself, shapes it, renders it, loves it so radically that he remakes it in his image" (*The White Album* [New York: Simon and Schuster, 1979], 146).

Far from attenuating his identity as a westerner, Humphrey's ties to the American South enrich his perspective. In his illuminating essay "More Freedom Than We Want: Corporate Life and the Literature of the American West," the southern critic (and native Oklahoman) M. E. Bradford argues that three important corporate myths shaped the life of eighteenth- and nineteenth-century America. These were the Puritan myth of New England, the Cavalier myth of the South, and the mercantile myth of the middle colonies. Curiously enough, the American West held essentially the same significance for the people formed by these three anterior myths. "Southerners and New Englanders and even commercial men felt about the West, as the West, qua possibility in more or less the same terms. To be unbounded in space and beyond the definition of familiar institutions was both exhilarating and frightening. Or rather, first exhilarating, and then frightening, once one had a taste of 'nature unimproved.'" Bradford goes on to say that, "like all heroic literature, the literature of the frontier carries with it at least the memory of the corporate life and accepts that memory as norm." It is the memory of a cultivated garden, now re-created as "a little town painted white but with the mountains not too far away and the spiritual presence of the great hunters and warriors never completely out of mind."[37]

The tension between individual freedom and corporate identity is at the heart of Humphrey's four western novels. The tragedy of Wade and Theron Hunnicutt lies in their adherence to a way of life that is entirely personal. Their beliefs and behavior make them icons for the community without ever being citizens of it. His admiration for the outdoor life notwithstanding, Faulkner always acknowledged the claim of domestic and social responsibilities and reserved his harshest judgment for those who ignored such obligations. If anything undercuts the moral vision of Humphrey's novel, it is the fact that he has kept too much of the admiration and too little of the judgment. But the tale itself is instructive.

The same is true of *Proud Flesh*, although the false god here is not the myth of the hunter-aristocrat but the most perverted form of mother love since Oedipus. Both the code of the hunter-aristocrat and family loyalty have value within a properly functioning community.

37. Bradford, *Remembering Who We Are: Observations of a Southern Conservative* (Athens: University of Georgia Press, 1985), 142.

When they are ends unto themselves, they become personally and socially destructive. Something of the reverse happens to the Cherokees. Here, the corporate identity of the tribe is shattered by government policy, and the journey west becomes not just the occasion but also the vehicle of their annihilation. Unlike the white pioneers, they never identify the West with freedom, nor are they ever bewitched by the siren call of untrammeled individualism.

It is in *The Ordways* that Humphrey strikes the most fitting balance between the needs of the individual and the demands of the group. In setting out after little Ned despite private misgivings, Sam Ordway affirms his loyalty to both southern and western codes of honor. But in eventually abandoning his quest, he affirms an even more fundamental obligation to the family he has left behind. The idyllic closing section creates a new community and an extended family—one that is large enough to include not only the newly recovered Ned but the recently deceased Will Vinson as well. Instead of a little town painted white with the mountains not too far away, Humphrey's image of a western home is of a goat ranch near the Mexican border. Never out of mind is the spiritual presence of a blind Confederate soldier who found his life by heading west, and the memory of a bereaved father who found his soul by heading home.

$$\scriptstyle\approx 12 \approx$$

Scum of the Earth

When his novel *All the Pretty Horses* hit the best-seller's list and won the National Book Award for Fiction in 1992, Cormac McCarthy suddenly became the hottest new writer in the United States. This reputation was solidified by the subsequent two books in his "Border Trilogy"—*The Crossing* (1994) and *Cities of the Plain* (1998). Seemingly everyone who was anyone (including O. J. Simpson in his jail cell) was reading this immensely talented novelist from the American Southwest. McCarthy, however, was neither a new writer nor a native westerner. His first published novel had appeared in 1965, and at least through the publication of his first western novel—*Blood Meridian*—in 1980, he was considered an obscure southern Gothicist with little more than a cult following. And all available evidence seemed to indicate that he preferred it that way. (When he won the National Book Award, he refused to attend the banquet, thus forcing his publisher to accept the award for him.) Just two years before McCarthy's big breakthrough into celebrity status, the following assessment of his early career appeared in the Spring 1990 issue of the *Southern Review*.

Cormac McCarthy may be the most highly respected unknown writer in contemporary southern letters. Vereen Bell estimates that McCarthy's five novels have sold no more than fifteen thousand copies in their various editions, and two of those novels *(Child of God* and *Blood Meridian)* are listed as "out-of-stock" by their publisher. If McCarthy has been shunned by the public, he has steadfastly resisted that sure refuge of the "serious" writer—academic patronage. (In fact, he flunked out of the University of Tennessee once and dropped out after a second try.) Although he has been sustained by private foundations, he seems never to have fed at the public trough, and he obviously prefers the company of skid row derelicts to that of professional literary types. He has guarded his privacy with the zeal of a J. D. Salinger or Thomas Pynchon without having their royalties as a buffer between himself and the critical establishment. When Mark Morrow finally tracked him down for a 1985 picture book on southern writers, he found McCarthy living in a ten-by-ten-foot room in the Colonial Motel on Kingston Street in Knoxville, his only visible possessions a portable typewriter and a '64 Rambler.[1]

But eccentricity is so endemic to writers and would-be writers that no one would give McCarthy a second look if weird behavior were all he had to recommend himself. It is the stylistic brilliance of his five novels that makes Cormac McCarthy a writer's writer and would do so even if he were as truly unknown as B. Traven. McCarthy possesses a southern feel for character and dialogue (rendered without quotation marks) and a not-altogether-southern eye for the mystery and otherness of nature. His sense of the comic reminds one alternately of Flannery O'Connor and the best of the current "grit lit" crowd.

However, it is his pyrotechnical use of language that is McCarthy's distinctive signature as a writer. His cadences and syntax inevitably remind one of Faulkner, but McCarthy's working vocabulary leaves even Faulkner in the dust. (One can imagine the college dropout taking a perverse pleasure in sending erudite professors scurrying to the dictionary to verify the meaning of some arcane term used with astonishing precision.) As John Ditsky notes, "Though doubtless operating under some degree of Faulknerian influence, McCarthy writes as though Faulkner had never existed, as if there were no limits to what language might be pushed into doing in the last half of the twentieth century." Consider, for example, a not atypical passage from McCarthy's *Outer Dark:*

> What discordant vespers do the tinker's goods chime through the long twilight and over the brindled forest road, him stooped and hounded the windy recrements of day like those exiles who divorced of corporeality and enjoined ingress of heaven or hell wander forever the middle warrens spoorless increate and

1. Morrow, *Images of the Southern Writer* (Athens: University of Georgia Press, 1985), 52.

anathema. Hounded by grief, by guilt, or like the cheerless ven-
dor clamored at heel through wood and fen by his own queru-
lous and inconsolable wares in perennial tin malediction.[2]

Only a college sophomore with a thesaurus or a supremely gifted
and self-confident writer would have dared construct such a paragraph.

The mixed blessing of Faulkner's influence has been a commonplace of southern criticism at least since the time that Flannery
O'Connor commented on the wisdom of getting off the track when
the *Dixie Limited* comes through town. As Louis D. Rubin Jr. points
out in his essay "On the Difficulties of Being a Southern Writer
Today; or, Getting Out from under William Faulkner," that sage ad-
vice has too often been ignored by writers who appropriate aspects
of Faulkner's style "to describe an experience that was not really
Faulknerian at all."[3] Although this specific observation was made
about William Humphrey, it could very well apply to Cormac McCarthy, whose first novel was published two years after Rubin's essay.
The echoes of Faulkner in McCarthy's prose serve not so much to remind us of stylistic similarities as to alert us to philosophical differences. For all the degeneracy and pessimism in his novels, Faulkner
was at heart a moralist who believed in an irreducible core of human
dignity. His work possesses a moral center, either explicit or implicit, that judges the evil and depravity of the world. In McCarthy's
universe that center either does not exist or cannot hold. Had Mc-
Carthy written *The Sound and the Fury*, Dilsey would have been gang-
raped by a bunch of Klansmen on the way home from church.

A good part of the difference between Faulkner and McCarthy lies
in the fact that Faulkner gives his characters a far richer interior life.
McCarthy's people more often resemble the Darwinian creatures
who inhabited the naturalistic novels of the late nineteenth and early
twentieth centuries. (Even in his primitive emotional state, Benjy
Compson seems less bestial than any half dozen of Cormac's cretins.)
As we read McCarthy's descriptions of his characters and their natural habitat, sometimes blending into each other, we see a humanity
that differs only in degree from the rest of the animal world. (When

2. McCarthy, *Outer Dark* (1968; reprint, New York: Ecco Press, 1984), 229.
3. Rubin, *The Curious Death of the Novel* (Baton Rouge: Louisiana State University Press, 1967), 284.

man and nature merge in Faulkner, as in *Go Down, Moses*, it is because nature has become more nearly human, not man less so.) When we do get inside McCarthy's characters, we find in *Sutree* a surrealistic dream world that exists outside the realm of reason, and in *Child of God* a cesspool of perversion that is not only unnatural but also a grotesque parody of much that is human. And as we move back to the outside world, we find not even the rational jungle of Darwin but an absurdist wasteland where chaos and pointless brutality take the place of natural selection.

In his first novel, *The Orchard Keeper* (1965), McCarthy made a point of continually violating the comfortable expectations of his readers. Vereen Bell has noted how the novel's shifting, almost random, point of view defies even the illusion of authorial control. McCarthy so consistently avoids the transitions and connections of a well-made novel that we suspect neither accident nor ineptitude but some more insidious design to be at work. This design extends beyond the form of the novel to the story being told. At first glance, the basic outline of that story is what one might expect from the first novel of a contemporary southern writer. A young boy grows up in a rural setting besieged by the forces of civilization. With his father dead, the boy's two primary role models are a wise and fiercely independent hermit, from whom he learns the ways of nature, and a sociopathic bootlegger, from whom he learns defiance of authority. Years earlier, the bootlegger had killed a man who tried to steal his car and then dumped the body in an abandoned spray tank in an orchard near the hermit's cabin. What none of the three major characters knows is that the dead man was the boy's father.

In a conventionally plotted novel, McCarthy might have had the young boy, John Wesley Rattner, torn between the two different forms of iconoclasm represented by the hermit and the bootlegger. Or he might have had the boy face a grave moral crisis by discovering that his bootlegger friend, Marion Sylder, killed the father he had sworn to avenge. Or John Wesley could have come to maturity by learning that his father was a tramp and a thief, not the sainted provider his widow made him out to be. McCarthy's steadfast refusal to turn any of these obvious tricks of plot may well be a higher form of realism, a fidelity to the disconnectedness of actual experience. The fact that this strategy is so disconcerting tells us something about the nature of art.

The greatest literature enables us to look into the very heart of darkness by making of the intolerable a thing of beauty. By giving coherence and articulation to human experience, art can make the fate of an Oedipus, a Kurtz, or a Benjy an object of sublime contemplation, an occasion for catharsis. In the hands of a clumsy or indifferent artist, the materials of tragedy degenerate into soap opera or pornography. This is clearly not the case with Cormac McCarthy. Neither clumsy nor indifferent, he is presenting reality with a deliberate paucity of narrative structure—either conventional or experimental. Even when literary things happen, it is with the inconclusiveness of real life. Rebellion leads to suffering but not to martyrdom. Words of wisdom are spoken without conviction and with no long-lasting effect. Epiphanies change no lives. The final scene of the novel shows a grown-up John Wesley sitting on his mother's gravestone, concerned only about the wetness of his sock.

If there is a message in *The Orchard Keeper*, it is profoundly naturalistic. The novel opens with a parable of three men cutting an elm tree that has grown up around a piece of fence. Obviously, this is a case of nature surrounding and obliterating a human construct. What is perhaps more significant, however, is the fact that the men assume that it is the fence that has grown up inside the tree. Not only are the effects of man less durable than the world of which they are a part, but human vanity frequently blinds us to that fact. At the end of the novel, we learn that the elm tree had been felled on the day that John Wesley had visited his mother's grave and that the iron embedded in the tree had been part of the fence surrounding the cemetery. When he leaves, John Wesley walks through the hole in the fence oblivious to what it might teach him.

Near the end of McCarthy's second novel, *Outer Dark* (1968), is an infinitely more grotesque instance of nature enveloping the merely human: "The tinker in his burial tree was a wonder to the birds. The vultures that came by day to nose with their hooked beaks among his buttons and pockets like outrageous pets soon left him naked of his rags and flesh alike. Black mandrake sprang beneath the tree as it will where the seed of the hanged falls and in spring a new branch pierced his breast and flowered in a green boutonniere perennial beneath his yellow grin." The difference between this nightmare landscape and the more pastoral image of the fence in the elm is a measure of the increasing horror of McCarthy's vision, or at least the increasing Gothicism of his technique. William J. Schafer sees *Outer Dark* (and McCarthy's work in general) as a testament of the "hard wages of original sin."[4] However, in a world where there is neither primal innocence nor a hope for redemption, original sin seems somehow too positive a concept.

If, as we have long believed, a sense of place is one of the glories of southern literature, McCarthy again frustrates our expectations, for the setting of *Outer Dark* seems to owe as much to Beckett as it does to Faulkner. (In commenting on the opening paragraph of *The Orchard Keeper*, John Ditsky notes, "If this is the South, it is the South perceived by Vladimir and Estragon.")[5] As in a dream, the locale of individual scenes is specific enough, often hauntingly so, without an identifiable context of period or region. We surmise only that we are someplace in the rural South toward the end of the nineteenth century. Beyond that, we know only that McCarthy's characters live in an outer dark of incest, murder, infanticide, and cannibalism.

The principal characters are a brother and sister, Culla and Rinthy Holme. Like a backwoods Adam and Eve (the comparison is William Schafer's), they couple and produce offspring—an infant whom Culla claims died at birth but whom he has really abandoned to the elements. When Rinthy finds no body buried in the child's ostensible grave, she correctly infers that the baby is still alive and in the custody of an itinerant tinker who sells household goods and pornographic postcards. Rinthy sets out in search of the child, and Culla in search of Rinthy. Although neither quest is successful, brother and sister continually cross paths with each other, the tinker and their baby, and three terrifying marauders whose behavior gives a whole new meaning to the concept of motiveless malignity.

Because he recognizes the taboo against incest (or at least against incestuous progeny), Culla is the more fully socialized of the two siblings. Rinthy is a far more innocent and elemental figure. She says, "I don't live nowheres no more. . . . I just go around hunting my chap. That's about all I do any more."[6] Her strong maternal instincts, in-

4. Schafer, "Cormac McCarthy: The Hard Wages of Original Sin," *Appalachian Journal* 4 (Winter 1977): 105–18.

5. Ditsky, "Further into Darkness: The Novels of Cormac McCarthy," *Hollins Critic* (April 1981): 3.

6. McCarthy, *Outer Dark*, 156.

cluding breasts that continue to lactate for her absent child, make Rinthy a positive symbol of the life force. However, her experience undercuts that life force at nearly every turn. Even when people take her in, which they are constantly doing, they are unable to help her find her child, and one of the homes where she briefly stays seems to be the very negation of family life. Although the husband and wife have produced five children, none lived to adulthood. The wife is reduced to churning butter to sell at the local stores (an ironic counterpoint to Rinthy's lactation). Not only is her husband unable to eat the butter, but he hurls an entire board of it at her in the midst of a pointless argument, as Rinthy beats a frightened retreat.

Culla encounters considerably greater peril in his travels. He sees graves robbed and men hanged from trees. In one unforgettable sequence, he crosses a river in a runaway ferryboat whose captain has been swept overboard. (During part of the crossing, Culla frantically dodges a berserk horse he cannot see, until finally the horse gallops to his death in the swollen river.) Upon attaining the other shore, Culla encounters the three marauders, who insist on his sharing a sinewy and indigestible meat that may well be human flesh. He is then forced to exchange his nearly new boots for rotten old ones and left to fend for himself in the night. When Culla Holme (now ironically homeless) takes shelter in an abandoned house, he is arrested for trespassing and is sentenced by the local squire to ten days' labor to work off a five-dollar fine. When Culla asks to stay on later for no more than room and board, the squire tells him to get out of town.

Culla faces additional danger when he encounters a group of hog drovers. After the hogs inexplicably stampede and plunge over a cliff, taking one of the drovers with them, the surviving men conclude that Culla has somehow been responsible for the catastrophe and decide to hang him. They are even encouraged in a roundabout way by one of the many false prophet figures who populate McCarthy's fiction—a parson who looks as if he could have stepped right off the pages of "Snuffy Smith." Culla escapes this bit of irrational and undeserved punishment by leaping into the river after the hogs. The presence of the parson and the obvious parallel to the biblical story of the Gaderene swine makes this incident something more than just another example of gratuitous violence in an absurd world. Again, the surface comparisons are meant to highlight differences rather than similarities. Unlike Christ, Culla casts out no devils. (In McCarthy's world, the demons are omnipresent and probably omnipotent.) He can save only himself, and that only by swimming with dead hogs.

McCarthy gives some sense of closure to *Outer Dark* when Culla Holme finally comes across the infant he has left for dead. The marauders have hanged the tinker (don't ask why) and stolen the child, and they seem to be waiting for Holme when he limps to their campfire after escaping from the hog drovers. Apparently having had a change of heart, Holme asks that the men give him the baby for his sister to raise. What follows is one of the most disgusting and harrowing scenes in contemporary literature:

> Holme saw the blade wink in the light like a long cat's eye slant and malevolent and a dark smile erupted on the child's throat and went all broken down the front of it. The child made no sound. It hung there with one eye glazing over like a wet stone and the black blood pumping down its naked belly. The mute one knelt forward. He was drooling and making little whimpering noises in his throat. He knelt with his hands outstretched and his nostrils rimpled delicately. The man handed him the child and he seized it up, looked once at Holme with witless eyes, and buried his moaning face in its throat.[7]

Although Holme has a too obviously symbolic encounter with a blind prophet a few pages later, the real end of the novel comes immediately after the butchering of the child. Arriving at the marauders' former campsite in the late afternoon (how many days later we do not know), Rinthy "trailed her rags through dust and ashes, circling the dead fire, the charred billets and chalk bones, the little calcined ribcage. She poked among the burnt remains of the tinker's traps, the blackened pans confused among the rubble, the lantern with its skewed glass, the axle and iron wheelhoops already rusting. She went among this charnel curiously. She did not know what to make of it."[8]

That Rinthy's quest for her child should end this way is almost as horrible as the murder itself. Not only is innocence incapable of overcoming evil, it is sometimes incapable of even perceiving it. However, nature itself outlasts both the good and the evil that men do.

7. Ibid., 236.
8. Ibid., 237.

McCarthy reminds us of this when, leaving the perplexed Rinthy, he describes the hanging tree growing up around the body of the tinker: "He took the sparse winter snows upon what thatch of hair still clung to his dried skull and hunters that passed that way never chanced to see him brooding among his barren limbs. Until wind had tolled the tinker's bones and seasons loosed them one by one to the ground below and alone his bleached and weathered brisket hung in that lonesome wood like a bone birdcage."[9]

If *Outer Dark* is a book of intermittent horror, McCarthy's third novel, *Child of God* (1973), is calculated to produce revulsion on nearly every page. To take only one example, the incest that precipitates the action in *Outer Dark* is an undramatized given (sort of like the adultery in *The Scarlet Letter*). In *Child of God*, it is a merely incidental perversion—graphically described. When the local dump man catches one of his slatternly daughters (offspring to whom he has given such names as Uretha, Cerebellum, and Hernia Sue) copulating in the woods, he chases the boy away and begins beating his child with a stick. "She grabbed it," we read. "He overbalanced. Hot fishy reek of her freshened loins. Her peach drawers hung from a bush. The air about him grew electric. Next thing he knew his overalls were about his knees and he was mounting her. Daddy quit, she said. Daddy. Oooh." When he ascertains that her swain did not "dump a load" in her, "he pulled it out and gripped it and squirted his jissom on her thigh. Goddamn you, he said. He rose and heisted up his overalls and lumbered off toward the dump like a bear." Walter Sullivan hardly overstates the case when he says of this novel, "In spite of the effective writing and the generation of dramatic tension, it is not a consummated work of art but an affront on decency at every level."[10]

But McCarthy's reputation as a serious artist is such that critics are inclined to give him the benefit of the doubt and assume that some higher seriousness redeems his gross sensationalism. Perhaps like Leslie Fiedler in *Freaks*, he is simply trying to define the human by the marginal rather than the central. In the second paragraph of

9. Ibid., 238.
10. Sullivan, *A Requiem for the Renascence: The State of Fiction in the Modern South* (Athens: University of Georgia Press, 1976), 71.

his novel, McCarthy describes his hideous protagonist as "a child of God much like yourself perhaps." Robert Coles finds this hint of theology quite convincing and says of McCarthy, "He is a novelist of religious feeling who appears to subscribe to no creed but who cannot stop wondering in the most passionate and honest way what gives life meaning."[11] While such a characterization accurately describes Coles himself, it begs several questions when applied to McCarthy. I am not convinced that Cormac McCarthy believes there is meaning in life or that the search for it is a worthwhile activity. Nevertheless, in a bizarre way, *Child of God* may be the most human of his first three novels.

As we have seen, *The Orchard Keeper* and *Outer Dark* both demonstrate the powerlessness of humanity to withstand the forces of natural mutability. The central action of *Child of God* is the effort of one seriously depraved human being to defeat those very forces. As dialectical opposites, love and death have always been closely linked in life and literature. Undying love and no-longer-living loved ones are the stuff of both sentimental tearjerkers and the most sublime novels and poems of the Western world. No human sentiment is more understandable than the desire that passion should transcend death itself. Yet, strictly speaking, this desire is profoundly "unnatural." Unchecked by a sense of reality, it can lead to morbid fixation and—at its most extreme—necrophilia. In fact, to some twisted minds, it may seem paradoxically necessary to kill the beloved in order to cheat death, or simple change, of its natural advantage. It was so for Porphyria's lover in Browning's poem and for Faulkner's Miss Emily. However, for sheer lunacy, neither of these lovers of the dead can touch McCarthy's Lester Ballard.

For Browning and Faulkner, necrophilia was the punch line (I hesitate to say climax) of the story, beyond which nothing need nor could be said. For McCarthy, it occurs at the center of the narrative, with its implications worked out in increasingly shocking detail. Before we even get to that narrative center, however, there is enough garden-variety depravity to titillate the prurient imagination. In less than fifty pages, Lester threatens to kill an auctioneer, spies on a couple in lovers' lane while spilling his seed on the fender of their car, kills a recalcitrant cow by throwing a rope around its neck and

11. Coles, "The Stranger," *New Yorker*, August 26, 1974, 90.

trying to pull it with a tractor, and strips the clothes off a woman who has been sexually assaulted and left by the side of the road.

We also learn that, as a child, Lester has bloodied a playmate who refused to fetch a softball for him and that he had walked into a barn where his father had hanged himself. In a particularly ghastly scene, he gives a captured robin to an idiot child of a girl he is trying to woo. After leaving the child with the bird for a few minutes, they return to find "its mouth was stained with blood and it was chewing. Ballard went on through the door into the room and reached down to get the bird. It fluttered on the floor and fell over. He picked it up. Small red nubs worked in the soft down."[12] Perhaps as a foreshadowing of Lester's future antics, the idiot has chewed the robin's legs off to keep it from getting away.

By the time Lester stumbles onto an abandoned car where a couple has been asphyxiated in the midst of coitus, less than ten pages after the incident with the robin, we are prepared for just about anything. McCarthy manages to heighten the ghoulishness of the scene by describing it in a matter-of-fact language that keeps our attention riveted to what is happening (here the resemblance is more to Hemingway than to Faulkner). While the dead man, his penis still sheathed in a wet yellow condom, appears to be watching him, Ballard kicks the man's feet out of the way, sniffs the girl's panties, and unbuckles his trousers. "A crazed gymnast laboring over a cold corpse. He poured into that waxen ear everything he'd ever thought of saying to a woman. Who could say she did not hear him? When he'd finished he raised up and looked out again. The windows were fogged. He took the hem of the girl's skirt with which to wipe himself. He was standing on the dead man's legs. The dead man's member was still erect."[13] Baroque language would have ruined the effect here. Like the sick jokes that began circulating in the late fifties and early sixties, this scene shocks precisely because it makes the horrible mundane, if not downright banal.

Lester is not only a child of God (whatever that may finally mean) but also something of a mad god himself, ruling a world of make-believe people. In addition to the human corpses he acquires, he has stuffed bears and tigers he has won at the fair. "As aberrant as Lester

12. McCarthy, *Child of God* (1973; reprint, New York: Vintage, 1993), 79.
13. Ibid., 88–89.

progressively becomes," Vereen Bell notes, "he is ruled at every turn both by unspeakable appetite and by a warped compulsion to domesticate it."[14] He plays house with his menagerie—first in a run-down shack and then, when that burns, in a cave. He even goes to town to purchase clothes, including black and red underwear, for his favorite corpses. It may be that Lester's behavior is most alarming when it comes closest to parodying the normal (just as the news that Ted Bundy collected cheerleader magazines seemed kinkier than if he had been exclusively a connoisseur of hard-core pornography). The point is not that there is no distinction between normality and abnormality but that in assaulting that distinction, mockery of the normal becomes a special kind of perversion.

To appreciate the particular quality of McCarthy's vision, one need consider only what other writers might have done with Lester's story. Flannery O'Connor would certainly have made a theological parable out of it. (Robert Coles notwithstanding, this is something that McCarthy does not do.) Faulkner might have turned it into another tale of the individual against the community. Richard Wright probably would have made Lester a black man who found necrophilia to be an existential political statement. And a liberal humanist such as William Styron could have shown how Lester's deprived background turned him into a criminal. Instead, we have a novel that seems to owe more to the tall-tale tradition than to any influence of the Southern Renascence. There is no single reliable narrative voice here, but seemingly omniscient accounts of Lester's behavior interspersed with first-person monologues from various residents of the area. After a while the wary reader begins to wonder how much of this he is to accept at face value and how much is pure fabulation.

In no facile sense are we to assume that Lester is simply a product of his environment or that he is really no different from ostensibly normal people. However, if McCarthy's mode of narration is meant to suggest that Lester has become a mythic figure for the community (that is Vereen Bell's contention), we have to wonder what it is about that community that causes it to make such myths. At least part of the legend of Lester Ballard is pretty conventional fare. Speaking of his ability to handle a rifle, a townsman observes, "I'll say one thing.

14. Bell, *The Achievement of Cormac McCarthy* (Baton Rouge: Louisiana State University Press, 1988), 61.

He could by god shoot it. Hit anything he could see. I seen him shoot a spider out of a web in the top of a big redoak one time and he was far from the tree as from here to the road yonder."[15] Lester is even barred from the fair because he has won too many prizes. But, of course, that note of diminution is itself telling. Rather than being a hunter of wild beasts, he is a winner of stuffed animals. In this modern-day parody of the frontier, it is only a matter of time before Lester's firepower and cunning are turned against his fellow man. And even then, his prey are not real live enemies so much as human trophies.

McCarthy also manages to draw subliminal parallels between Lester and the community through scenes that eerily resemble each other. After Lester bags his first corpse and tries to carry her up to the attic, he discovers that she is too heavy for him. So he brings in some lengths of old plow line, which he pieces together before the fire. "Then he went in and fitted the rope around the waist of the pale cadaver and ascended the ladder with the other end. She rose slump-shouldered from the floor with her hair all down and began to bump slowly up the ladder. Halfway up she paused, dangling. Then she began to rise again."

After Lester's underground cache of loved ones is discovered, a rope is thrown into the cave. "When it descended they made it fast to the rope about the corpse and called aloft again. The rope drew taut and the first of the dead sat up on the cave floor, the hands that hauled the rope above sorting the shadows like puppeteers. Gray soapy clots of matter fell from the cadaver's chin. She ascended *dangling*. She sloughed in the weem of the noose. A gray rheum dripped."[16] These, however, are not the only dangling corpses in *Child of God*.

Early in the novel, one of the townspeople surmises that Lester "never was right after his daddy killed hisself." This citizen was one of two men who cut the body down. "I seen his feet hangin," he recalls. ". . . The old man's eyes was run out on stems like a crawfish and his tongue blacker'n a chow dog's. I wisht if a man wanted to hang hisself he'd do it with poison or somethin so folks wouldn't have to see such a thing as that." Much later in the story, an old-timer

15. McCarthy, *Child of God*, 57.
16. Ibid., 95, 196; emphasis added.

recalls a public hanging from around the turn of the century. Obviously not sharing the squeamishness of the present generation, a crowd of spectators had streamed into town to see two malefactors brought to justice. It was the first of the year, and the streets were still decorated with holly boughs and Christmas candles. As the old-timer remembers it:

> People had started into town the evenin before. Slept in their wagons, a lot of em. Rolled out blankets on the courthouse lawn. Wherever. You couldn't get a meal in town, folks lined up three deep. Women sellin sandwiches in the street. . . . [The sheriff] brung em from the jail, had two preachers with em and had their wives on their arms and all. Just like they was goin to church. All of em got up there on the scaffold and they sung and everybody fell in singin with em. . . . Whole town and half of Sevier County singin I Need Thee Every Hour. Then the preacher said a prayer and the wives kissed their husbands goodbye and stepped down off the scaffold and turned around to watch and the preacher come down and it got real quiet. And then that trap kicked open from under em and down they dropped and hung there a jerkin and a kickin for I don't know, ten, fifteen, minutes. Don't ever think hangin is merciful. It ain't.[17]

These men had been White Caps, a vigilante group to which Lester's grandfather belonged.

Lester Ballard, who has defied the forces of mutability with such monomaniacal zeal, finally cheats the hangman. Never indicted for any crime, he is confined to a mental hospital in Knoxville near a man who used to open people's skulls and eat their brains with a spoon. (They did not converse because Lester had nothing to say to a crazy man.) With journalistic specificity, the omniscient narrator tells us that Lester contracted pneumonia in April 1965 (the only way we have of dating the story). When this ailment proves fatal, his body is shipped to the state medical school and reduced to spare parts.

The dissection is described with clinical detail. (John Ditsky is reminded of the dissection of Gary Gilmore in Norman Mailer's *The Executioner's Song*.) Then, "at the end of three months when the

17. Ibid., 21, 167–68.

class was closed Ballard was scraped from the table into a plastic bag and taken with others of his kind to a cemetery outside the city and there interred. A minister from the school read a simple service."[18] There is a certain poetic justice in the exploiter of corpses becoming an exploited corpse. At a more general level, however, Lester's end is simply another instance of the human person being reabsorbed into an indifferent nature. In that sense, this child of God is indeed like all of us.

When we get to McCarthy's fourth novel, *Sutree* (1979), we find three characteristics not evident in his previous work: a protagonist of obvious intelligence with a recognizable interior life, an affirmative sense of community, and a benign view of nature. The reason for these differences may simply be that McCarthy began *Sutree* before any of his first three published novels. Both thematically and technically, *Sutree* makes a good deal more sense if we see it as an earlier rather than a later product of McCarthy's muse. There is much of the apprentice novel about it and very little that resembles either *Child of God* or the more recent *Blood Meridian*. In fact, it seems hardly a novel of the seventies at all, but rather the sort of tour de force we might have expected in the sixties from an extremely gifted young man trying his damnedest to write like Faulkner, think like Steinbeck, and live like Kerouac.

Throughout a good part of the nineteenth century, southwestern humor featured a cultivated, upper-class observer thrown among barbarians. The humorists used this observer's superior sophistication as a means of judging the rabble while affirming conservative social values. In the character of Cornelius Sutree, we have a representative of the upper class among the dregs of humanity. Sutree, however, is there by choice. Like many another sixties dropout, he finds life to be more authentic in the gutter than in the mansion. His entire life, and McCarthy's entire novel, is as much a social and political statement as the work of the southwestern humorists. The difference is that McCarthy's vision is radical and proletarian rather than conservative and aristocratic. This is most evident on those few occasions when Sutree comes in contact with the world he left behind.

The most sustained of such encounters occurs when word arrives

18. Ibid., 194.

on skid row that Sutree's little boy has died. As this is the first inkling we have had that Sutree has left a wife and child behind, it comes as no surprise that he is not welcomed home with open arms (closed fists is more like it). When he appears on the scene, his mother-in-law begins clawing and kicking him and tries to bite his finger off. His father-in-law clobbers Sutree in the head with his shoe and then goes into the house to fetch his shotgun. Later, the local sheriff, who could have walked off the set of any B movie about the South, buys Sutree a bus ticket and tells him to get out of town.

In the midst of all this rancor, Sutree manages to visit his son's open grave and pile dirt in with his bare hands while holding the cemetery tractors at bay. Given the man's obvious grief and his ill-treatment by his in-laws, it would take a hard-hearted reader not to sympathize with Sutree. Since McCarthy tells us nothing about Sutree's married life and makes his antagonists into cartoon figures, we are not supposed to wonder why he abandoned this child he now seems to love so much. Nor does he seem to feel any guilt for having done so. Sutree's world is one where emotion crowds out moral responsibility. It reeks of a sentimentality lacking in McCarthy's other, harder and bleaker, novels.

Fortunately, we do not read Cormac McCarthy for dropout sociology any more than we read the southwestern humorists for conservative politics. For whatever reason Sutree may have taken up residence among the derelicts of the Knoxville waterfront, his adventures there hold our interest. Like the inhabitants of Steinbeck's Cannery Row, his cohorts are an assortment of whores, pimps, gamblers, and sons of bitches. By far the most memorable of these is a backwoods simpleton named Gene Harrogate.

We first see Gene when he is arrested for sexually violating a patch of watermelons. Such wanton destruction of property earns him a stint on the chain gang (he would have been charged with bestiality had his lawyer not pointed out that watermelons are not beasts), where he meets our hero, Cornelius Sutree. After becoming a free man (he prolongs his stay by refusing to work in the prison kitchen), Gene goes from one harebrained scheme to the next, until he is finally carted off to the penitentiary for stealing money from pay phones. The only other one of Sutree's associates who is almost as bizarre is a "pale and pimpled part-time catamite" named Leonard. When Leonard's father dies, the family does not tell anyone and keeps the body in an icebox for six months to keep the old man's welfare checks coming in.

Finding this book's humor its greatest virtue, I am simply not convinced that there is enough to admire in its unfunny moments to warrant its incredible prolixity. Published after such a superbly crafted novel as *Child of God*, *Sutree* seems particularly lugubrious and overwritten. No doubt, the rhetoric and vocabulary are meant to impose some sense of order and beauty on a world distinctly lacking in both. I fear, however, that McCarthy is simply asking language to do more than it is capable of doing. With Faulkner, one has a sense that the ornate language is matched by a largeness of vision. In McCarthy's work, absence of vision—a resolute inner dark—would seem to be the point. One cannot illuminate that darkness with fancy talk any more than one can permanently light up the night sky with Fourth of July fireworks. It is a good show, but the stars are a better guide.

The linguistic thickets in McCarthy's most recent novel, *Blood Meridian*, are not as formidable as in *Sutree*, but the moral landscape is considerably more harrowing. Having left his native South, McCarthy writes about a region that is native to the American imagination—the Wild West. As one might expect, however, McCarthy's West is not the mythic land we have come to know from pulp novels, movies, and television. Ever since Columbus's discovery that the world had a West, a new life (if not necessarily a new Eden) has seemed distinctly possible just beyond the horizon. Living in a country much larger and younger than those of Europe, Americans have tended to mythologize their experience in terms of space rather than time. Even though Frederick Jackson Turner announced the closing of the frontier a century ago (some four hundred years after Columbus had opened it), a belief in limitless space, personal freedom, and a second start remains an intractable part of the American dream. Only in recent decades have we seen a substantial body of literature that can be regarded as antiwestern.

In his 1968 book *The Return of the Vanishing American*, Leslie Fiedler argues that such writers as John Barth, Thomas Berger, Ken Kesey, David Markson, Peter Matthiessen, James Leo Herlihy, and Leonard Cohen were creating a new literary genre by exploiting and lampooning the pop western. At the same time, the arbiters of middlebrow culture were also doing their best to debunk the West of our collective imagination. I can recall reading in magazines such as *American Heritage* that Wyatt Earp was not really (in that marvelous redundancy) brave, courageous, and bold, but a cowardly bully who pistol-whipped drunken cowboys. Calamity Jane (or was it Belle Starr?) was not really a tomboyish actress whom one might one day marry, but a hideously ugly slut who copulated without regard to species or level of consanguinity. Even the movies got in on the act, giving us everything from the gentle spoof of *Cat Ballou* to the gut-bucket nihilism of Sam Peckinpah. *Blood Meridian* is very much in the Peckinpah tradition. In fact, it might even be regarded as a novelization (grotesque word for a grotesque phenomenon) of Peckinpah's West.

Set in the American Southwest and northern Mexico during the middle of the nineteenth century, *Blood Meridian* is loosely based on history. It follows a young man—known only as "the kid"—from his home in Tennessee to East Texas shortly after the Mexican War. From that point until the end of the book, some 330 pages later, we follow the kid's picaresque adventures among cutthroats so vile that they would make a modern-day motorcycle gang look like a boys' choir. Although the titular leader of these freelance killers is Captain John Glanton, the metaphysician of the group is a hairless behemoth named Judge Holden. Rather than seeing violence as a means to an end, the judge regards brutality as its own justification. Throughout history, he argues, men have fought for a wide variety of causes and values. As a confirmed skeptic, he does not pretend to know whether any of these causes and values have objective validity. What is universal, however, is the act of fighting itself. Men make something valuable by fighting for it. According to this twisted logic, not only are all wars holy but only war itself is holy.

Obviously, the pervasiveness of human evil is McCarthy's central point. (One of the book's epigraphs is an excerpt from the *Yuma (AZ) Daily Sun*, noting the discovery of a 300,000-year-old skull that "shows evidence of having been scalped.") "To a remarkable degree," notes Vereen Bell, "the evil of suffering, which in *Sutree* merely impinged upon human life, in *Blood Meridian* has metastasized and become human."[19] The problem is that the sustained and senseless violence of this book can shock for only so long before it begins to

19. Bell, *Achievement of McCarthy*, 124.

numb. The killing and maiming are finally so repetitious that action becomes the cause of boredom rather than an escape from it. In setting this tale in the American Southwest, McCarthy proves conclusively that it was not the Nazis who invented the banality of evil.

Whether Cormac McCarthy will continue to be "unknown" or eventually find a place in the mainstream of modern American (or at least modern southern) literature remains an open question. His books are too difficult and eccentric to woo readers away from Danielle Steele and James Michener, and unlike Harry Crews (the only other serious contender for "most degenerate southern writer"), he continues to shun the vulgarities of self-promotion. If McCarthy is to be discovered, it must be by the academic and critical establishment he has so far shunned. Although it is difficult to imagine a younger Malcolm Cowley preparing a Viking Portable McCarthy, Vereen Bell's recent book *The Achievement of Cormac McCarthy* (published as part of Louisiana State University Press's Southern Literary Studies) is an important first step toward canonization. The only problem is that Bell's book seems addressed to an audience that already understands and appreciates McCarthy's work. At present, that audience is probably too small to be anything other than a literary cult.

One cannot help admiring any contemporary writer of fiction who possesses sufficient self-confidence to go against the minimalist grain. Also, there is something refreshing about a novelist who still writes from experience rather than from graduate courses in the Theory of Fiction. Of McCarthy's five books, however, only *Child of God* seems likely to outlive him. It is the sort of book that astonishes by testing the very limits of nihilism (pushing the outside of the envelope, as Tom Wolfe's test pilots would say). Such books (Joan Didion's *Play It as It Lays* is another) ask us to believe that the alchemy of style can transform patently offensive material into an object of aesthetic contemplation. The result is what Yeats might have called a terrible beauty, with the moralists among us italicizing the adjective and the aestheticians the noun. Whatever else one might say of him, the author of *Child of God* is a master craftsman with the courage of his perversions. But that distinction is probably not enough to earn him a place among the immortals. I suspect that Cormac McCarthy is what Faulkner would have been had *Sanctuary* been his greatest novel.

Index

DATE DUE
